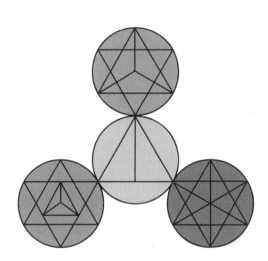

SIMRAN

KNOWING

The 7 Human Expressions of Grace

REDFeather™
MIND | BODY | SPIRIT
An Imprint of Schiffer Publishing, Ltd.

Cover design by: Brenda McCallum
Interior design by: Melody Gallipeau and
Christopher Bower
Type set in Desire/Garamond

ISBN: 978-0-7643-6516-4
Printed in India

Published by REDFeather Mind, Body, Spirit
An imprint of Schiffer Publishing, Ltd.
4880 Lower Valley Road
Atglen, PA 19310
Phone: (610) 593-1777; Fax: (610) 593-2002
Email: Info@redfeathermbs.com
Web: www.redfeathermbs.com

For our complete selection of fine books on this
and related subjects, please visit our website at
www.redfeathermbs.com. You may also write
for a free catalog.

REDFeather Mind, Body, Spirit's titles are
available at special discounts for bulk purchases
for sales promotions or premiums. Special
editions, including personalized covers, corporate
imprints, and excerpts, can be created in
large quantities for special needs. For more
information, contact the publisher.

We are always looking for people to write books
on new and related subjects. If you have an
idea for a book, please contact us at proposals@
schifferbooks.com.

Other REDFeather Titles by the Author:

Living: The 7 Blessings of Human Experience
ISBN 978-0-7643-6271-2

Being: The 7 Illusions That Derail Personal Power, Purpose, and Peace
ISBN 978-0-7643-6371-9

Other Schiffer Books on Related Subjects:

Dancing with Riches: In Step with the Energy of Change Using Access Consciousness® Tools, Kass Thomas,
ISBN 978-0-7643-6154-8

The F.A.S.T.R. Process: The Secret of Emotional Power, Liz Barallon,
ISBN 978-0-7643-5851-7

FSC
www.fsc.org
MIX
Paper from
responsible sources
FSC® C016779

KNOWING

THE 7 Human Expressions of Grace

SIMRAN

Dedicated to
the awareness of sacred beauty within each human being,
and the expressed embodiment of the Divine.

In LIVING your Communion, Devotion & Humility to life. . . allow
KNOWING to come forth through your innate BEING of innocence and curiosity.

YOU ARE THE GATEWAY FOR . . .
7 BLESSINGS OF HUMAN EXPERIENCE.
to experience and express . . .
7 HUMAN EXPRESSIONS OF GRACE.
in order to absorb and dissolve
7 ILLUSIONS THAT DERAIL PERSONAL POWER, PURPOSE, AND PEACE.

```
      0
      0
      1
     1 1
    1 0 1
   1 1 0 1 1
    1 0 1
     1 1
      1
      0
      0
```

THE SELF-REALIZATION TRILOGY

BOOK 1—LIVING: THE 7 BLESSINGS OF HUMAN EXPERIENCE

BOOK 2—BEING: The 7 ILLUSIONS THAT DERAIL
PERSONAL POWER, PURPOSE, AND PEACE

BOOK 3—KNOWING: THE 7 HUMAN EXPRESSIONS OF GRACE

CONTENTS

manifestation. 191

oppression. 219

remembering.

Being is becoming.
Becoming is *KNOWING*.
***KNOWING* becomes *BEING*.**

This book (KNOWING)
illustrates your multidimensional journey within SELF.
These writings support awakening to your humanity and an
expanded experience of your spiritual senses, vibration, and frequency.

Each section has correlations to Self and self in the books titled LIVING and BEING.
Within the multidimensional grids shared, and also listed in the back of the book, You are
privy to a universe of inner fulfillment that correlates to experience, expression, and creativity.

LIVING depicts your layers of unconscious duality that determine experience and expression.

BEING depicts your layers of subconscious vibration that impact experience and expression.

KNOWING holds layers of humanity, sacred experience, and a doorway to divine expression.

You are a rippling, layered, vibrational consciousness consisting of many dimensions.
Become present to each lens of Self/self/SELF that You look through, live from,
and express as, moment to moment.

Human Grace opens the way for Divine Grace to enter.
Be gentle... kind... and compassionate...
when engaging with self... Self... and SELF.

The SELF-REALIZATION SERIES of
LIVING ... BEING ... and KNOWING
is dedicated to the
GOD
within You/you/YOU.

Namaste.

1
0 0
0 0 0
0 0
1

acknowledgments.

In Love . . . Of Love . . . With Love . . . As Love . . .

You are . . . I am . . . We are . . . **experience experiencing itself, as many parts of ONEness.**

Deep gratitude for those who willingly continue this path, devoted to the journey of the soul. It is not easy, or brief, but serves in the most profound of ways. To my friends, family, sisterhood, and brotherhood: thank you.

To my family at RED Feather/Schiffer Publishing, *thank you* for midwifing the Self-Realization series.

Jeff Spenard, Ryan Treasure, Jeff Gerstl, and my family at Voice America . . . it is an honor and pleasure to have cocreated *11:11 Talk Radio* since 2009. *Thank you* for collaborating each week.

Grady Query and Mike Sautter, there are not adequate words to express my respect, admiration, love, and immense gratitude.

To my sacred sisterhood . . . your connection during these pivotal years of change have held me. I love you.

To my family—Raj and Ajit Randhawa (Mom and Dad), Mitti and Sonya Randhawa, Michael and Nikki Haley, Gogi and Amber Randhawa. My heart is grateful for the love and support.

Tuck Self, your continual advocacy and laughter-filled friendship bolstered my strength and faith in some very difficult moments. Larry Reed, I cherish you, and this series of books is dedicated to your loving memory.

Sage and Krish, I love you unconditionally and completely.

We are *ONE* family . . . in remembrance and reunion.

***YOU/I/WE/THEY* are *ONE* . . . and the same.**

knowing. *How do i/eye/I say thank you?*
I see those around me.

Knowing. *I acknowledge those who held me.*

KNOWING. *I AM eternally grateful.*

preface.

**Awaken to the sacred intimacy of pure presence.
Become deeply vulnerable to the innocence of your human experience,
the essence of Divine Knowing, and the tender kiss
of grace that exists between them.**

Life is designed to stretch you. This book series is that embodied practice, guiding you through patience, presence, and love. This threshold, between the visible and invisible, stewards your multidimensional nature into integrated awareness. In book 1, *Living: The 7 Blessings of Human Experience, Self* represents the robotic, asleep, unconscious, conditioned, and homogenized dream walker, adorned in identities and attempting to make sense of life.

Book 2, *Being: The 7 Illusions That Derail Personal Power, Purpose, and Peace, self* represents the obsessed nature of personhood, ignorant of its vices and unconsciously obedient to shadow, animal, and monster expressions. These aspects act out your deep cravings and hunger. This dimension of *You* experiences life in the gray zone: numb, disconnected, and deeply distracted. This version of *you* is possessed by your inner demons.

Book 3, *KNOWING: The 7 Human Expressions of Grace,* is a return to humanity, your humanity. It portrays an intentional, devotional, and committed walk through the valley of shadows and death, while also *remembering* your eternal and divine nature. We are not taught to let ourselves feel. Imagine committing as deeply to the darkness as *You* have to Light. *Why?* An intentional, conscious commitment such as this shifts experience and expression from horizontal *Living/living* to vertical alignment. There is much to learn within darkness. This is the bridge between "life as a *living* hell" and "*Living/LIVING* as heavenly aliveness"; the narrow passage from underworld to sacred oversoul. It is time to remove the shame of being human, or having feelings and openly expressing them.

This *Self-Realization series* is written so *You* recognize which dimension of *You/you/ YOU* expresses and creates within each given moment. In order to illustrate your multidimensional aspects of *Being/being/BEING,* certain words are italicized as (1) all lowercase, (2) first letter uppercase and the remaining lowercase, or (3) all uppercase. Lowercase designation refers to the shadow-animal-monster state. First letter capitalized, with remaining ones lowercase, illustrates your unconscious-conditioned-robotic expression. All capital letters represents a more aware-sacred-embodied humanity. When two have been combined, your energy encompasses both spectrums.

When all three are written—such as *Self/self/SELF*— the entirety of your expression is present. All dimensions of *You* exist simultaneously, although one prominently leads. For a detailed understanding of this wording style, go to the section titled "Glossary of Terms" at the end of this book. Otherwise, disconnect the mind and trust your intuitive nature to connect with the text as written. Let its medicine work with each level and dimension of *You/you/YOU*.

Within this book, *you/i/we/they* and *you/me/us/them* are also used because there is no separation. *We* cocreate as one entity—the collective—even though *you/i/we/they* appear as separate individuals. If something is true for one of us, it will be true for all of us. *You/i/we/they* are the village that is not currently present, nor has it ever been. If *it takes a village to raise a child,* evidence shows that *you/i/we/they* are quickly destroying all of ours. Let this personal growth become sacred activism that leads toward a golden era of peace.

Book 3—*Knowing: The 7 Human Expressions of Grace* —is a return to the extrasensory and intimate experience of dissolving as you meet your true humanity and begin KNOWING the divine in form. Herein is something *beyond the illusion*, yet woven within it. In succumbing to life and having no control, human grace can be activated. Through deep, contemplative presence, integration, and reflection, *You/you/YOU* become the offering on the altar of Divine Grace.

This *Self-Realization series* is a palpable reminder that Source embarked on a multidimensional experience through *You*. This meandering of *Self/self/SELF* is an intentional, integrative relationship that requires your highest commitment and communion. There are many ways to read these books. (1) Choose a section that corresponds to the "*blessing/illusion/grace*" current life experience you are encountering. Each section stewards you to higher octaves of experience. (2) Focus on the bold quotes. Let nuggets inspire moments of contemplation, meditation, or mantra in an intuitive and mystical approach. (3) Read one paragraph, or one page, daily and allow concepts to sink in. Chew on them. Marinate in inquiry, discussion, or journaling to expand awareness. (4) Let the section titles and italicized subquestions deepen personal exploration. (5) Use the book as an oracle by randomly opening and receiving your message. (6) Read from beginning to end. Then begin again, moving more slowly. (7) Take all three books of the series, reading correlating sections as illustrated in the multidimensional grids. Regardless of method, these are your "how-to" manuals for living, being, and knowing; for slowing you down and deepening your state of presence.

Ponder, contemplate, and meditate on *You*. . . all of *You/you/YOU*.

This trilogy birthed out of my own seven-year experience of deconditioning after experiencing grief, loss, and trauma. These writings are not philosophy, theory, or channeling. I lived what I am sharing. My story is irrelevant to your growth, but the wisdom gained can catapult *You* farther and faster. Focus on your life story. That is the setting for these multidimensional layers. Let nothing distract *You* from this work. It is the most important work *You* can do for yourself and our world.

My spiritual quest has been written throughout two trilogies. The first set of books— ***Conversations with the Universe (CWU), Your Journey to Enlightenment (YJTE),*** and

Your Journey to Love (YJTL)—share early mystical encounters, vulnerable insights, empowering steps, and personal wisdom. *CWU* reflects the mundane and mystical occurrences as signs, symbols, and synchronicities. It depicts a multitude of ways in which the world speaks to you, about you. *YJTE* illustrates breaking away from conformity and homogenization through twelve steps of love, courage, and commitment, to reawaken the divine child within. *YJTL* is the intimate embrace of self as the ultimate soulmate, by unconditionally loving the shadow, human, and divine child. These earlier books are wonderful adjuncts and supportive prerequisites for this new trilogy but are not required. The insights within them will enhance your experience and accelerate your ability to see life in a completely new way. They can be powerful follow-ups to the *Self Realization* trilogy. Trust your intuition to guide your steps.

Let go of what *You* know for all that *you* don't.
Let life be in celebration of *YOU*,
your union, and communion.

Wherever *You* are—whatever *You/you/YOU* are encountering—let this series steward the ascension *You* have been yearning. Place your story and circumstance within the framework of this soulful pilgrimage. Integration occurs in *KNOWING. . . your presence is enough.* This book is likely to be a slow read; one that is to be sipped and savored. *You* may find yourself chewing on one or two pages a week, perhaps one or two paragraphs a day, or one to two lines at a time. The material can be dense because it cuts to the core of feeling things we do not always want to feel. But this is soul work. The ego will fight, resist, and get distracted. Meet *Self/self/SELF* through your devotional, disciplined commitment to the journey of your soul. *You* are being guided into an experience of silence. . . presence. . . and embodiment. Experience *KNOWING*.

Your *knowing* is wishing. . .
until embodying *KNOWING*.
Let intuition guide each step,
on the inside and out.
The path *You* travel is uniquely yours.
What is the point of being human
if not embracing humanity?

knowing.
Why am i/eye/I here?
I/eye/I don't know.

Knowing.
I Know I want to KNOW.

KNOWING.
I AM in the KNOW.

one.

What do eye/i see?

Open to incandescence. . .
your expression of Essence.
Life is the soul's expansion of illumination.
A skintastic suit for Divine Cosmic Awakening. . .
In Laughter, Of Laughter, With Laughter, As Laughter.
The Universe has a sense of humor.
But *You/you/YOU* missed the cosmic joke!
***YOU* are the *YOUNIVERSE*.**

There comes a point when every individual finds themselves on their knees. In that dark of night, it becomes difficult to see. Hope fades away. Faith becomes lost in the rubble. Often, it is a period of isolation and deep grief, where *being* alone feels overwhelming, and *Being/BEING* alive even more so. During these periods, everything *You/you/YOU* have known about yourself is rocked to the core, breaking apart any sense of confidence or *Self* that exists. This obliterating moment is where loss, betrayal, abandonment, injustice, and failure culminate in a tsunami experience. It appears as if life is shattering. However, the jagged edges of your million pieces that lie scattered all over the floor reflect something. Within the sharp and hard edges of your *Being/being/BEING*, glimpses of internal fractures, holes, and conditioned patterns can be found. These parts of *You/you/YOU* are what brought *You* to ground zero.

Believe it or not, what occurred is one of the best things that could happen for *You*, personally and soulfully. These moments hold great opportunity for revealing your tender humanity, which has long rested inside the center of your guarded heart. *You* are about to begin an incredible experience of discovery. What will *You* find? Something larger than *You/you/YOU* could ever fathom. It is sweet, delicate, sacred, and strong. It tastes like transformation. It smells like change. It sounds like courage and feels sacred. But. . . it is a mystery; a deeply hidden *One/ONE*.

**You/you/YOU are the "pupil" in the black void of space,
centered within a pool of white light,
from where YOU gaze upon an infinite creation of your own design.**

The time in front of *You* requires a deep dive into times that have passed, because *You* still carry them. Pushing forward leaves little space for awareness. Pebbles, rocks, and boulders are *being* carried into each new moment; chained to your ankles, carried on your back, lodged in your throat, and held tightly within your hands. *You* venture into the future dragging baggage by both hands, as *You* walk backward into each experience. Your future cannot be *light* with weight unconsciously carried: mental, emotional, familial, ancestral, social, collective, etc.... This does not even account for your additional wardrobes: masks, identities, roles, and personas. For these reasons, life feels tiresome, and certain moments seem heavy. This is *living/being/knowing* unconsciousness.

When things are extremely unbearable, many push past the soul's sacred calls. Unfortunately, *you/i/we/they* are conditioned to believe that getting on with life is more important than *Being/being/BEING* with what life presents. Society models pushing forward, getting over things, and quickly moving past chaos, challenge, conflict, achievements, milestones, and successes. For most, life is more centered upon goals than the journey; upon image rather than presence. Being dismissive about life's profound moments wanes fulfillment. Casually tossing feeling experiences aside for the next need... gratification... goal... or thing... results in an experience of vacancy, meaning *You* aren't where *You/you/YOU* are.

**The moment *You/you/YOU* think there is nothing to see...
is the moment *You/you/YOU* miss what *Is/is/IS* in front of *You*.**

Unspoken beliefs regarding time limits for handling emotion, pain, and suffering hinder higher aspects of *You* from coming forward. Those venturing beyond socially acceptable timetables tend to be regarded with sympathy and pity, instead of honoring the strength to be fully human in the face of where they are. What *You* are unwilling to reveal to yourself creates restlessness in being real with others. Denial and deafness do not support *Self* awareness or spiritual understanding. Ignorance and neglect create weariness within the soul, even if external masks portray differently.

Forging on is a survival tactic. This might be a way to survive, but it is not the way to thrive. Instead, this version of fear, fight, and flight produces the walking dead. Such an approach only prolongs pain and discomfort, causing people to seek other distracting coping mechanisms. Resorting to medications, numbing agents, avoidance techniques, or addictions produces other challenges, suffering, and dysfunction. Issues become compounded, which further create similar echoes of experience. By not facing what is inside, life must provide other eruptions to facilitate uncovering what has long been denied.

What if our most-heart-wrenching moments are calling for presence? What if pain, grief, and loss are the body's signals for respite? What if the soul longs for periods of communion, where the only meaningful work is that of immersing in compassion, listening, and presence? Rarely have any of us been taught to sit with *what is*, to really *hold it*, and *wrap it in love.* In prior experiences of pain and hardship, *You* have likely done what others have: lightly feel, push down, move past, and scab over. Those around *You* might have said— *"Focus on something else," "In time, this will pass; just stay busy," "Stay positive,"* or *"Suck it up, Buttercup."*

Conditioning dissolves with expressions of human grace.
The flowering of humanity opens the way for receiving Divine Grace.

You have put on facades to others. *You* have encountered those who pretend. This is how *you/i/we/they* project *our/their* discomfort; through denial and avoidance. This sort of denial gaslights those around us. Our younger generations are shown that numbing, hiding, and pretending are normal, healthy ways for handling uncomfortable, emotional experiences. Have *You/you/YOU* given in to, or offered, platitudes out of your discomfort in situations? This occurs when not wanting to see other's pain, or feel one's own.

The time has come for an alternative path; a necessary pause... for as long as needed. This means stopping *everything*. A conscious pause is spiritual convalescence in advocacy for humanity. This awakens true aliveness. Time, with timelessness, is necessary to become aware of pain and suffering being held. Spaciousness dissolves conditioning by providing a landscape in which to feel. Your discomfort began from the moment *YOU* were conceived in consciousness. Space is required for dismantling generational tendencies and long-held identities, while also absorbing unconscious physical, cellular, generational, ancestral, and collective energies that exist. Every ache, pain, and condition stems from memory lodged within.

When present with suffering, conditions are ripe for reuniting what is separate. This moment is the moment for bridging individual unconsciousness and collective conscious presence. That occurs only within the present moment, through deep intimacy with *Self.* This is the devotional path of the soul. The ego will want nothing to do with that; it is interested only in gaining significance in the outside, illusory world.

You can more quickly and powerfully effect outer change by doing inner work. *You,* your body, and all of life are the harmonic convergence that creates the interconnection of collective *MIND/BODY/SPIRIT—IS*ness. *ThIS,* amid the full spectrum of your humanity, has a substantive effect upon generational and collective healing. Bridging these individual and collective multidimensional layers integrates the ascension of the lower *self* with the descension of the higher *SELF,* into the unification of cosmic wholeness.

You/I/We/They are signs, symbols, and synchronistic
messes/messages/messengers of how the world speaks to Us about Us/us/US.

Devotion requires radical honesty, absolute bravery, and wholehearted willingness. Time and presence create conditions for opening the heart. *You* cannot merely think the heart open. *Opening* means sinking into the well of grief, and slipping into your fractured spaces. The sadness *You/you* desperately want to avoid offers a great and holy baptism where, if willing to drink of its waters, *YOU* shall be resurrected. This is an unconventional method of letting go, because it asks *You* to loose your grasp on reality, while also staring directly into it.

The seven human expressions of grace gently walk *You* through the shadows of death to dissolve your *self* of the purgatory embedded within the folds of illusion. However, it is necessary to have someone, an animal or constant companion, throughout the process, so to remember what is real. *LOVE* is real. Your *animal/companion* must be *One/ONE* who loves *You* deeply and can see your Essence, despite circumstances. They must commit to being your sacred witness and vision keeper. This means they hold the vision while *You* cannot. It also means they can be present, without the need to interfere with your feeling process. This unconditionally loving act not only serves *You* in remembering *what-you-are* but also catalyzes soul expansion. *You/you* have not met the true *YOU* yet.

Life is a deeply personal walk. It began long before *YOU* become *You/you*. Awareness of *YOU* originated within the cosmic sphere of Divine imagination. Consciousness receded as *You/you* were imprinted through a variety of dimensional environments. Conscious awareness did not go anywhere; it remained within *You/you/YOU*. This presence relaxed deeply inside but has always been available and accessible. Now, *You/I/We/They* must return to this original, relaxed, natural awareness and access our innate divine power.

To get a true sense of. . . *WHAT YOU ARE,*
understand. . . *Who You Are,* and. . . *how you are.*

Your life was designed to teach *You/you/YOU* about patience, trust, love, and presence. Do not run from what *You* are given. Slowly breathe in presence. Sip of patience. Savor the moment. Each experience presents an invitation for bestowing human grace, especially those of pain, challenge, hardship, and tragedy. Individuals embarking upon the courageous walk of uncovering Essence change their world on quantum levels. Rather than the complex interference of conditioning, belief systems, personal will, or continuous action. . . a simpler path is available. Transformation and transmutation are a result of noninterference, nonaction, and presence. Embodiment creates a visceral experience of the distinction between force and power.

You will see that your story is irrelevant, yet integral. You will discover that bodily senses are inextricably linked to human vices but must be fully experienced to open to your subtle senses. When experiencing subtle and gross body sensations—and subsequently transcending them—*You* naturally rise through stages of enlightenment detailed in many esoteric and sacred texts. The miraculous is always available to *You* through the practical, devotional embrace of everyday, ordinary experiences. Are *You* ready to *know* what makes life hard? Would *You* like to *Know* your human graces, and *KNOW* an experience of greater ease? The secret lies in fully absorbing the essence and energies of your experiences.

Treasures hide in plain sight,
amid daily happenings. . .
from the numb and painful. . . mundane and tragic. . .
to beautiful and blissful. . . sensory and nourishing.
Your richness is alchemically sealed within a story of time.
You are Pandora's box.
Light, peace, and joy live inside as precious gems.
Be opened. . . Be open. . .
and set the *SELF free/Free/FREE.*

knowing.
How do things change?
i/eye/I need to change.

Knowing.
I have everything within me to change the world i/eye/I see.

KNOWING.
I AM here. I AM here. I AM here.

NOTES

---

echoes.

What follows me?

Every moment is an echo of prior experience.
Each action and reaction has a cascading effect. . .
rippling from center,
and returning to Source.
Echoes reverberate in seven-year increments.
The farther the echo,
the larger the impact,
and louder its emanation.
Life is designed to bring *You/you/YOU*
back to the origin point
in each string of echoes.

Things that occur are not random. Your life is filled with echoes. A symphony of sound and energy will unfold as echoes of experience collide. Each new stanza of life appears different; yet, each chorus echoes a repeating theme or message. Echoes are incredibly subtle. However, once aware, they become loud and clear. When life's echo moments appear, an experience will look, feel, vibrate, and have the energy of an originating moment. You will see this by the energy and feeling that is invoked from within *You*.

Life's blessings—especially those of a challenging nature—are born of stories, which consist of rippling and converging echoes. Dense echoes carry the residual energies of betrayal, deceit, doubt, and inauthentic living that have been long held. Life also reveals echoes of empowered living. Moments of joy, cycles of success, and great achievements create energetic imprints within life's rhythmic experience. Echoes can last for extensive periods, over an entire life, or across many lifetimes if not dissolved.

Sacred echoes are catalytic moments of truth, wisdom, and sovereignty that produce leaps in consciousness. These "aha moments," "awakenings," and "profound moments" are never singular. They are shifts and expansions that build upon prior awareness. Sacred echoes can be momentary or long lasting. Unfortunately, most do not sit within any of these experiences long enough to gather the magic they offer.

**The future—yours and seven generations forward—
is dependent upon how *You/you/YOU* engage with and purify "this" moment.**

Life's echoes continue until dissolved through awareness and pure presence. When a moment in time is fully cleared and integrated, it is said to have healed seven generations forward and seven generations back. This cannot be done by the mind. It is possible only through disintegration within the body's cellular memory. The concept of generational healing implies ancestral family or legacy children. However, each experience can have its own generational rippling; a seven-year span that echoes. Clearing requires deep inner work and focus. We cannot think or wish away accumulated density. The mind will trick *You* in to believing that is possible, but your body is a storage facility of time. You will have a physical release when something has been cleared: that of the body, through emotion or shifts in dis-ease. In choosing emotion as your release valve, *You* can avoid physical issues and disease.

Healing family generations—forward and back—occurs after first acknowledging, embracing, and dissolving your personal lineage of connected echoes, meaning those stemming from the earliest point of *your life* to the latest experience of *your life*. This is why remaining present to your inner work is important. *You/I/We/They* remain unconscious to how we powerfully impact our world, and other people, when not present with ourselves.

**YOU are the pond. . . *you* are the drop.
You are the echo. . . your life is the ripple.**

Just as a drop of water within a pond creates expanding waves, so does each experience occurring from in utero to age seven. Echoes stem from physical memory during this age stage. These are gross, visceral sensations. Reoccurrences of charged, unintegrated experiences echo in seven-year cycles, building within the layers of each subsequent *body/band/veil* that forms around *You*. These *bodies/bands/veils* include your emotional body, mental body, energetic body, etheric body, auric body, and so on. These bodies are your inner experience that mirrors as outer experience.

This spectrum of *bodies/bands/veils* from conception through in utero create echoes. It houses the conditions and conditioning for social aspects of your life experience. These timeless *bands* include your climactic body, cultural body, ancestral body, collective body, universal body, galactic body, and so on. These soul *bodies/bands/veils* record historical experience that weave into your lifescape.

An echo is the pure reflection of a vibration or sound meeting itself after traveling outward. *You* create echoes all the time. So does everyone else. This is why there is too much noise. *You* are part of everything that existed before now; the reverberation of a divine drop cast in curiosity and discovery eons ago. As echoes, *you/i/we/they* collide and dance like raindrops of intermingling concentric circles on a pond. Each creates an effect that impacts those surrounding it. Life is, and has always been, *Self/self* calling unto the *SELF* in this manner. This is the great illusion. . . because, *You/you/YOU* and *eye/i/I* are reaching for the same. . . *ONE*.

You must choose to *KNOW.*
But, *You* **must** *Know* **to choose.**

To be in full receptivity of *Self/self/SELF*-awareness, follow your life path completely, consciously, and devotedly. Take nothing as insignificant, or for granted. In this way, every human thread powerfully weaves into the soul's grand design. Do not stop, deny, discount, or ignore any part of your journey before its rightful conclusion or *You* will tread the same path again, within this life or another. Living fully within the mystery requires wild abandon. When absorbing the parts of *You/you* that are deadened, struggling to survive, or just getting by... *You/YOU* become free. To absorb means to dissolve back into yourself.

Human beings become fragmented, compartmentalized, and disjointed through early life experiences, generational legacies, and collective energies. Do not release anything. That action magnifies afflictions. Instead, these experiences and expressions must be brought back into *You* through absorption and integration. That which became separated into *You* and *you* and *YOU* must reunite. Only then can *You* truly "let go" of your illusions. Aches, pains, ills, and illusion create the perception of separation. Bring your *Self/self/SELF* home; absorb all pieces that were cast away. The same is true for aspects of connection, wealth, joy, and sacredness. These too have been denied, feared, and abandoned. Your goodness must be absorbed, or this remains at the surface.

Illumination sits inside your cells. Alchemy resides within your body. It exists in areas that your ego does not want seen, heard, or acknowledged. A world within worlds has forever hummed deeply inside. The persistence of a timeless and immortal memory continually pulses within your cellular structure. A sacred romance began eons ago when *THE ONE* separated into two, and two became many. All of life arose from that originating revelation; expanding and contracting through constructs of oneness, duality, and multiplicity. Time and illusion flooded in, expanding and morphing possibility into infinite degrees. Everything that occurred since then is merely echoes of that cosmic moment of separation. Yet, the real remained consistent, ever present, and witnessing... as silence, space, and stillness. This is where *You* must go. First, discover all of the noise, busyness, and clutter your life holds. Then, make your way to divine emptiness, nothingness, and *BEING nowhere/now-here.*

Your life is a bridge of oneness...
Awaken to *KNOWING.* **.. life is a dream of your own making.**
Let this recognition resound of truth.
With this, all noise will cease; only pure silence will remain.

knowing.
What can i/eye/I do about the darkness and evil in the world?
I do not have to believe the monstrous world i/eye/I see.

Knowing.
I embrace the shadow, animal, monster, and human parts of me.

KNOWING.
Light is within me.

NOTES

whispers.

What beckons?

**You chose the scenic route
and strayed from the straight and narrow path.
A curvy road filled with detours, exit ramps, and stops.
Adventure unfolds upon windy roads.
It beckons. . . flirts. . . teases. . . and tantalizes.
Do not fret, worry, or struggle. . .
even these lead home.
Life guides your way. . .
as magical signs, sacred symbols,
and timeless synchronicity.
Life is speaking to *You/you/YOU*. . .
about *You/you/YOU*. . .
always leading toward *YOU*.
Whispers will point *You* toward remembering. . .
You/you/YOU are playing a game. . .
of hide-and-seek.**

Earth is not a school. If it were, it would be a mystery school. Earth is a playground for aliveness to emerge and expand, through *You*. Earth's playground of dimensional reality is for exploration and discovery. Every individual is born with a body of grace. It is yours to find and activate. *You* are infused with integral elements for engaging divine alchemy. However, specific conditions—and conditioning—are required for *You/you/YOU* to access them. Receiving human grace impacts your cellular structure, alchemically initiating an inner awakening. Discipline and devotion must expand and deepen for the full disintegration process to initiate this receivership of *SELF*.

The sacred is within everything. *You/I/We/They* are the *I AM* presence. . . in every way, shape, and form. The *I-to-WE* experience brings about this expansive realization. This cannot be an intellectual concept or process. It requires embodied experience. In the instant *You Know/KNOW* this, nothing can ever be the same. Perspective and perception will be altered completely.

You/you/YOU are a faceted crystal that siphons light through multiple faces. *YOU* encompass many lenses through which to see, feel, and imagine. Your *True Love's Kiss* is to be tendered, for awakening the *ONE*. This kiss does not come from the outside, another person, an event, or a touch. It occurs within *Self/self/SELF* as *remembrance*. Through internal atmospheric pressure that has built over time, remembering unfolds. In forgetting original *SELF*, *YOU* expanded the experience of form and density into a multiplicity of forms and duality.

You/you/YOU are the prayer,
and the pray-er. . .
for a sacred and divine revelation to come.

The Grace of:	The Remembering	Knowing
The Illusion:	What has to dissolve?	Aliveness
True Love's Kiss:	What nature is required?	Creation
Aura of the:	What is emerging?	Unification
Fragrance Emitting:	What is the inhale?	Truth
Flavor of:	What is the exhale?	Energy
Melody Through:	What is harmonizing?	Growth
Visceral:	What is being absorbed?	Wisdom
Alchemy:	What can be transmuted?	Infinite Presence
Essence as:	What may be embodied?	The Void
Forgiving:	What is for giving?	Awareness

From the infinity of timelessness
to the beginning of time,
each moment, action, reaction, and inspired action
has been a *Divine/divine/DIVINE* child's play,
initiated by the *ONE/One/one* who first made sound.
Beginning with the *Word/word/WORD*. . .
whose casting is your magic wand of creation.

The *aura* is an emission of light that surrounds *You*. As your frequency heightens, through the absorption of anything denied or held separate, higher levels of light emanate *Being/ BEING*. The aura reflects your radiance, from the awareness of divinity inside your cells. This illumination creates changes within your body, brain, and life experience, producing the heavenly fragrance *You/you/YOU* are to emit.

Fragrance pours forth from within. Each individual gives off a unique scent. The sense/scents of discernment gauge people, places, and things via the odor or fragrance being emitted. Your animal nature's sense/scents of smell intuitively guide awareness as to what is safe or unsafe, healthy or unhealthy. However, *You* have forgotten how to tune into these instincts: animal, human, and divine. As *You* cultivate your sense of discernment for fear, greed, hate, kindness, love, and purity. . . gut instincts strengthen the use of your senses in unique ways.

Individual smells are as discernible as apple pie, cologne, burnt, or garbage. For example, people associate Mother Mary with the scent of roses. Sometimes this fragrance exists despite no roses being present. Mother Mary's essence of unconditional love hangs within the air. *You* have a Divine fragrance; your blend of pure expression. As essence awareness is more present within *Self/SELF*, your personal fragrance becomes enhanced. *Scent-sitivity* facilitates inspired action, direction, and attraction.

Flavor represents the palpable *manner/manna* of your embodied nature. Flavor is the seasoning of your distinct expression, which comes through your experiences.

Melody reflects the rhythm and fluidity of your soulful expression. It is your energy, heart, gut, and mind in alignment with one another. As these harmonize, the soul more easily expresses its true voice, tone, and flow.

Visceral relates to the palpable sensation and texture of what is residually held within your physical form. It is often lingering echoes from early life. This cellular and physical imprinting of pain, trauma, and discordance requires attention and transmutation. When old energies dissolve. . . greater freedom, naturalness, peace, and ease are experienced. It is necessary to transition from *being* "embedded" energy into *KNOWING* "embodied" experience.

Essence is the infinite space and presence of your Divine nature. This is accompanied by innocence. *Essence* is remembered through consciously *LIVING/BEING/KNOWING* an awake and aware state that encompasses truth, purity, and lightness.

In *KNOWING* every other as *You/you/YOU*, no separation can exist, or disconnection. When that holy vision dawns within your consciousness, body, and nature. . . nothing can wound, rile, empower, or inspire *You*. No craving, desire, or aversion can possess *You*. No teacher, healer, or other can give *You* anything; nor can *You/YOU* give another what they believe is missing. Union, communion, equanimity, and oneness reveal these *Truths/TRUTHs*. This flowering of Divine consciousness is the ultimate whispering of *BEING*.

Moments tick. . .
the mind talks. . .
the past echoes,
the future cries out.
You are all of it.
You are none of it.
You/you/YOU are *Oneness;*
every *One/one/ONE* and every *Thing/thing/THING*.
You/you/YOU are *LIFE,*
the paradox of *life,*
the experience of *Life*. . .
and the expression of eternal aliveness.

knowing.
Why is this happening?
i/eye always give myself exactly what I/eye require to grow.

Knowing.
I Am doing the best I can.

KNOWING.
I AM essential to life.

complexity.

What do you have to dissolve?

Many lives and many masters converge
as the unified experience of *You/you/YOU*;
expressing emotionally, spiritually, mentally,
energetically, physically, and conditionally.
As *You* journey within this grand realm. . .
your tree of life will form.
This intricate symbol is *You/you/YOU*.
As sands of time pixelate your human experience. . .
a holy design is laid down.
Depicting a *memory-all* of your expression,
life's sacred mandala is created
and dissolves each time *You/you/YOU* find completion.
Your incarnation is a beautiful layering of light, sound, and color
contrasted by shadow, distortion, and complexity,
casting expressions of change, life, birth, death, and rebirth.
The cascade of divine inspiration
is an intricate, but exquisite, fragmentation of wholeness
that yearns for original simplicity.

The nature of exploration is to travel. . . in and out, up and down, back and forth. With each human expression, the world becomes more complex. Progress and innovation arise out of curiosity and creativity. Yet, in these creative expansions, an unlikely slew of problems also unfolds. Each new endeavor creates more and more and more, ultimately leading to complex systems and structures. It is all divine expression, the yin and yang of creative capacity. Expansion produces ingenuity. The potential to simplify and solve the challenges is born again and again.

Infinity allows for complexity, as a possibility, within the grand design of life. In order to *Know/know/KNOW* itself, infinite creative capacity expresses all forms that can be imagined. Nothing can be created externally unless it is first envisioned internally. Through a multiplicity of genomes and DNA configurations. . . organisms and species. . . creatures and forms. . . the seen and unseen. . . life awakens into morphing creations of matter, time, and spacial configuration, the complexity of which is intriguing, inviting, and inspiring. In the midst of it all, the contrasts created are triggering, stirring, and mesmerizing. Complexity will suck *You* into its black hole; within it, worlds upon worlds form. A black hole, whether the void of endless vice or that of creation, eternally exists inside *You*, not outside. *You* are a complex *Being/being/BEING* within the simplicity of eternal space.

You were born unto life to fulfill its longings.
Do not bamboozle yourself into believing life is not
subject to your shortsighted ones.

Complexity brings with it pressure, impatience, and tension. What was a simple idea can become too much: too much to deal with, too many people, too much stuff, too many issues, too many problems. There become too many layers, too many steps, and too many ties that bind. When *too much* is too much, it is because invisible strings of attachment have formed. These create the tension *You* feel, and the contrast experienced. *You* find yourself amid boxes, ceilings, and compartments. Mounds of clutter create further chaos. *More* is not necessarily better; it is more. How does it happen? What began as a one-celled organism has evolved into an entire world that now creates AI, space stations, and technology capable of more than ever thought possible. It's exciting, yet it's burdensome. It's thrilling, yet tiring. It's what *You/you* want, but *You/YOU* don't.

Life is dynamic, unpredictable, and multidimensional. Consisting of interconnected relationships and parts, life builds from inspiration, action, and reaction. Energy fluctuations, along with accompanying feedback loops, create the patterns and rhythms of our world. Each movement changes, expands, and increases. While at the same time, the complexity that built what is in front of *You*. . . also destroys it. The systems and structures that come into existence are bound to fail from the moment they are born. The cycle of life always includes death. Creative capacity, curiosity, and innovation eventually will destroy what was. Like a beautiful, shifting kaleidoscope, beauty abounds within our endless cycles of birth, death, and rebirth, eternally manifesting and dissolving through a space-time continuum.

Life's creative exploration never had anything to do with _You_.
It was born of a *simple* desire for experience.
Do not make life more complicated than that.
Everything is simply experience.

You/i/we/they are incredibly complex creatures, composed of rhythms and systems. The body is a high-tech piece of equipment with many levels, layers, and sheaths, seen and unseen. Within *You* exists the capacity to create anything, and *You/you/YOU* do. However, things become difficult and complex due to the meanderings of your *Mind/mind*. Little do *You* realize the simple and profound power of *MIND*. Through this magical portal, the power of *Knowing/knowing/KNOWING* can, and will, create anything *You* focus on. This is divine genius but, when wielded unconsciously, takes on a life of its own. When human beings think too much, duality and density taint the creative meanderings of genius. Too much thinking leads to psychosis of the *Mind/mind*, meaning an endless loop of thoughts or continual processing of information. Repetitions within *Mind/mind/MIND* create belief on conscious and subconscious levels. Belief systems are another trap of complexity.

Sometimes, life feels hard. Life challenges, obstacles, crisis, and chaos can bring things to *the head*. Frustration, stuckness, helplessness, or hopelessness hover like dark clouds. With this turmoil, it becomes difficult to see... to hear... and *KNOW*. When too many obstacles hinder pathways, solutions and exit strategies are not easily discerned. With every path blocked, little room for possibility remains. A way through will not feel easy. This can occur within one area of life or touch every corner of experience when in psychosis.

Complexity exists due to the willful and controlling manner in which your life is *Being/being* lived. Our complex world churns with self-centered willfulness, rather than our natural capacity for joy, play, and imagination. *You/you* are the artist; life is your art form. And, until now, unconsciousness and conditioning have been your mediums.

YOU are light. Yet often, *You/you* are dense as a doorknob.

Stories are the riverbanks that guide history's future, but they are irrelevant to higher mastery. Stories depend upon time. They need past, present, and future. They require characters, heroes, and villains. Stories strengthen your false *Self/self*. The false *self* is not a *wrong self*; it is simply identification with a lower master. This occurs when living upon the horizontal spectrum of time. Horizontal living remains focused on *story*, which has ties to lower vibrational energies. *You* always have a choice... to remain within the complexity of story, or to move toward the simplicity of presence. With *self-grace*... stories, shadows, and energies that veil your world are absorbed. *Mind/mind/MIND* concocts these colorful stories and never-ending movies, recording and storing them. The ego requires these, not the soul.

Presence comes through your soul nature. This higher place of mastery does not get hooked by contrast, positivity, negativity, or duality. Each step of experience is approached with devotion. *Living/LIVING* a consciously aligned life is of utmost importance for the soul-focused individual. This expression of *SELF* embodies vertically aligned words, thoughts, and actions. Devotional presence makes way for spiritual maturity through periods of aloneness, silence, contemplation, and meditation. These disciplines awaken *Mind/MIND* and cultivate greater light from within.

With simplicity, less is more. There is less of everything else, and more of *You/YOU*.

Life does not see complications, problems, or complexity. *You/you/YOU* do. Life celebrates all that manifests as your reality. It is not concerned with the direction of an expression, or the outcome. There is no attachment to the degree of light or shadow emitted, or interference with what manifests. Life expresses infinity to experience creation to the nth degree. That, in itself, is the embodiment of simplicity. Complexity and simplicity are *One/ONE*; merely different points of the same spectrum. Here is the paradox: *one* can't exist without the other *ONE*. Even this thought is both simple and complex. It encompasses *KNOWING* the end as the beginning. To know the simple as complex, span from beginning to its farthest reaches. To return to simplicity, go back to *all it was born of*.

The complexity of life comes from your *Mind/mind/MIND*. The thoughts *You/you/YOU* think impact the material world. Worry, fretting, and anguish amplify negative creation. Ruminating over worst-case scenarios, doom-and-gloom possibilities, and failure brings forward all manner of complications. Through these as focus and vision, *You/you* only create more to worry, fret, and anguish about. This is your use of *knowing,* rather than the command of *KNOWING.* The best antidote for any type of complexity is space. Making space allows room for something different to enter. However, making space is a process of depth. This cannot work if performed only on the surface. Clear your schedule and freedom would exist immediately. Clear your emotional baggage, and you will feel as light and light. Clear the *mind* of what ails it, and the body can be freed from illness and dis-ease.

Complexity and simplicity coexist. Paradox requires both within this realm's land of opposites: holding *what is true* and *what is false* simultaneously. Life utilizes contradictions for your experience, and its own. Complexity will pull *You/you* into its trap. Simplicity will guide *You/YOU* out. Complexity will be the death of *You/you.* Simplicity will bring rebirth.

Any thought, word, action, or belief
that anchors doubt, disharmony, ill, or dis-ease is a lie.
Such delusions within an individual and collective psyche
are inherited, are inflicted, or come through being interfered with.
These are not truth,
but the story that was made true.
Emotional legacies weave through time by way of blood,
burrowing into the bodies of offspring and generational legacies.
They live inside endless permutations of life,
until an emerging soul is courageous enough
to bless, transform, and transmute these. . .
through the alchemical process of uniting
demon* and *GOD.
Stop everything. . . Be still. . . Be present.
Heal *Self/self/SELF.* . .
and free your generations to come,
and those that have gone.
Become simple minded.
Become simple hearted.
Simply be. . .

knowing.
Why does life have to be this hard?
i/eye don't have to make life hard.

Knowing.
I look for ease within the contrast.

KNOWING.
I AM the grace of simplicity.

the grace of simplicity.

What is the remembering?

Invite the grace of simplicity. Consciously initiate this.
Let the kiss of the storm invoke the aura of mastery.
The fragrance of beauty reveals your truth.
The flavor of gentleness expands your energy.
Through anticipation, the visceral memory of rage dissolves into balance.
The essence of clarity brings forth alchemy of mind, taking *You/you* to higher ground.
Receive this gift of human grace. . .
KNOWING. . .
your presence is enough.

In the face of extreme challenge, all manner of discord and dis-ease arises. Friends and family might cut and run. Money depletes. Your external world falls apart. *You* are stretched more than you have ever been before. In those moments, *You/you/YOU* might not want to be *here* anymore. *You* find yourself on your knees, praying to be *taken out* because life is overwhelming and painful. The dark night of the soul looks and feels this way. The valley of shadows and death cloaks your life in darkness, failure, or breakdown. However, these arise as opportunities for up-leveling. The contrast surrounding *You* stems from false, misaligned, and hidden parts of *You/you/YOU*. These have to be acknowledged for them to dissolve. Your *tower moment is pointers* for awakening to aspects of *You/you/YOU* that make life complex. The soul is calling *You/you/YOU* to simplicity. Right now, *wake up. . .* not to something larger than *You*, but to what is too small about *You/you*.

Amid the rubble of your insecurities, doubts, and delusions lie the conditioning *You* are constrained by. Life is required to fall away when *You* are not living authentically. Up to now, your experience has been based on others' projections. *You* are *living* who *You* must be, rather than *what YOU are*. Shine the light of higher consciousness into your inner world. Through the grace of simplicity, clear the clutter that exists within your life, your experiences, and *Self/self.*

When life brings crossroads, a fork in the road, or an ending. . . listen for the *small* voice that got *You/you* to this point. The ego loves complexity. That is its playground. Go inside your heart. Hear *SELF* whisper, or scream, *"Let go."* Beware, your *ego* will do everything to drown out, divert, or override this message. But the message will be heard time and time again. And, if continuing not to listen, *You* will create greater complexity in your body, your life, and your relationships. Life's rhythmic stops and starts have purpose. Let the "re-*mind*ers" encourage *You* to stop. . . and simplify.

With the blessing of life, and within the illusion of time, *You/you/YOU* create complexity; to discover the grace of simplicity, as a way of awakening your humanity.

Trigger moments are wake-up calls asking *You/you/YOU* to pause. . . reflect. . . and shift. These are indications of complexity, externally and internally. When wake-up calls occur, the invitation for a more natural, organic expression of *Self/self/SELF* is available. Life will always create circumstances that support *You*, or bring forth those that clear what does not serve *YOU*.

Until *internally* at peace, *You* are not free. Even if out of sight out of mind, these energies *will* remain until neutralized. Clear your triggers; otherwise *You/you/YOU* energetically attract experiences and people that vibrate at that same level. Casually dismissing or outright resisting a challenging person, place, event, or experience only reincarnates the same thing in another way. This is an especially important point to consider when clearing your space of material things, because all things hold energy until dissolved. This also relates to relationships carrying emotional baggage, homes where emotionally charged experiences have occurred, and workspaces where businesses have been before. Triggers occur because energy has been spiked.

You cannot leave until you can stay. You cannot stay until you can leave.

Notice the subtle rumblings of thought and emotion that surround material items. Consider the density that sits within your home, workspace, and relationships. Be aware of any negative associations that rise. Let your feelings, thoughts, and sensations expand, so to be recognized. Material possessions can offer insight into withheld emotions and belief systems that subconsciously run your life. Residual energies reside in the things that surround *You* on a daily basis, positively or negatively affecting your mood, attitude, and energy. How *You* are triggered illustrates your emotional, energetic, and mental ties. Each triggering item possesses *You/you*. Subtle sensations and discordant memories signal that internal work is necessary, so *You* dissolve and absorb any attachments.

Notice the memories or emotions that are activated by particular items. *You* might be unaware of associations to pain or trauma if feeling numb or repressed. Holding ont o things with negative attachment keeps discordant energy resonant within *You,* your space, and your subconscious mind. However, do not release in haste. Nothing should be discarded casually or quickly. Keep things until *You* are clear of the feelings being evoked. Do not take action until neutrality and appreciation for the person, place, or thing has been achieved. Once neutral, keep or give away the item with love, care, and grace. In this way, no residual energies remain. By sorting and clearing your material world, psychological and emotional attachments loosen their hold on *You/you/YOU* and your life. That sense of lightness allows a more authentic *YOU* to begin emerging.

The deceptive intelligence is sneaky. Sometimes *You* may believe attachments are dissolved when they are still present. Be cognizant of holding ont o items once they have been cleared of residual attachment. If they are not needed, do *You* need to keep them? Do not keep jewelry, clothing, or other things that sit unused, packed away, or preserved. If *You* are not using it regularly, get rid of it. The Universe needs space to bring new things into your life. Clear all clutter. This includes papers, books, and clothes. *You* will feel lighter and clearer. Your space will feel more open, and *You* will more easily experience flow.

It is beneficial to release the old and make space for the new. Having too many things in your space, or excess clutter, creates health issues. Clutter manifests as sinus issues, aches, joint pain, illness, and dis-ease. Hoarding creates congestion and stagnancy. Keeping things, but not using them, is linked to the shadow energies of greed and fear.

Unconditional love is supreme simplicity.
It holds nothing. . . expects nothing. . . demands nothing. . . and requires nothing.

The Grace of Simplicity	The Remembering	Knowing
The Illusion—Complexity	What has to dissolve?	Aliveness
True Love's Kiss—The Storm	What nature is required?	Creation
Aura of the Master	What is emerging?	Unification
Fragrance Emitting Beauty	What is the inhale?	Truth
Flavor of Gentleness	What is the exhale?	Energy
Melody Through Movement	What is harmonizing?	Growth
Visceral Memory—Rage	What is being absorbed?	Wisdom
Alchemy of Mind	What can be transmuted?	The Void
Essence as Clarity	What may be embodied?	Infinite Presence
Forgiving Complexity— For Giving Simplicity	What is for giving?	Space

Spiritual simplicity looks like big things leaving your experience: physical items, jobs, people, money, etc. Embodied simplification encompasses the subtle leaving *You*: energy, emotions, visceral sensations, fears, and attachments. Subtle purges offer higher dimensional experiences, creating greater awareness of your multidimensional nature. Continued praxis of dissolving what no longer serves allows clarity to rise. The distinctions among mind, ego, personality, and identity become more discernible. Through ongoing *Self/self/SELF*-reflection, less and less purging will be needed. Your devotional commitment to simplicity will bring ongoing awareness and insight.

By releasing what owns *You*, other voices within will begin speaking. *You* will notice that words of caregivers, family, friends, society, and fear course through your mind. Just listen. Do not follow any impulses. Realize how life has been based upon the thoughts, words, needs, and projections of others. Stay in the body and listen with ever-present inquiry. In releasing your complex quilt of thought forms, layers of conditioning will begin falling by the wayside. As this happens, contemplate who *YOU* are, what *YOU* want, and what true fulfillment is for *YOU*. Aim for the *Truth/TRUTH*. Through presence, something new opens and *You/YOU* will be renewed.

Simplicity is simple. . . it requires very little.

Simplicity is the first step of the deconditioning process. Initial phases of release often occur in bulk, but energetically and emotionally, a full cycle can take up to seven years for completion. If not present to your false selves, visceral energies, and suppressed emotions. . . dis-integration can take longer. When devotional and loving, expansion can occur in an instant. Life is dramatically impacted by your level of presence. As your physical space clears, *You* may have less materially but will feel richer than ever before. A renewed experience of freedom, ease, and weightlessness will wrap itself around *You*. Rise to a new vantage point. Embrace a higher vision. Simplifying your life is the beginning. . . of the end.

Be the ever-present champion, sister, brother, friend,
and fellow traveler of all others in this great reunion.
But do not carry their baggage; do not even carry your own.

You must step out of time, and away from issues of the past. Do not push toward the future. The illusion of time must dissolve so that *You/you/YOU* are present to what is in your face. . . your space. . . your mind. . . your heart. . . and your energy. *You* have accumulated a great deal over time. This stage of humanity has to do with listening to your world, your experiences, and your heart. Through listening, sense how and when *You* swim upstream, against the current. Clear actions of efforting, strain, stress, and struggle. There is no need to hold on to any of that.

The grace of simplicity comes with timelessness. Timelessness is a great healer and transducer. The gift of timelessness clears not only inner and outer clutter, but also ancestral and physiological time. Let life show *You* where to apply grace. Lean in. Clear *inner, outer,* and *under* worlds, so that whispers of longing and fulfillment are heard through the grace of simplicity.

You **have been asleep. . . awaiting the kiss of true love. Life's soft vermillion grazes**
your skin. . . beckoning *You* **to follow the road less traveled.**
You/you/YOU **are not alone.** *You/you/YOU* **have never been.**
Awaken to the one who dreams, and see the watcher.
Lean in. . . love and be loved. Be held softly. Be hugged gently. Be kissed tenderly.

knowing.
How do i/eye make things simpler?
eye/i/I can choose the path of least resistance.

Knowing.
I Am discovering how to let go.

KNOWING.
I AM weightless.

...

TRUE LOVE'S KISS—THE STORM

What nature is required?

Swept away by this kiss of true love. . .
your atmosphere is electric and defining.
Your clouds of consciousness are richly charged,
sparking thoughts within your dark, gray matter.
As thunder booms, discordant sounds release,
bringing lightning bolts of insight that illuminate peace.
Sacred waters stream forth in sadness, joy, grief, and relief.
In the dark night, be the rod of understanding,
by *Knowing/KNOWING* the *God/god/GOD You* are commanding.
Be the breaking through of divine light. . .
reclaim your sacred and solemn birthright.

Mother Nature is like any mother. . . she loves, nurtures, disciplines, and expresses when her children act up. If *You* do not come *in* now and then, nature will create a way for *You/you/YOU* to. Personal storms assist the return to naturalness. Each one comes bearing gifts of growing instinct, increased intuition, and new aliveness. *You* are nature. *You* are the waters of emotion. *You* are the electricity of thought. *You* are earthen grounding, where sustainable change is possible. *You* are separation and oneness, dancing through inner climate change of your emotions.

Each storm is a rite of passage that opens *You/you/YOU* to mentally, emotionally, energetically, and physically growing beyond current conditions. Storms catalyze inherent gifts, skills, and talents. These unfold as *You* move through the storm, empowering your ability to live, be, know, and thrive. Storms are experiences that sometimes stun, leaving *You* speechless. Other storms bring *You* to the ground, requiring everything in your life to rebuild. At times, storms are the emergence of your unconscious, reactive, explosive aspects, mirroring any shadowy, lowbrow ways. As *You* discover the beauty of being *lost at seeing*. . . *YOU* also are becoming the lighthouse. In time, *You* will celebrate these tumultuous moments for the higher consciousness expansion, personal growth, and spiritual maturity they provide. Gratitude for each emerging storm arises when able to see the whole picture.

In engaging the path of seeker, emotional obsessions abound;
storms, big and small, hide within your earthen ground.

You/you/YOU might be feeling the early stages of clouds rolling in, a full-blown
storm, or experiencing an ending. Something new potently hangs in the air, causing
the atmosphere to smell fresh, but also, another deluge appears to be on the way.

Although the desire to lunge forward into the new is near, be with the friction that *You* feel in your atmosphere. Let it bring *You/you* its gifts. Otherwise, in leaping quickly forward, *You* take the storm into "the new."

Be aware and beware; the external storm experience has enough power to make the false real. Do not become ensnared within darkening clouds of thought spurred by the outside. Do not be enveloped by negative currents in your world, no matter how these flirt, tease, cajole, or taunt. Do not mistake the density as real or believe it to be true. In doing so, life will manifest more of the same, and with greater intensity. Instead, let the external be a pointer. Allow it to guide *You* toward internal storm conditions, feeling places within the body that are wrought with booming thoughts and charged with electricity. Feel the thundering rain that wants to beat from inside *You*. Hold that place. Precipitation may stream through the windows of your soul. Ride each wave, allowing recognition to bring calm. There is no need to shelter from the storm. It is *You/you*. Instead, quell your internal atmosphere by standing in reverence for its power. Emergent thoughts will pop powerfully, giving rise to the discordant energy within.

Everything is inside *You/you/YOU*.
What manifests externally is the mirror of that.

Inner storms flurry with reactionary thoughts and emotions. They seemingly strike out of nowhere. However, these moments reveal your reactivity…restlessness…misdirection…and escapism. They illustrate the lower vibrations weighing down your life. Storms also hold breakthroughs of awareness, and bursts of insight that cleanse your space. Most importantly, they create the path to mastery: mastery of mind, mastery of emotions, mastery of energy, mastery of the physical, and mastery over the spiritual.

In staying present to the storm, *You* may find yourself steeped in puddles of regret, resentment, and righteousness. Slothfulness may assault *You/you/YOU*. Ancient shadows of greed, vanity, lust, and jealousy may surface. Do not ignore these subtleties. These elements block your life, love, ease, and freedom. These are the clouds that repeatedly hang over your head, heart, and life. Breathe through all that rises. Remain still, as a sacred witness.

These energies not only are inside *You* but also encompass the friction resting within the collective field. Breathe with these energies; breathe for the world's collective unconscious to become conscious. Bring the world into the shelter of your heart. Remove the heavy cloaks of those who most offend and anger *You*; invite them to sit and stay awhile. Recognize these close and distant relatives for the truth they bring. Respectfully be with them for the duration of their stay. Get to know this band of weary travelers. They seek your companionship, friendship, and love. They have arrived at your door, to meet their brethren and be led to higher ground. *They* are *You/you*. You are *Them/them*. See them this way, or they cannot leave.

Life's reflections are your storm-tracking system.
Let it be your barometer for pressure building inside.

Even if the storm relates to people and things outside *You*, pay no attention to their words or actions. Clouds of anger and reaction will appear; let them, but take these inside to naturally subside. Lightning strikes and thunder claps will initiate the impulse to *do something*! However, any outside activity is merely distraction from the real issue. Do not do anything; be still. Let impulses pass without interference. When the wind whips your emotions higher, go inside the body and ground *Self/self* until they settle down. Hold space while the elements of your nature rant and rave. . . scream, cry, and sigh. Do nothing; commit to the storm.

Your current experience is a manifestation of a prior state. Be present to what is in front of *you*, so that any beliefs beneath surface awareness transform. Subconscious beliefs and vibrations manifested your current reality. Unless brought to awareness, cloudy thoughts will continue bringing storms. Center into feeling *self* and *Self*, while aspiring toward the embodiment of *SELF*. Inquire upon *Knowing* and *Being* your next best expression. Higher octaves of *You/YOU* require space, practice, and focus.

As the storm within subsides, note the subtle trembling that begins within your ankles and feet and rumbles through different parts of your body. Notice how *You* are shaken to your core. This is your distrust: of *God/god/GOD*, life, others, and *Self/self/SELF*. *You* cannot feel this subtle sensation unless very still and quiet. It hums within your organs and shivers inside bone. It is explained away as stress and inflammation. But this keeps the body constricted, and your life restricted. Sink down and feel ungrounded. Your roots loosen with each storm that occurs. Do not hesitate to fall apart. Crumble. Pause. Let the ground deepen *unknowing* and cultivate new *Knowing/KNOWING*. In time, *You* will rebuild trust, with *Self/SELF*, others, life, and a new understanding of *God/GOD*.

There is nothing and no one outside *You/you/YOU*.
Life is a projection screen.

At times, storms feel everlasting. However, their purpose is to bring up everything that is unlike *LOVE*. Insights shall rise through your mental fog with patience and time. When swells ensue, exercise your ability to remain calm. Do not amplify issues with fear, worry, and identity-driven freewill choices. Free will creates added turbulence. This unconscious interference often creates additional steps. Breathe. Life knows how to navigate what is coming.

As the storm subsides, breathe in the fresh scent of *mourning,* so that remaining heaviness clears. Inner work and pure presence can clear any storm, inner or outer. Learn how to ground within chaos. Discover how to steady yourself in times of turbulence. Continually clarify the *eye/i/I* at the center. Tame *Mind/mind* and heart. A neutral space is the most powerful antidote to what is polarized.

In developing mastery, life will feel lighter, clearer, and stronger. Dive into the heart and womb of your creations. Everything is energy. All is connected. Either feel and absorb what exists internally, or fully experience the world's mirror of what *You/you/YOU* hold. Your outer life is an obstacle course that guides, empowers, and strengthens mastery. Be with the conscious and unconscious. Release the complexity of external circumstances. Embody internal simplicity.

May the storms that follow be of heart-pounding love, and lightening laughter. May your inner and outer fires burn with presence and purpose. May rising waters flood forth with generosity and compassion. May winds blow in positive change. May the *eye/i/I* be seen with love, compassion, and unity. May *You/you* realize all that has been denied, so that *You/YOU* are illuminated by all there is to receive. May your conscience be clear. . . and all discordance be cleared. May Divine Will bring interference to its end. See, hear, feel, acknowledge, and *KNOW* the *TRUTH* of *BEING,* by raising a cathedral of Holy Spirit within your earthen temple.

The outside is merely a gauge for up-leveling mastery.
It reveals your weather changes.
Be the calm center of every experience.
Don't be the storm, or the chaos within it.
Otherwise, *You/you/YOU* are part of the problem.
When *you* become problematic. . .
remember,
You/you/YOU are also the solution.

knowing.
How do eye/i/I move through a storm?
eye/i/I can come inside.

Knowing.
I Am able to navigate the weather that rises.

KNOWING.
I AM nature.

. . .

AURA OF THE MASTER

What is emerging?

Catch sight of the truth. . .
It's right in front of *You.*
You/you/YOU have long held your own tail. . .
devouring yourself each step of the way.
End your chase.
What *You/you/YOU* seek is within your grasp.
It has always been.
Stop.
There is no point in running,
and nothing to run after.
There is no end to achieve,

or a beginning from which to start.
***You/you/YOU* are the journey**
of a continuous experience;
the eternal and everlasting experience. . .
of unfolding mastery.

Long ago, *You/you/YOU* were imprinted with illusion: false ideas. . . false perceptions. . . false beliefs. . . a false *self/Self*. *You/you* fell into a black hole of deception, where lies upon lies built an illusion of smoke and mirrors. This created hard edges, boxes, constructs, and conditions. It left little room for other things to enter, reducing your presence and awareness to truth and wisdom. *You/YOU* took on animal fever. Shadow faces hid within your brush, with life. The innocent *child/cub* became wounded.

The human *self* is raw, animal and reptilian; a usurper of power, while also feeling oppressed. An aspect, deeply hidden within *You*, is a feral creature, filled with pain from experiencing a world gone mad. It writhes. It hungers. It hunts. It hums with an undercurrent that is a kill-or-be-killed instinct. All people have an animal *self*, either feral and hungry, or regal and free. *Living* in survival mode encompasses the former. Survival is fueled by adrenaline and fear. To be regal and free means healthy fear is present, but greatly superseded by inner power. Watch animals. They are present. They remain in the present moment. *You/you/YOU* have forgotten this great power. *You* do not access this deep instinctual nature. By living beyond the present. . . instinct, sense discernment, and intuitive timing fade.

Reflect the energy of Spirit to expand the aura of Master.
In raising your vibration, our global reflection of energy also shifts.

Even when expressing inauthentically, a way is still made to experience authentic humanity. Through darkness, the auric field builds in mastery by surmounting all that life brings. *You* must become your own mama bear, or king of the jungle. Living awake, aware, and mindful of *Self/self/SELF* is a daily practice for attaining mastery. This is not possible without feeling and absorbing your depths of withheld ignorance and pain. In the raw experience of facing and absorbing emotions, the transition from an active, unconscious, animal nature into a conscious, receptive, *divine* expression begins. Spiritual maturity awakens through understanding, ahas, and insights. Leaps of consciousness come with presence to your experiences and expressions. In reclaiming your birthright, *You* return to the garden of eden with the softness of humanity, purity of the child, and awareness of a Master.

Mastery is not a ladder to climb.
It is the consistent practice of reflection, remembering, and alignment.

Mastery is an experience of absorption—reclaiming all that was denied—so that *ALL* of *You/you/YOU* dissolves into pure awareness. Experiences are manifestations of conscious and unconscious selves. *You/you/YOU* are not yet aware of the magnitude of your pretending. Much of life has been your lie; your personal bondage and *Self/self/SELF-* imprisonment. The truth is *You* were designed to live as pure, unfettered experience.

Mastery is gained through the knowledge and acceptance of your experiences and expressions. Let life be your mirror, guide, teacher, and guru.

Mastery is intimately tied to alignment; that of thoughts, words, and actions. Be cognizant of the words *You/you/YOU* speak. Clear them of negativity and false prophecy. Your word is a scepter that creates not only your life, but also worlds of illusion and disillusionment. Your experiences are a result of the declarations, beliefs, and words spoken from childhood forward. What *You* command materializes as reality. Contemplate what *You/you* declared as a child. . . a teen. . . and a young adult. What do *You* continually proclaim? What do *You/you/YOU* constantly complain about? Or criticize? How do *You/you* keep ill, lack, drama, and limitation alive and prospering? Intentions, words, declarations, commandments, and prayers are prophecy of what is to come. Watch your words become your wand.

Today's encounters appeared out of yesterday's notions.
Today's proclamations create tomorrow's potions.

Alchemize your old world into a new one through the alignment of word—spoken and unspoken. The unspoken word is as powerful a creative element as the spoken one—if not more so. Listen to the ghost whispers of your mind, and those of the deceptive intelligence. Listen to how *You* judge, defend, criticize, and create. Hear your inner-voice expectation of others. Hear the repetitive, old, and negative beliefs that loop. Begin by being aware of and realigning what is held in the conscious *Mind/mind/MIND*. Now, imagine what might be buried within the subconscious mind.

Curiously and enthusiastically dive into absolute alignment. As *You* upgrade, embark upon the next stage of mastery: inspired action. Do what *You* say, and state clearly what *You* will do. The mastery of inspired action utilizes intention for weaving trust, faith, and goodwill toward visions and outcomes. With mind, heart, body, and soul. . . let each action be wholehearted in commitment. Mastery does not mean perfection. It is steady commitment and focus to *Living/LIVING, Being/BEING,* and *Knowing/KNOWING* the highest expression of *SELF*. For this to occur, your thoughts, actions, words, and energy must be aligned.

The final step in mastery involves aligning your energy to what is said, thought, and done. Speaking beautiful words, without being cognizant of discordant energy, creates blocks, challenges, and obstacles. Pursuing a vision while holding the energy of bitterness, jealousy, or rage can only create a misaligned outcome. Acts of service performed from an energy of lack, self-need, or sense of hierarchy cannot prosper or fully serve. Although your conscious mind believes words *Being/being/Being* espoused, experience will mirror what is present within the layers of *Self/self/SELF*.

Mastery is a minute-by-minute, day-by-day endeavor of consistent, subconscious exploration and conscious absorption. Mastery attunes to higher *Being/BEING*. Integration is richer than just intellectually understanding. The reconciliation of all layers brings about mastery and manifestation. This means the energetic, emotional, mental, physical, and visceral vibrate in alignment. Transition your field of consciousness into a light-spring of new blossoms that are fresh with color, fragrance, and aliveness.

There is great simplicity when recognizing what no longer serves. This is *Mastery*. There is great simplicity in understanding what *You/you/YOU* do not want. This is

Mastery. There is great simplicity in discerning what *You/you/YOU* do want. This is *Mastery.* There is great simplicity in creating space for what feels good. This is *Mastery.* There is great simplicity in receiving what *You/you/YOU* are calling in. This is *Masterful.* There is great simplicity in ascending beyond what *You/you/YOU* have created up to now. This expands your aura of the Master.

Only the ego proclaims what it has done, or that there is something to do.
This is the small, forcing the great.
Mastery never speaks, so not to interfere with the perfection that *IS*.
This is the power of the great through the small.
Uncertainty will court *You/you/YOU* in a way that certainty never could.
Embrace uncertainty.
Let this be your divine lover.

knowing.
How do i/eye master this myself?
i/eye can master moment.

Knowing.
I Am here for mastery.

KNOWING.
I AM a Master.

. . .

FRAGRANCE-EMITTING BEAUTY

What is the inhale?

This moment came
from the consciousness of your past.
How *You/you/YOU* experience and receive it
creates what happens next.
Do not focus on doing;
deepen into the beauty of *Being/being/BEING*.
Let the richness this moment brings
create wealth with seeing.
Life is wise.
It knows how to catalyze.
Life is already awakened to the gift of *You/you/YOU*.
Fully awaken to your due.

Life does not judge your experience. It does not expect anything of *You/you/YOU*. Life breathes *You/you/YOU* in, inhaling your colorful bouquet of expression. Life does not discard any part. It delights in all that *You/you/YOU* embody, in birth. . . through life. . . with decline. . . as decay. . . amid death. . . rising into rebirth. . . and in reclaiming renewal. It is present to experiencing your growth, expansion, wonder, and exploration. Life seeks your perspectives, perceptions, projections, and feelings. It is your embodied, unique expression. *You/you/YOU* need do nothing for life. You can actively do more nothing, because life knows what to do. Let its design lead. After all, *You/you/YOU* are an expression of its magnificence, a divine blueprint, never to be replicated or repeated. Life *IS a* design. . . a destiny. . . a deity that lives inside *You/you/YOU*.

**Through growth as contemplative mastery, awaken your beauty;
dissolve the black hole of slothfulness.**

Divine grace lies within the inhale of your own sweet notes. Be filled by what is sensory, aesthetic, aromatic, and harmonic. Experience and express the scent of love and acceptance. Let the blending of these waft into every space *You/you/YOU* wander. Become a creator of divine beauty, utilizing the hues, tones, and textures of each experience. Allow beauty to be experienced in, as, and through *You/you/YOU*. Let beauty express, in contrast to any darkness encountered, and within the darkness too.

There is a path before *You*, one that has already been traveled. It is in time, and beyond time. It is occurring, has already happened, and is yet to occur. The *KNOWING* of this lay beyond intellect. This beauty resides deeply within remembrance; *You/you/YOU* leave this behind as your legacy. . . prophecy. . . and Divine creation. Beauty is an aspect of your inheritance. This need not have a form, but *You/you/YOU* will create a multiplicity of forms. When life is fragrant with the beauty of your presence, everything *You* touch shall flower with your creative essence. Manifestations shall abound. *YOU* will remain in the atmosphere, long after *You/you* have left.

**Self-image. . . holds the fragrance of divine ownership, as a vessel of Spirit.
Self-value. . . holds the fragrance of divine inheritance; the richness of Holy Spirit.**

For the purposes of initiating *Self*-grace, use a peyote candle in your space to support root energy. Known as a sacred mother plant, peyote is a woody fragrance used in practices such as meditation, chanting, or various cleansing ceremonies. This also provides shamanic energy for awareness and clearing. Peyote works by interacting with the neurotransmitter serotonin in your brain, to alter thinking and perception. It smells of moss and grass, and experience with this plant is a communion or religious sacrament. Many traditions sees it as a plant that supports being able to "converse with God." It is recommended to consult an expert when using as a psychedelic, because various experiences will occur.

Having a warm, inviting, and complex nature, woody scents are particularly good for transitioning for shadow work, for dark-night-of-the-soul periods, and into fall and winter. They are tools that mother and nurture the human spirit, due to their natural depth and sensuality for work involving *Self*-trust, *Self*-acceptance, *Self*-worth, and *Self*-value. Burning wood as incense is one of the oldest and most common religious and spiritual traditions, since aromatic properties, and benefits, date back many thousands of years. Common fragrances include sandalwood, cedar, pine, and teak.

Self-acceptance. . . holds the fragrance of worthiness, of Divine Ancestry.
Self-trust. . . holds the fragrance of _KNOWING, ONE_ness with _DIVINE BEING_.

Life is a Divine Mother, unconditionally loving and cherishing all that she holds. She neutrally guides and teaches while *You* move through phases of stretching, contractions, growth, receiving, and release. Life is a womb space of cycles and rhythms. She brings forth endless dreams of life, death, and rebirth. Life breathes with *You*. Every person—friend or foe, every experience—painful or joyful, and every expression—challenging or easy. . . opens your experience to the essence of this unconditionally loving, Divine Mother.

Nestle in. Get close; suckle from the breast of experience. Let life feed, nurture, and rear *YOU*. Holy creation is infinite in its beauty. Life is the love from which *YOU* were cast. Let the fragrance of beauty invite, invoke, initiate, illuminate, and express the creative and abundant Divine feminine power that is the essence of life. . . through *YOU*.

Become aware of how beauty is always present. When creating beauty through words, thoughts, actions, and creativity, *You/you/YOU* amplify the signature of divine creative capacity; through *You* the beauty of *God/god/GOD* expands. All experience births from this space of aliveness, in which beauty begets more beauty. When initiating beautiful experiences, that legacy that ripples throughout the fabric of *your/my/their/our* reality.

Peyote is a divine mother messenger that means "to glisten."
You are a plant. . . here to glisten.

Life is a secret garden, fragrant with your divine presence. Breathe in your beautiful *Self/self/SELF*. Become the landscape of creativity that continually expresses your heavenly fragrance. Let your heart blossom with the soul's fragrant beauty. A subtle mist appears *dew/due* to your embrace of experience, emotions, and feelings. This flowering—vulnerable, tender, and soft, yet strong. When imbuing your fragrance of beauty, nothing can be seen, touched, or created that does not carry your signature of *BEING*.

As *You* move into each day, inhale your sweet fragrance. Revel in the beauty of *Being*ness, which emerged from nothing to become something. . . many things. . . anything. . . all things. To blossom can appear a trillion different ways. Your flowering is *One/one/ONE* in that trillion; a unique and spectacular *ONE*! Life is gently unfolding through *You/you/YOU*. . . and a beautiful flowering it is.

Celebrate all that has been,
all that was, all that is in process, and yet to come.
You/you/YOU are life's celebration of itself.
Let the beauty of that remembering,

be the awakening of your becoming.
Such fragrance is within *your/our/their/my*. . . midst/mist;
it is heaven. . . scent.

knowing.
How do i/eye find good in this moment?
i/eye/I start with where i/eye/I am.

Knowing.
I bring beauty to each moment.

KNOWING.
I AM beautiful.

. . .

FLAVOR OF GENTLENESS

What is the exhale?

Be gentle. . .
with your words, thoughts, and actions.
Be gentle. . .
with yourself, others, and life.
Be gentle. . .
in your choices, imaginings, and leaps of faith!

While the world may appear insane at times, each individual has the opportunity to choose sanity or insanity. *You/I/We/They* have a daily choice as to the state of presence and compassion held. Those that cannot see, hear, and acknowledge another's pain are unable to acknowledge themselves or their own pain. The degree to which *You/I/We/They* ignore *Self/self/SELF* is indicative of the *ignorance*, apathy, and indifference within the world. Positivity and spirituality can become masks if not aligning and realigning through daily practices. Life is energy; *yours/mine/theirs/ours* collectively.

Your unwillingness to ground, and become still, reveals the excess of processed ideas, techniques, and packaged goods *You/you/YOU* have bought into. The addictive sweetness of positive thinking, the tartness of negativity, and smorgasbord of self-help, personal growth, and multimedia distractions keep *you* craving. Ignorance burns inside with its unpalatable taste. The additives of substance abuse and slothfulness increase hunger, so that *You/you/YOU* never feel fully satisfied. There is no richness to ground in, if continually living on the surface and within illusions, even those appearing shiny and sparkly. However, those who influence *You/you* are under the influence of their own shadows.

As *You* endeavor upon truth in questioning,
restore gentleness through the key of devotion.

Living/LIVING with the flavor of gentleness means accessing, holding, guiding, and feeling into what is called for in each moment. In moving through pain, trauma, and turmoil... the flavor of gentleness becomes a salve, and balm, within your understanding. Unawake and unaware of the bigger picture, your tending must be gentle and soft. Handle yourself with care. Experience everything... but do so gently and mindfully.

You/you/YOU are fragile, yet strong. *You/you* are a wounded animal... an injured soldier... a fractured piece of rare crystal. This does not mean *You/you/YOU* are broken, or can be. Fragility means *You/you/YOU* are vulnerable, which can become a weakness or be cultivated into a strength. *You* may be a bleeding heart, a sensitive with the ability to grow compassionate presence. The subtle and small are important for this essence to express through *You*.

Begin loving yourself in gentle ways. Let practices of *Self*-love seep in. Receive acceptance like warm oil coating the skin. Let your breath drip in like molasses. Let each footstep land softly upon the ground, every single one kissing the earth as if for the very first time. Just as the arms sway by your sides, imagine your hands gingerly grazing the skin of your experiences. Deepen your intimacy with each moment and be gripped by what lay in its wake. Breathe, as the body moves gently with all that it feels. Listen to your breath. Be with yourself. Let the stale and stagnant energy move out of your *Being/being*. Let each exhale distill life one molecule at a time. Breathe. Find your heartbeat in the space between what *you know* and what *You/YOU* don't yet *Know/KNOW.*

Cultivate the flavor of gentleness through a regular practice of walking. Move everything *You/you/YOU* feel inside through your feet. Pound the pavement with your sorrows, complaints, dreams, and desires. Let gratitude flow down your body and out through your toes. Allow prayers to course through your bloodstream and pool within your soles, so to bless every place *You* step. Walking will teach *You* to speak softly... move intently... act slowly... and breathe deeply. Every single day, walk. Walk. Walk. Walk. Be silent when walking. Walking supports your root energy center. Trust also grows with strengthening the legs and feet. Find places in nature, but if *You* cannot, then walk where available. Walking sends an energetic and physical message to life; things are moving. Anchor in the new, while releasing the old with each step. In this way, your stillness becomes movement.

Do not make life too real, or *You* separate from the mystical. Life is magical, occurring in the spaces between what can and cannot be seen. Its aura is subtle. Life's effervescence is woven into *You*, and *You* within it. Drink of life's sacred chalice; this is your holy grail. *You/you/YOU* are the elixir. Become intoxicated. Taste and savor your experiences and expressions. As *You* do, life partakes of *You/you/YOU*. All the while, be gentle with how *You* view... respond... and react to time and circumstance. Be gentle of Spirit... with Spirit... in Spirit... and as Spirit.

Be gentle...
with your life, your body, and your self.
Be gentle...
in your movements, gestures, and responses.
Be gentle...
in love.

Be the flavor of gentleness.
Let that taste linger. . .
for all eternity.

knowing.
How can i/eye be gentler to myself and others?
I/eye/i can choose gentler experiences.

Knowing.
I season every experience with gentleness.

KNOWING.
I AM the gentleness of Spirit.

. . .

MELODY THROUGH MOVEMENT—ANTICIPATION

What is harmonizing?

Reality is not real. . .
it is a changing blend of illusion, expression, and experience.
Illusion is a byproduct of creativity.
Heaven is a byproduct of creativity.
Remembrance brings *You* to the real.
***You/you* are nowhere, no one, and nothing. . .**
***YOU* are everywhere, every-*One/one/ONE,* and every-thing.**
This is remembering. . .

Life is meant to be an experience of harmony. Your experience should be an ebb and flow of thoughts, feelings, and creations that feel good. That is your natural state. However, that is not how *You* live a lot of the time. Rather than approaching life with arms wide open, *You/you* have become guarded, afraid, and resistant. It is as if "a heart wall" has formed. This barrier does not allow a natural movement of harmony to flow through your experiences. Rather than receiving the bountiful good that is available, *You* repel it, only receiving experiences that prove your need for walls, barriers, and safeguards.

Dissonance is a lack of harmony. Discord causes *You/you* to get busier or find things to distract yourself with. . . *squirrel!* Through past conditioning and conformity, *You/you/YOU* moved out of your natural melody. A combination of bodily sensations, harsh thoughts, low energy, and dense emotion built inner discord. Forward movement becomes sabotaged by fear, conditioning, and *Self/self/SELF*-betrayal. Areas of stagnancy result from pushing against your natural rhythm. Certain patterns, mannerisms, and behaviors keep negative experiences in place, while conditioning creates an urge to move, get busy, or get on with life. This helps *You* avoid what feels bad, but it also pushes away what feels good.

Wisdom through inquiry shifts *Being* teacher to *BEING* example.
Don't tell others how to heal; show them what that looks like.

You must stop and rest. This occurs in degrees. Stopping and pausing are also movement, but a different sort. These moments allow activity beneath the surface to come into awareness. Just as life rests in the cold earth during the winter season and appears dormant, on the surface, nothing seems to be happening. Underneath, life hums, balancing energies of decay and new growth. But also, new life is preparing to unfurl and flower. Birth, life, death, and rebirth require the ability to rest, relax, sleep, and reawaken. This is where *You/you/YOU* are. Balance the energies of your life, as your surface world experiences a season of winter.

All noise must stop. This *is* life purpose, and of great value. Balance what is out of balance. Stillness is movement. Life is always vibrating, even when appearing to do nothing. Willingness to be present with your interior is activity. Do not engage outer life until *You* receive a clear message to do so. Your body will signal when it is time to venture out into the world again. Have no worry; there is always enough time for everything *You* desire. Hibernate. Do the inner work. Rest is far more valuable than pushing, productivity, or pressure could ever be. For now, stop and rest. Only from a place of silence can a clear, new melody begin. For harmony to return, the melody of your soul must be remembered. This occurs when creating balance between *Self* and life. Your cave and cauldron will hold everything as *you* boil, simmer, and stew. As shedding and death of identity occur, life will offer the nutrients required to renew *You*. Harmony comes by dissolving discord.

You may be surprised by how much stress, tension, and constriction has built within your physical structure. Tiredness will bear its weight upon *You/you*. Notice how *You/ you/YOU* force yourself forward. When doing so, your body might feel like it has been run over. During deep pauses, it is normal to feel at odds with yourself, to not know who *You/you* are, or why this is happening. Fluctuations of emotion and thought rock *You/ you/YOU* back and forth. Life brings forth challenges, so *You* remember your original state of relaxation in mind, body, and spirit.

What does it mean to rest?
What would true relaxation of mind, body, and spirit feel like?

Attuning to a higher resonance requires tuning in to your soul. This can feel challenging when *YOU* are used to *Being/being You/you*. Releasing activities that have become customary can make *You* feel uncomfortable, and out of control. Anxiety might arise, as can despair and depression. Stay with it. Feeling your emotions and experiences is how you detox, dissolve, absorb, and integrate them. Energies that are buried inside are going to rise to awareness in body and mind. When this happens, it is because they call for your presence. With presence and time, they will dissolve. This requires your devotion and discipline. However, it is not something *You* "do." Rest, relaxation, and naturalness have to organically settle. With deep breathing, space, and care. . . these deepen.

Are *You/you/YOU* in or out of tune with the Divine orchestration of the Universe?

Your experiences illustrate how tuned in *You* are to the sacred voice of your soul. Sometimes You/you will feel completely human; other moments the crescendo toward divinity will make *You/YOU* feel otherworldly. Each state has its own set of notes. Each lyric of life builds upon the strings and strands of time. *You* are the instrument. Your expression is a specific note. Your life is the song. Attuning to your natural movements, melodies, and rhythms equilibrates *Being/BEING*.

"Har" means God. Harmony represents chords of ascending progression in Divine movement. The natural melody of life rests behind everything. Allow life to move *You*, rather than driving, pushing, or forcing your way. Initially, this will feel unnatural because few of us have been taught to relish space, boredom, and intentional play. Increased levels of relaxation come through play, natural living, and organic expression. Play is natural creativity. It is the way of the universe, and *what* created all things.

***KNOW* your good,
and *You* will *KNOW* your *God/GOD*.**

Anticipation is the right use of control. It can alleviate conditions of discomfort, restlessness, or victimhood. Be sure to anticipate positive outcomes and high vibrations, not negative, low ones. The energy of anticipation redirects focus, giving the ego something to do so that it does not create interference. Anticipation of positive outcomes makes uncertainty more manageable by offering hope. It is a great amplifier of harmony and is also beneficial for the brain. Anticipation also teaches patience and brings awareness to doubt. Let this movement course through your blood, bones, and tissue.

Anticipation is expectation, excitement, faith, and suspense. This attitude and liberty creates a foundation for shifting into higher experiences of life. It is the starting point for recognizing yourself as a cocreator for achieving a higher octave. This is the first step in harnessing the law of attraction. Through anticipation, begin stirring the energy. Like Merlin, take what exists and let that be your tool for creating magic. As *You* lasso creative power, your muscle of *Knowing* builds. This buoys your energy into alignment, awakening higher vibrational play with your universe. Deepen into divine *KNOWING* by awakening your melody of movement. Engage greater authority and empower *Self/self*. Let anticipation become your spiritual discipline; an act of daily preparation.

**Life is a dance.
Experience is the dancer.
You/you/YOU are the music.
Humanity is the movement
that unites heaven and earth.
The Divine is always strumming its rhythm within you.
Get quiet and still enough to hear it.**

knowing.
What's possible?
eye/i/I/ don't know, but eye/i/I am willing to ask.
Knowing.

Life is always serving me.

KNOWING.
I AM the dreamer and designer of my life.

. . .

VISCERAL MEMORY

What may be absorbed?

Let the past go.
Forgive, even forget.
Begin anew.
Take nothing in thought, word, or deed.
What was. . . is dead.
In keeping it alive,
nothing new can be born.
Live your genius.
Be free. . . of *self/Self*.
BELIEVE. . .
There is a far greater *YOU* than *You/you*.

Life is an outward expression of what rests microcosmically within, revisiting times and themes in order to create higher, ever-expanding cycles and echoes. Experience is derived from what *You/I/We/They* consciously and unconsciously believe. They are also driven by inherited collective and ancestral memory that is embedded within cellular memory.

Some memory stems from fight, flight, or freeze—spanning as far back as early childhood, in utero, or generational legacies. These can be positive or negative memories. Those of celebration, connection, and love exist. But also, dense energies such as trauma, grief, and rage are given to *You*. As life unfolds, *Your* relationships and experiences illustrate the vast library of memories that lie within the subconscious mind and cellular body. During triggers, and with space, these may begin surfacing. Life is composed of repeating echoes, memory, and history. There is nothing new; only energy that is either stored or repurposed until conscious, dissolved, and/or absorbed.

Embedded within your physiology are subtle layers that *You* are to discover. Through gentle absorption, dense visceral memory is uncovered. *You* undergo the process of spiritual alchemy. Through the journey of *Self/self/SELF* realization, neutrality and breathing become two great allies. They cultivate balanced composure, while also providing a foundation for focus. These and other skills support life in being mastered. Neutrality is especially valuable for staying the course toward new creation and manifestation. You will experience the peaks and valleys of waves that ebb and flow inside. These visceral energies are your deepest layers of discord. Some of these energies have been there since the beginning of time. Devotion to *Self/self/SELF* leads to the awareness of visceral conditioning created within this incarnation and accumulated through history, culture, lineage, and collective memory.

Rooting out the cause of painful sensations can become a distraction. The ego will keep searching for quick fixes or seek to make meaning of the uncomfortable, as a way to avoid fully feeling. Finding reasons and projecting the cause of discomfort onto someone or something are ways ego attaches to story. *Mind/mind/MIND* tries to justify and understand "*why*." However, this type of mental action is merely distraction. The preoccupation with "*why*" keeps veils present and truth hidden. With distraction, the potential for absorption, transmutation, and alchemy eludes the moment. Rather than following the mind's wild-goose chase, stay present with the body. Stay focused on what *You* are feeling from the neck down. Deeply experience what is *Being/being* felt; let sensations become the language of memory.

Cultivate listening as *You* invite unification with the wound;
deep presence is required to access your visceral memory of rage.

The body's natural intelligence brings attention to what is out of alignment. This rises as strange sensations, random emotion, and twinges of abstract pain that are often without cause or explanation. Visceral memory sits within your blood, bones, and tissue. This cellular energetic is the stagnant, dense energy that *You* cannot feel when active, busy, or hurried. Visceral memory builds slowly; it is the long-held, suppressed emotion of time. These gross sensations arise when given extended stillness, silence, space, and time. Multiday, all-day meditation periods, while you remain extremely still, will allow you a palpable understanding of the gross energies trapped inside your cells.

You are required to feel if truly desiring to *Know/know/KNOW* your *Self/self/SELF*. Unless deliberately choosing to pause and be present, *You/you/YOU* will unconsciously slip into repetitive behaviors, addictive patterns, and distraction mechanisms. Denial is another way *You* avoid feeling this storehouse of deep pain and ancestral memory. Feeling is just that: feeling. Sensation is simply… sensation. Humanity encompasses both; otherwise *You* possess no true humanity. These arise so that *You* are aware of your energy. It is not required that they shift. Awareness is most important. For the energy to dissolve, these sensations require full presence. That process does not require your control, nor does it encompass any "doing."

When present, without attachment to feelings changing, absorption occurs. This is different than release. Rather than letting feelings go, they dissolve by being held with love. Dissolved energy is taken in and absorbed. It is integrated but is actually the dis-integration of stuck energy. This type of integration creates space for Spirit to more deeply enter awareness. This supports embodiment of both, fragmented energies and higher *Self/SELF*. *You* learn to address energy and emotion in a healthy way. Emotional intelligence is strengthened by managing and mastering emotions. In doing so, *You* build the wherewithal to dissolve discordant energies that have collected over time. This is not only personal energies, but also ancestral and collective energies. Fully owning sensations creates greater health and limitless soulful expansion. Releasing feelings without accepting them results in fragmentation and dis-ease.

Visceral memory belongs to time.

You/you/YOU were born to remember
YOU are timeless.

Your deepest visceral memories will be of grief, separation, and rage, with rage and hate being the most intense. These energies rumble beneath the surface of all human beings. *You/you/YOU* carry the memory of suppressed ancestral pain and generational trauma. Unconscious rage is the most active and tangible. This visceral memory has existed from the time *You/you/YOU* were a toddler, if not before incarnation. It subtly reveals in the terrible twos and tiresome threes. Early on, when rage shows itself through tantrums, it is often shut down. Because of this, *You/you* learn that rage is inappropriate. Each time *You* are not allowed to feel your rage, memory is stored and ancestral visceral imprints are strengthened. With suppression, conformity takes root, resulting in codependence. People pleasing is replete with unconscious rage, which, ironically, builds more unconscious rage.

Suppressed rage can express itself physically, as rashes, burns, cuts, or bruises. The unconscious *Self/self* will express itself in many ways. Pimples, blisters, and boils reveal withheld rage and anger. Addressing issues only through medical means keeps rage rumbling as an undercurrent. Memories rage when *You* do not listen. . . feel. . . or sense.

Rage is the expression of your caged, feral animal *self*.

The heart chakra remains blocked when carrying rage. This keeps *You/you* from loving and being loved. Until taking ownership of your circumstances and manifestations, *You/you* will project rage onto others. If objectively listening, *You/you/YOU* will hear your distortions of reality, self-inflicted lies, and self-betrayal. Listen to your rage. It will tell *You* of its stories, wounds, and hidden belief systems. It will scream at the injustice it has experienced. It is calling for your love. It seeks your forgiveness, and it seeks to forgive. . . *You*. . . the world. . . life. . . God.

Residual energies are a result of separation. These are the veils. The body is the last great frontier of consciousness. It is the bridge between animal expression and humanity *Being*. The grace of simplicity catalyzes profound shifts, by clearing emotional and mental clutter held within the physical. Life will look and feel different when *You/you/YOU* do. With the embrace of each visceral sensation, greater aliveness is revealed.

Each individual is a repository for life's unfelt and unhealed traumas, betrayals, pains, ecstasies, and pleasures. Cherish the body for all it holds and carries. Initially, *You* may cling to the pain, rage with it, cry with it, and snuggle into its familiar memory. But do not hold tightly to any of it. Be sacred witness to these temporary visitors. With time, each sensation *You* meet will receive your embrace and be transformed by it, making *You* feel more whole.

Breathe in.
Contemplate daily.
Seek no answers.
Look for no endings.
Release the need for meaning.
Broaden the mind.

Open your heart.
Breathe out.
Breathe in even deeper.
Cleanse your conditioning.
Heal your human condition.
Seek feeling.
Melt into each moment;
that is all there is.
Drop thought. . .
Nestle into the heart. . .
Love the body. . .
Romance the soul.
Create space for *LIVING, BEING, KNOWING*.
Breathe out.
You are beginning.

knowing.
What does "this" remind me of?
It reminds me of everything eye/i/I don't want..

Knowing.
I can feel all parts of myself.

KNOWING.
I AM everything

. . .

ALCHEMY OF MIND

What can be transmuted?

Two become one. . .
amid fire and flame.
What was once divided,
now becomes the same.
What was dual in creation
shifts into union through communion.
Reduce everything *you know* to ash;
be free of mental constriction and live unabashed.

You/you have been devoted to lower *Self/self*, its drama, and illusion. . . knowingly or unknowingly. Dysfunction has been your drug. *Mind/mind* has been the addict. Illusion is your addiction. The storyline *You/you* carry, while wandering through the wilderness, must be laid to rest. Place it within the fire. Let it burn to ash. Watch it smolder and witness the darkness burn away. Bless it for *Being/being*, and kiss your storms goodbye.

Within *You/you/YOU* is the capacity to alter your world. The same power that created your conditions can change them. Give yourself space. Spend time alone. Walk... walk...walk. Utilize contemplation. Create more "empty" time in the outer world, so that *You/YOU* embody the timelessness of your inner world. False mind and ego must be extracted for a higher *Mind/MIND* expression. Become sovereign within. The only necessity is space. With open space, something new can enter... be it healing, an answer, awareness, or inspiration. Space is not physical; it is the land of no where, no time, no thing, no mind, no one, knowledge, know-ings, and know-bility. Enter this majestic landscape, leaving all else behind. Life will hold no real meaning until *You* are able to meaningfully hold your own presence.

Criticism, condemnation, and judgment are signs of a negative attitude.
Complaining, impatience, and regurgitation of story
energetically project your negativity.

Your gold is buried deeply. It rests within the densest, darkest, heaviest spaces. Sticky shadows of jealousy, anger, guilt, shame, fear, inferiority, and depression are the materials of alchemy. If in denial of this darkness, *You* cannot change anything. Life will merely reflect your misalignment, in large and small ways. That can appear as relationship failure, ill health, career issues, and waning finances. Manifestations in the material world point to aspects of *Self/self/SELF* calling to be transformed. This is the path of Mastery.

Big *Beings/BEINGs* will encounter big things. *YOU* are that! Do not shy away from what is yours to do, nor deny it. The Master mines every crack and crevice for the gold it holds. This will likely take *You/you/YOU* down... down... down until *You/YOU* bring the ego to its knees. *Mind/mind* is the mountain that must be ascended. As *You* venture into the winding pathways of *Mind/mind*, keep rising to higher ground. Do not stop until *KNOWING* the pinnacle of higher *MIND*.

The ego will attempt to lead *You/you/YOU* into fantasy, drama, and illusion. Do not let it. Your task is to focus on what *IS* real, not on the illusions *you* made real. The ego is a frightened and feral part of *You/you*. It puffs itself up with pride, image, and false identity. It is so clever and convincing that *You/you/YOU* willingly are abducted, time and time again. But through these machinations of ego, blazes appear. Experiences stemming from childish immaturity and reactivity fan the flames of drama and trauma. Yet, that same fire can also be used to cleanse and purify *Being/being* of its illusions.

Hear thyself;
let gifts of signs, symbols, and synchronicity awaken clarity.

The beginning stage of alchemy is *calcination*, where fire is used to burn everything that once was. Charged experiences, difficult circumstances, and painful moments are your fires. In the wake of these moments, the ego will fight to hang ont o the constructs it created. It will clamor for survival. These are the challenging experiences *You* walk through, which become catalysts for your transformational process. The return to wholeness rests within the darkest parts of *You/you/YOU*. Utilize the elements within—fire, water, earth, and ether—to cure *You/you/YOU*.

Fully face your challenging and painful experiences. They reveal the *Mind/mind/MIND* that created them. That is your starting point of transformation. Your *golden essence* is buried inside your problems, chaos, challenges, obstacles, and difficulties. *You/you/YOU* must bear the heat and fire of your own damnation to find it. This means sitting within the cauldron of spells that *You/you* cast upon your own life. Seek out your negativity. Dip into your density. Look for the resistance, triggers, and discord that have dug in. Your *prima materia* is unique to *You/you/YOU*.

As your inner world purifies, the real *YOU* has space to grow and mature spiritually. Remove the moldy, stinking thinking that has grown within your moist spaces of long-held sadness, grief, jealousy, and anger. Wisdom rises amid the evaporation of emotional density. This supports higher ground in forming. Each stage of spiritual awareness builds an aspect of your new foundation. Cultivate the soil of your awareness as wisdom lifts *You* to higher ground. Lower *Mind/mind* must be alchemized to higher *Mind/MIND*. This requires the sacrifice of your lower base thinking as *prima materia* for transformation. Alchemy transforms base, lower *Mind/mind* into higher ground and higher *Mind/MIND*.

Alchemy, in its highest form, is a psycho-spiritual practice where all things come together as *One/ONE*. Alchemy of *Mind/mind/MIND* occurs when purifying the mental body of its weight. A purge must take place to transform the pathology of your psychological sphere. Within this inner sanctum, cultivate the power of *MIND* over matter. Although these seem separate, they are linked. The principle of "*as above so below*" applies. Through accessing higher MIND, *You* gain command over manifest "reality." Shift your focus and vision to higher vibrational thinking. Transcend the level at which *You/you* have been *Living/living*. Begin cultivating, seeding, and harvesting Higher Ground.

There is nothing out there.
Everything is a manifestation of your consciousness.

The Law of Polarity or Law of Opposites underlies all manifestations. One opposite cannot exist without the other. In *Knowing,* everything manifest has poles, opposites, and extremes; your current experience can be approached differently. Through positive affirmation, and in anticipation of your desired outcome, begin shifting your thoughts, words, and imaginings. Envision a new experience on the horizon, one that is opposite of your current circumstance. Begin anchoring a state of *Mind/MIND* that sees and believes. Shape the way in which *You* perceive. Follow your bliss; find what makes *You* happy. This changing of *Mind/mind* will lead to more-pleasurable opportunities, experiences, relationships, and clarity.

Love is the most powerful purifier
in all of creation.
It dissolves everything
unlike itself.
Make space
for aliveness. . .
and the presence of
Divine Go(o)d.
Believe. . .
what *you* cannot see.
Trust. . .
that *You Know*
what *YOU KNOW*.

knowing.
What am i/eye thinking?
i/eye watch my mind run in circles.

Knowing.
I Am a work in progress.

KNOWING.
I AM clarity.

. . .

ESSENCE AS CLARITY

What may be embodied?

Where are *You*?
You/you/YOU are everywhere.
What are *You*?
You/you/YOU are everything.
Who are *You*?
You/you/YOU are all that is.
How?
You/you/YOU experience and express.
Why?
You/you/YOU unfold, dissolve, and transform.
When?
Then. . . There. . . Now. . . Always.

Attitudes stem from deeply unconscious patterns. Subtle attitudes remain present long after the conscious *Mind/mind* believes things have been released. Negativity is the first of seven energy attitudes that permeate until brought into complete awareness. These attitudes create the energy and identity of victimhood, which perpetuates story, oppression, and suffering.

Negativity, the first attitudinal energy, appears in many ways: the need to be right, having to win, out-of-control emotions, blame, and reactivity. This energy and these behaviors must shift to transcend your current state of *Mind/mind*. Regurgitating stories, complaining, and seeking answers outside yourself facilitates behaviors connected to negativity. Unconscious patterns, of being hard on yourself or projecting onto others, compound negativity. All of this stems from confusion, which is simply the forgetting of *Truth/TRUTH*.

Forgiving complexity creates the inspiration for giving simplicity to *Self*.

Your need to move, act, or run in the moment is not coming from clarity, nor will it bring any. Quick movement is reactionary. It merely creates more interference and confusion. Reaction is the ego's engine for fight or flight. When in a reactive state, simply feel what is present. Allow the fog to roll in. Feel the confusion. Sink into being offended. Accept the anger and aggression that builds. Notice the unconscious emotional energy that rises in the heat of a triggering moment. This is your steam; it comes from the raging waters of your ocean. *You* are feeling the fire that singes and burns. Reaction has a seductive pattern of rising, projecting, and fracturing. The conflict existing between mind and heart creates this friction. As pressure builds, irritation becomes a catalyst for unveiling subtler emotions. These dense energies block your understanding, choice, and awareness. Your presence burns away beliefs, thoughts, and conditioning that pose barriers to authenticity and inner authority.

What stands in your way are illusions that *Mind/mind* created. Nothing is really there. Confusion cannot be processed away. That only creates further psychosis, which leads to more processing. Seeking answers from others creates more noise, thus bringing on more confusion. Let your *Mind/mind* chatter and confusion come. The mind must tire to lay down its burdens. Getting to this point can feel exhausting. In truth, *You* have exhausted the ego.

Seek not to know "what," but "when."

Sit in your fog until *You/you* see *YOU* again. *YOU* are a lighthouse; let that inner light navigate the fog and storm. Clarity sits inside every cell but must be rooted out of *You/you/YOU*. Let insight come slowly. Sip it like scalding tea. Savor inquiry. Gently play with each moment. The present moment is the key to clarity in many others. Clouds of confusion, doubt, and insecurity will be dissolved only by wading through them. Confusion creates the perfect pressure for clarity to eventually bubble up.

Confusion is not driven by "*what*," but "*when*." This is an important distinction, regardless of the issue or question. The "*when*" is a moment in time that initiated the confusion. Although your confusion appears to regard a current situation, it is based on something in the past. Once pinpointing the "*when*," "*who*" and "*what*" become clear. Challenging issues and upset appear to be about "current problems." However, the upset is never about the current issue but, instead, is a trigger of something and someone long before. By discovering the "*when*," and then the "*who*," creating reaction within *You/you/YOU*, greater *Self/self/SELF*-realization is made available. Confusion happens when *You/you* are not clear on *YOU*. Hear thy *Self/self/SELF*. Clarity comes when thinking stops. Discover the power of the pause.

Get lost in confusion.
Let that build in intensity, so that *Self/self/SELF* is clearly seen.

You live in a world of diversity. This is a beautiful thing. *Your/our/their/my* unique pieces create this beautiful world tapestry. The more diverse the world, the greater clarity *You/YOU* can achieve regarding your place within it. When *You* get clear, others are supported in *Being/being/BEING* clear. Sometimes that means "the other" is part of your tribe. In other instances, "the other" is your opposite, adversary, and enemy. Both experiences present opportunities for growth and expansion. Through diversity, *You/you/YOU* can also discover commonalities within your differences.

Individual *Truth/truth/TRUTH* consists of many parts. The ego's truth will be loud. It uses deceptive measures to push its agenda, overcompensate for fear, and convince others of its position. The ego focuses on outer world needs. Additionally, there are many versions of truth. The higher *SELF* whispers *TRUTH*. It patiently waits for *You/you*. This part of *You/you/YOU* is unconditionally loving. Higher *SELF* points and guides in soft and gentle ways, nudging *You/you* inward to find *Truth/TRUTH*. Your multidimensional levels of *Truth/truth/TRUTH* contribute to the that of the world. Collective *Truth* is built upon individual *Truth/truth/TRUTH*s coming together. This is the reason for such contrast. Our world is a mixed soup.

Do not wait for clarity to come. . . it waits for *YOU* to rise.
Clarity is always present. *You/you/YOU* are not.

Clarity in "response ability" requires *conscious choices*. Every time *You* say *yes* to something, be clear on what *You* are saying *no* to. Each time *You* say *no*, understand the foundational *yes* that lay beneath it. Clarity will not be logical or intellectual. It will rise from *Truth/TRUTH* embedded in *Being/BEING*. Clarity sits within a future *You* are not privy to, but in the process of creating. As a conscious creator, it is important to hone discipline, intuition, and imagination. This awareness stems from *Mind/MIND*. However, clarity can also be found within feeling, longing, and belonging. It is in discovery of the gentlest, softest, tender sensations. Clarity requires ownership. True clarity is borne of experience, and a space beyond experience. It comes in the wake of mastery, after dissolving story and memory. It is born of chaos, confusion, smoke and mirrors. The heart may or may not yet know what it wants, but with your willingness to sit in all that is present, clarity shall emerge. *Not knowing* is a vital part of *KNOWING*.

Something bigger is always happening. Hold space for that emergence. There are many moments where *You/you/YOU* won't see anything, and then a single moment where *You/you/YOU* see everything. In an instant, clear *KNOWING* cuts through the fogginess of mind.

KNOWING arises out of timelessness. A foundation upon which to stand will begin to build. Until then, do not act or move. Do not "do" anything. This is another type of clarity; it reflects the humility of trust and faith. When doing ends, *Being* begins. When thoughts cease, peace comes. When emotion stops, feeling starts. When clutter is gone, clarity comes.

Deepen. . .
into the ache.
Open. . .
to all possibilities.
Clarity requires. . .
Ownership.
Responsibility.
Choice.
Trust.
Anticipation.
Faith.

knowing.
Why am i/eye confused about this?
My confusion is a step toward clarity.

Knowing.
I Am getting clearer day by day.

KNOWING.
I AM lucid and clear.

. . .

FORGIVING COMPLEXITY—
FOR GIVING SIMPLICITY

I forgive life for feeling hard.
I forgive this earthly dimension for being complicated.
I forgive time and red tape.
I forgive the continual hoops I have to jump through.
I forgive myself for creating a complex world.
I am for giving simplicity.
I am for giving ease.
I am for giving an experience clear of obstacles and negativity.
I am for giving high-vibe creative expression.

I am for giving attention to mastery.
I give presence to the simple things in life.
I give way to what feels easy.
I give in to the unknown.
I give Essence.
I give to my human *Self* the grace of simplicity.
I alchemize mind with the aura of the Master.
I alchemize beliefs with the fragrance of Beauty.
I alchemize thinking with the flavor of Gentleness.
I alchemize doubt with the melody of Movement.
I alchemize confusion with the Essence of Clarity.
I am *ONE* with *DIVINE PRESENCE*;
I transform and transmute complexity through the grace of simplicity. . .
I open to the absorption of all visceral memory and residual rage.
May *DIVINE ALCHEMY* smolder through my mind and dissolve the slothful *self*.
May I adorn the raven's wings
so to bridge the illusion of the mental plane with the reality of Divine Mind.
I fly with faith toward a heavenly embodiment.
I am for giving the raven's gifts of prophecy and insight,
metamorphosis and transformation. . . shape-shifting and clarity.
May these gifts of *KNOWING* be granted by *DIVINE GRACE*.
I AM the mastery of *GOD*.
I AM the beauty of *GOD*.
I AM the gentleness of *GOD*.
I AM the sacred movement of *GOD*.
I AM the conduit of *GOD*.
I am the clarity of *GOD*.
I AM.

. . .

UP-LEVEL TRUST

TRUST shifts your POINT OF ATTRACTION

self ——-> *Self* ——-> *SELF*

Be present. Gradually, shift into higher octaves of presence, awareness, and perception. Move up the vibrational ladder. Feel your way and ascend to a new reality.

The first human expression of grace establishes a new foundation upon which to engage with the world. This requires trust; recognizing that your perception and perspectives create the life You will encounter. To create a gentle and generous life, You/you/YOU must become trustworthy and trusting. Discover how to become the God of Higher understanding so that an innate trust in all of life unfolds.

Up-level trust—through grounding—in the truth of who *YOU* are. As *You* anchor within yourself—and specifically the GOD within *YOU*—your ability to create a life of meaning, purpose, and fulfillment unfolds. *You* are an ever-expanding, energetic expression of creative capacity. Awaken your *knowing... Knowing... KNOWING.* Give life something to respond to.

living.
———————————————————

acknowledgment
(slow down and feel.)
———————————————————————

eye/i want to find myself. eye/i want to know myself. eye/i want to live my life purpose.
eye/i'm not where eye/i want to be, but at least eye/i am asking questions and seeking answers.
eye/i want to feel something; anything. eye/i want to have emotions; especially good ones.
eye/i want to care about something. eye/i want to not feel so tired. eye/i want to stop being bored.

being.
———————————————————

acceptance
(bring attention to your breath.)
———————————————————————

eye/i feel... lost, wandering; confused. eye/i feel... chaotic, anxious; overwhelmed.
Sometimes, eye/i feel... apathetic, indifferent; complacent. eye/i feel... bored and restless.
Other times, eye/i feel... angry, very angry. At times, eye/i feel rage; and it scares me.
eye/i feel... afraid. eye/i feel... scared; scared of the future, of people, of the world.

knowing.
———————————————————

anticipation
(breathe slowly, deepen into your body.)
———————————————————————

eye/i may feel lost outside, but eye/i am finding places of comfort inside. In becoming aware of
what does not feel good, eye/i know the opposite is available to me. It is okay to feel this way
because eye/i am getting to know myself better. eye/i have an opportunity to see life differently.
eye/i learn to breathe, as eye/i become aware of my fear. eye/i step toward moving beyond it.

Living.
———————————————————

appreciation
(pause and be present to what the moment is asking.)
———————————————————————

I am grateful for the morning sun. I am grateful that I am willing to grow.
I appreciate that I get up and face each day, even if I don't feel like it. I appreciate the signs
that cross my path. I appreciate the ability to ask questions, even if I don't immediately receive
the answers. I appreciate being able to hear myself. I am grateful to be able to breathe.

Being.

————————————

satisfaction
(connect mind to heart to gut to ground.)

————————————————————————————

I feel satisfied with taking small steps. I feel satisfied with being able to contemplate my next best step. I feel satisfied with choosing what I can. I feel satisfied with how I start my day. I experience great satisfaction when eating a good meal. I feel satisfied when walking in nature. I feel satisfied dancing. I experience satisfaction with doing one small thing for myself each day.

Knowing.

————————————

adoration
(inhale deeply and absorb what is present.)

————————————————————————————

I love myself a little more each day. I love the way it feels to stretch and grow. I love knowing that contrast means the opposite is on the way. I love that I am lost, because it means I will be found. I love that I am wandering, because it keeps me wondering. I love that I am feeling things I never felt before. I love that I can always look up. I love that I am learning to be accepting of where I am. I love that I can be with emotions that I could not handle before.

LIVING.

————————————

celebration
(rise above and rejoice.)

————————————————————————————

I celebrate emotions ebbing and flowing. I celebrate waking up each day. I celebrate where I am in my journey. I celebrate that I attract experiences that help me discover my gifts. I celebrate signs and symbols appearing on my path. I celebrate the mastery I am leaning into. I celebrate seeking. I celebrate the interesting books, teachers, and methods that help me grow.

BEING.

————————————

exaltation
(ground in sacredness, devotion, and equanimity. . . unconditionally Love!)

————————————————————————————

I AM listening. I AM hearing. I AM acceptance. I AM seeing. I AM acknowledgment. I AM feeling. I AM Knowing. I listen intently. I hear reverently. I see sacredly. I acknowledge instantly. I accept fully. I feel intimately. I Know completely. I touch. I taste. I smell. I sense. I discern. I vibrate. I hum. I expand. I contract.

KNOWING.

————————————————

jubilation
(exhale your newly created vibrational reality and. . . believe!)

——————————————————————————————

I AM growth. I AM potential. I AM Creative Capacity. I AM the unfolding. I AM transforming. I AM the drop. I AM the wave. I AM the ocean. I AM the sky above. I AM none of it and all of it. I AM BEAUTY. I AM POLARITY. I AM MASTERY. I AM TIME AND I AM TIMELESS. I AM CREATIVITY. I AM EXPLORATION. I AM CLARITY. I AM SPACE.

When creating your own ladders of creation. . . always begin exactly where *You/you/YOU* are. Be truthful with how *You/you/YOU* feel. Be authentic in what *You/you/YOU* are thinking and feeling. A new human builds from the ashes of your old life. Let your words be the transformation and transmutation that lead to ascension. *You* are the bridge between where *you* are and where *You* want to go. Absorb the whole of *You/you/YOU* each step of the way. *You* are growing into *KNOWING* as *You* move up the ladder of consciousness, and into rainbow light. What *You* place into the universal vortex remains in escrow. Belief amplifies the energy and creates physical awareness. *KNOWING* creates change, transformation, and miracles.

attachment.

What has to dissolve?

The enslaved become sovereign
when no longer attached to their slavery.
The victimized become empowered
when no longer attached to their oppression.
Those at war find peace
when no longer attached to their fight.
***You* will find freedom**
when no longer attached to your story.
Each attachment dissolves
when identity ceases.
Every dissolving. . .
is a sacred rite of passage.

The ache of attachment is excruciating. *You* do not know how to let go; nor do *You* really want to. It can feel betraying to move on from people, places, and things, even when they are unhealthy, toxic, or abusive. No matter how much it hurts, *You* hang on. At times, the pain of attachment is felt physically. *You* cannot move forward; nor is there desire to do so. Attachment is a knife that cuts both ways. *You* feel it; the other feels it. Attachment is a tug of war, one drenched in codependency. In reality, all attachment is really fear. . . the fear of leaving, the fear of being loved, and the fear of shining brightly. Through attachment, your ego keeps *You* small; where settling for mediocrity and continually betraying *Self/self/SELF* becomes the norm.

Fear of the unknown keeps *You/you* attached to "what happened" and "what did not happen." This creates dense emotions that infiltrate all of your experiences. Angst. Anxiety. Frustration. Resistance. Grief becomes a hole that cannot be closed. Anger feels like a volcano that will not be soothed. Heartbreak is a chasm that might never be filled. Cries. Pain. Suffering. It hurts intensely. The heart aches deeply. Emotions are directly related to attachment.

There is a low growl deep within.
It is the sound of your animal; wild, feral, wounded, and hungry.
When it sinks its teeth into something, it will hang on until death.

As *Mind/mind* regurgitates *would haves, could haves, what ifs and whys. . .* days, weeks, months, and years can tick by. Weighed down by secrets, deception, manipulation, and corruption, vines of attachment grow strong and thick. The trauma of circumstance leaves individuals in bondage and enslaved by them. Everything will remind *You* of the past, what is no longer present in your life, or what coulda-shoulda-woulda been your future. With attachment, *You* cling to memories that never were. . . experiences *You* will never know. . . and special moments that *You* make up are going to be missed. Attachment is followed by collateral damage: lovers *you* couldn't fix, friendships gone awry, relationships encumbered with expectation, and family members that refuse to change.

The great hindrance of complexity is that *You/you/YOU* unknowingly become tied. People, places, things, beliefs, patterns, behaviors, dreams, goals, regrets, failures, successes, image, etc. . . . have strings of attachment. Your perspective on "what life should be" convolutes things. *What ifs* run wild. Attachments, causes, and your need to change what is warps reality into an abstract designs of shadow and light. *Self/self/SELF*-obsession. . . *Self/self/SELF*-absorption. . . and codependence are swamps that suck *You/you* in.

Life is unpredictable,
although constrained by order-generating rules of man-made and cosmic law.
Hang on for dear life.
But, be assured, all of eternity has *YOU* in its heavenly grasp.

Hiding within is a hungry, angry, frightened, and feral shadow animal. It wants meat and holds the attachment-based energies of revenge, regret, repression, and remorse. *You* may not have known an animal is crouching and present during your most emotional moments. *He/She/It* comes to remind *You* that other animals rest in your midst. Those who hurt and challenge *You* are not human. They are hungry animals, ready to pounce and kill. Human beings become worse than animals when acting out from attachment. Beware of them, but be aware of your *self*.

Your words, texts, and venomous sprays will betray *you*. The wanton desire for someone to pay or be punished illustrates your animal behaviors of hunger, greed, and lust. *Praying/preying* in this manner results only in your own punishment and imprisonment. Notice your animal when angrily desiring another be held accountable. Such vices will turn on *You*.

Cultivate compassion for the animal inside. *It* has been caged for too long. *It* does not need taming; it needs to be freed from your attachments. *You* and the animal have often curled up together in preparation for the hunt. Free this animal by awakening to your shadow expressions, projections, and hostilities. Your animal nature is another layer to accept, embrace, and absorb. *He/She/It* is here to teach *You/you/YOU*. Feel everything. Seek discernment, and detachment.

Slip into the unknown.
Something bigger. . . better. . . and more bountiful is always waiting.

Your specific pattern of connecting and clinging is your attachment style. Different attachment styles include insecure attachment, dismissive-avoidant attachment, and fearful-avoidant attachment. An insecure attachment style is an anxious-preoccupied expression that holds a negative view of *Self/self/SELF* and positive view of others. Here, change is resisted in order to remain small. With a negative view of *Self/self/SELF*, *You* do not stand in your power, or any unknown possibilities. If others are superior, *You/you/YOU* get to hold ont o victimhood.

The dismissive-avoidant attachment style possesses a positive view of *Self/self/SELF* and a negative view of others. This attachment of superiority creates an identity that is *self*-serving, arrogant, and entitled. Change is resisted out of fear of intimacy with *Self/self/SELF*.

Fearful-avoidant attachment relates to individuals having unstable or fluctuating views of *Self/self/SELF* and others. Any level of attachment creates passive-aggressive tendencies between staying and going. This friction eventually wears away and tears apart the existing reality. Fear of uncertainty is the primary place of resistance. Fearful-avoidant attachment is always based on a lack of trust or truth.

Regardless of style, attachment is attachment. If leaving a person, place, or thing without having healed, *You* have not really left. The ego convinces *You* of being complete, but your past will follow like a shadow. Reactivity creates escape into other relationships, activities, or modes of distraction. It may appear as if *You* are moving on, but the prior scenario with recur with a new person, place, or thing.

Each situation must be mastered before leaving it. However, in abusive situations, physically leaving is required. Whether staying or going, it is necessary to reach neutrality regarding the experience and person(s) involved. Be present with your emotions, thoughts, and energy until pain, discomfort, and negative thinking are no longer present.

Processing and regurgitating stories is futile.
This type of attachment prolongs suffering and compounds stress.

Be present to how *You/you/YOU* are tethered, and whom *You* are tied and bound to. When energy is focused upon another, *You/you/YOU* amplify their circumstance and reduce your power. This not only creates energy leakage inside *You/you/YOU* but also creates a hole within them. Nothing and no one outside of *You/you/YOU* requires saving. Remain focused on *Self/self/SELF*.

In being attached to a person, place, or thing. . . *You/you/YOU* make their life, circumstance, or situation about *You*. This *Self/self*-absorbed position stems from your need to control or need to be needed. This does not help. Instead, it traps the other in their condition. Recognize how *You/you/YOU* use others to distract from disowned parts of your *Self/self/SELF,* by way of control, interference, or projection. Attachment reveals your nature of codependency. Attachment to another's healing is your need for purpose and significance. Attachment to another's happiness is a way to ignore your life.

Anything or anyone that creates reaction is your healing work, not theirs. Instead of projecting your actions and emotions onto another's life, return to your inner world. Focus upon your own life. Instead of interfering, honor the sacred walk of every other. Allow others the dignity of fully experiencing their landscapes of horror, atrocity, humanity, alchemy, and divinity. Hold vigil and vision for their empowerment. Every human *Being/being/BEING* is Divine. Each person expresses sacredness in their own way—channeling it, living it, experiencing, receiving, and giving it. All are equal; see no hierarchy.

**You/you/YOU have chosen life to move through stages of awareness,
from completely unconscious to consciously devoted.**

The stronger the attachment, the more powerfully the person, place, or thing owns *You/you/YOU*. The tighter your grip, the greater your experience of codependence and enmeshment. Although attachment appears with things in the outside world, your attachments originate inside *You/you/YOU* and are primarily based on identity. The attachment to identities and what those encompass in terms of image, beliefs, role, and material accoutrement are what create complexity of thought, expectations, and emotional reactivity. Dissolve the energies of each identity and their stories. Identification is intimately connected to attachment. When identity is locked in story, perspective, and illusion. . . complexity builds. When *You/you/YOU* become aware that story is the hotbed of most attachments, *You* can begin dismantling it. The more deeply embedded the identity, the stronger the attachment and subsequent pain.

Cutting cords does not detach *You/you/YOU* from a person, place, or thing. This protocol leaves open connections flailing in the wind. These openings behave as portals for other "like" energies to attach. *Self/self/SELF*-reflection dissolves attachments. Presence of feeling—related density pain, loss, angst, desire, etc. . . . . dissolves energetic cords. Acceptance absorbs dense energy, alchemizing it for other uses.

At the root of all attachment are beliefs on spirituality, faith, and religion. These create the guidelines *You* live by. Loyalty to religion, culture, and family not only creates your most profound attachments but is also what derails *You*. When unwilling to detach, *You* remain in a state of wanting, lack, and *SELF*-denial. This often results in praying, pleading, prostrating, and weeping. Ultimately, your life is based on attachments connected to the *God/god* of your understanding, whether that is a punishing God, loving God, judgmental God, external God, or God within. This "God" reflects as your thoughts, parents, friends, social and cultural mores, doctors, government, religion, etc. . . . Face your *Self/self/SELF* head on; there is nowhere to run or hide.

Cutting a cord only creates a live wire that creates another shock.

As *You* plunge into your shadows of attachment, belief systems will surface. Layers of negativity and discordant thinking become more and more apparent. Your attachments may even have attachments. Through presence, discoveries regarding your perceptions, patterns, and behaviors will rise. *You* will see the numerous ways attachment appears. *You/you/YOU* may be attached to being right. . . to justice. . . and to details. *You/you/YOU* may be attached to what is hidden, and to having control. *You/you/YOU* could be attached to image, perfection, and identity. Perhaps there is attachment to being successful, seen, heard, or acknowledged. Your attachments will trip *You* up, create delay, and destroy fulfillment. Through a daily practice of inquiry, contemplation, quiet meditation, absorption/awareness, appreciation, and anchoring into new creation. . . balanced equilibrium with your surroundings can be attained.

When closed off from possibility, *You/you/YOU* will experience detour after detour. Attachments keep you tied, bound, and stuck. Attachments are not of true *SELF*. These places of friction are pointers. Resistance exacerbates challenges upon this terrain, creating additional winding pathways and unpaved unknowns. But even these scenic routes lead back to the *high way*. All of your steps are training for future destinations. Resist nothing; embrace everything. Then, return to the sacred sanctuary of your high heart. Rise into the cathedral of your consciousness. Bear witness from your highest point of *BEING*.

The physical body is a sponge,
soaking in every experience, environment,
energy, and imprinting.
Beware. . . and be aware;
the enemy is *in-a-me*.
Do not take a lifetime to give back
what has been collected.
Become a sieve of what is good for *You/YOU*.
Do not be attached to what is not yours.
Do not even be attached to what is.

knowing.
What am i/eye attached to?
i/eye keep myself bound because of my attachments.

Knowing.
I Am aware of my behaviors; I can change them.

KNOWING.
I AM the witness.

NOTES

the grace of detachment.

What is the remembering?

Invite the grace of detachment.
Consciously initiate this.
Let the kiss of floods invoke the aura of your light body.
The fragrance of union reveals truth.
The flavor of tenderness expands your energy.
Through appreciation, your visceral weight of frustration dissolves.
The essence of tranquility brings forth alchemy in the body,
placing *You/you* on sacred ground.
Receive your gift of human grace.
***KNOW*. . . your presence is enough.**

Explore life's array of landscapes as distant lands. Take in the sights, sounds, smells, tastes, and touches of aliveness. Fully imbibe every destination. Every valley will move *You/you/YOU* deeply inside yourself. Each mountain will lead *You/you/YOU* high above where *You/you* ever imagined possible. Swamps will bring forth the beauty of your murky and hidden depths, while the ecstasy of aliveness beneath the surface brings about new expressions.

When life brings low points, kneel and kiss the ground. When it lifts *You/you/YOU* up, embrace the sky. Sink into each experience as *You* would a pristine pool of water. Dive in, swim around, and play at the bottom of your sacred pond. Kick, splash, and float. Then, get out. Clean yourself up, and ground in appreciation for the intimacy and embrace of your deep ocean of consciousness. Your sacred depths are filled with all manner of experience, expression, awareness, and wisdom.

Within the blessing of challenge and the illusion of duality,
***You/you/YOU* created attachments;**
in order to discover the grace of detachment, for awakening to your humanity.

Each experience of life is leading *You* toward the spiritual mastery of detachment. This is not unattachment, apathy, disconnection, indifference, numbness, or not feeling. It is not separation or complacency. Detachment is full immersion in an experience without attachment to the outcome, or any agenda. Inner communion is the primary focus, while also fully allowing the external experience as it unfolds. Face and deeply feel your life circumstances, and this will dissolve and absorb the energies of attachment. Feeling every emotion in its magnitude—without needing to shift the feeling, experience, or outcome— brings forth incredible growth, and opportunities for wisdom. Human beings incarnate to understand, experience, and integrate the physical world. *YOU* came for duality; *Knowing* it teaches the truth of *Oneness/ONENESS*.

Treks into your dark wilderness shall bring forth a band of wounded children, led by the youngest among them. This babe in the woods holds two great secrets: your darkness and your light. *He/She/They* holds tightly to a sacred gem. This soul stone is your sacred wound, the origin point of your echoes. *He/She/They* also hold a crystal goblet, that of your Essence. This is the holy chalice of *GOD BEING YOU*. This mystical, magical wounded child *BEING/being* is your yin and yang, requiring attention at different moments. Both are always with *You*. Initially, they behave as children do, getting lost in time and play. Fully immersing in creations they have cast, your holy angel and divine devil imaginatively create in the light of day, and dark of night. Somewhere in time, duality became your reality.

You/you/YOU inadvertently cling to souvenirs: injustices, wounds, grievances, and memory. This is extra baggage; it only slows your travels. These trinkets are fool's gold. Do not make them more valuable than they are. Empty yourself of what *You/you/YOU* hold, grabbed, and cling to. Cultivate compassion and empathy for your wounded parts, and what is bound to be. All of it is necessary to make history.

The Grace of Detachment	The Remembering	Knowing
The Illusion—Attachment	What has to dissolve?	Aliveness
True Love's Kiss—The Flood	What nature is required?	Creation
Aura of the Light Body	What is emerging?	Unification
Fragrance Emitting Union	What is the inhale?	Truth
Flavor of Tenderness	What is the exhale?	Energy
Melody Through Balance	What is harmonizing?	Growth
Visceral Memory—Frustration	What is being absorbed?	Wisdom
Alchemy of Body	What can be transmuted?	The Void
Essence as Tranquility	What may be embodied?	Infinite Presence
Forgiving Attachment— For Giving Detachment	What is for giving?	Neutrality

The pull of attachment, to things outside *You,* relates to what *you* are tied to internally: mentally, emotionally, and energetically. *You/you* call attachment love, but it is far from that. Love based in attachment is dense, shadowy, and dark. It will always be a double-edged sword that creates bleeding hearts.

Sanskrit has two words that translate to *love.* However, they are vastly different, and the distinction between them is detachment. *Kama* is self-centered and personally attached, usually with romantic tendencies. This love is merely a facade, implying that there is no happiness without togetherness. Selfish attachments are sticky. They can be smothering and dominating and are generally codependent.

Prema is pure love, where the desire is happiness for all. This is higher love that sees through the eyes of the divine. There is no attachment, only love, and it is unconditional. This is true love. The entanglement of personal motives is not a factor. Detachment is foundational in this gift of pure love and freedom. Love is given space for pure expression with no expectation of return. When cultivating the grace of detachment, prema is to be given to *Self/self/SELF.* Then, it can be bestowed upon others, creating a foundation for embodying unconditional love.

Attachment is when you are too focused on what is outside.
Detachment is when your focus returns to what is of import on the inside.

Your greatest attachment is to *Being/being You.* Life knows how to dissolve and decondition your constructs of identity. It will create circumstances that require surrendering anything less than the bigness of *YOU.* Detachment returns *You* to the child *self,* disentangling threads of history and conditioning collected along the way. In experiencing the full gamut of emotions, awareness comes and attachments dissolve. In unwinding the wound, unconditional love reawakens. That embrace of the playful Divine child will open the way for the great to express through the small. It is possible to be present, conscious, and aware, regardless of where life takes *You.*

Through devotion and discipline, begin exploring inner space. Bring the essence of love and being loved without conditions to all things, including yourself. This stage of *knowing* acknowledges the river of life, the direction it is flowing, and the landscape surrounding it. The landscape may be overgrown, messy, and still beautiful. Witnessing the space is all that is necessary. When focusing upon the river, ask, "*Will I move with the river, or against it?*" Your choice determines the next experience. Either complexity or simplicity will unfold. The moment of choice occurs in a blink of an eye but sets off a cascade of events through time.

Life knows where it is going; *You/you/YOU,* not so much. Even so, life will lovingly guide. Embody a conscious approach to life and living. Every soul is capable, including *You.* Embodying detachment integrates the energies of unconditional love and spiritual generosity. Detachment also expands the skills of discipline, focus, and vision. With humility, follow the direction of Spirit whenever it whispers, remembering it is the sacred river in which *YOU* flow.

Your stories will mold *You/you/YOU*.
Your beliefs will hold *You/you/YOU*.
Your questions will guide *You/you/YOU*.
Your words shall create *You/you/YOU*.
Your thinking will play with *You/you/YOU*.
Your integration will enrich *You/you/YOU*.
Your embodiment will define *You/you/YOU*.
Your disintegration will return *You/you/YOU*.
you are the *You* that *YOU* have been waiting for.
Now. . .
Go find Your *SELF*!

knowing.
How do i/eye let go?
i/eye am afraid to let go, and yet i/eye will, little by little.

Knowing.
I Am feeling my feelings, as I let go.

KNOWING.
I AM present; I AM capable.

. . .

TRUE LOVE'S KISS—THE FLOOD

What nature is required?

Let melancholy reveal the storm.
Let it flood *You* with emotion.
Drown within your depths.
Know your vast reservoir. . .
and ponder the small puddles too.
Dip within the trickles that whisper of secret longings.
Breathe. . . and bathe these lost dreams into belonging.
Be inspired by the strength. . . courage. . . and vulnerability
that peer from beneath your misty windows. . . of soul.
Be stilled by Great Spirit; receive your anointing.
Be drenched by all that showers; let life's waters fill *You*.
Be cleansed through and through.
Let joy now paint the picture. . .
that reigns within *YOU*.

There come precious, beautiful, human moments where it is necessary to tear... cry... wail... anguish... grieve... cleanse... and clear the space. When these happen, let the tears roll. Mourn what must be mourned. Cry every last drop, especially when it feels as though the tears will never end. *You/you/YOU* have held much; even more than *You/you/YOU* are conscious of. Life will bring experiences that support this process. If *You/you* repress what needs to be felt, life will create experiences that support this process. *You* will experience storms, which subsequently bring the flooding of all that is held. Your body *Knows* what to do in these moments. It is organic and wise. It sees possibilities that *You/you/YOU* cannot discern from your current position. Let go, and let it flow.

Grief in the body stems from long before your current experience. This moment of grieving likely reopened old wounds. Grief is years, lifetimes, and generations in the making. Emotional density builds until the perfect moment of complete release. This the sacred flood. Dip into your heavy spaces. Honor your times of purging. Do not judge yourself, the emotions, or your experience.

Grief comes with loss, discarded dreams, and abandoned visions. Transformation occurs within the cocoon of grieving. Tears collect when they are stuffed, swallowed, and held down. Withholding is an act of *Self/self/SELF*-betrayal and only builds more sadness. When *You/you* repress what needs to be felt, experiences of flood are created. Blocked emotion creates sickness, depression, dis-ease, and increased aging. Heartbreak, grief, sadness, rage, anger, envy, happiness, joy, and peace require commitment. Presence and *Self/self/SELF*-love are necessary for navigating tumultuous waters.

In engaging the path of rebel, secret obsessions abound, creating floods, big and small, that have hidden within your earthen ground all along.

Floods are part of your nature. Waterfalls are as well. Aspects of *You/you/YOU* have become frozen in time. Tears smooth the rigid walls that barricade your mind and heart. Release softens the hard edges of your persona. When hardened edges give way, torrential waves of time release. These sacred waters bring forth rich cleansing. Your inner rivers have the power to heal and nourish your creative heart. They precipitate a beautiful new life. Drench your *soil/soul*. Open to your *current* experience and receive the *dew/due* of your holy spirit. Revitalize your foundation, so that *You* move toward sacred ground.

Floods appear quickly but need time to subside. Tidal waves result after tears have steadily risen over the years but have not been allowed to flow. Beginning low in the belly, waves build in pressure as they move toward the heart, throat, and eyes. *You* will experience a bulging feeling in the neck. This blocked sensation is the ego's attempt to build an energetic dam to keep *You/you* from shedding what must release. Tightening within the throat will ensue as swells below intensify. As it becomes difficult to breathe, *You* feel weak in the knees and struggle to stand in the buoyancy of your moving waves. In an exact and perfect moment, tears rain down, first as a trickle. A heavy downpour follows. Hang on tight while the flood rushes through. Grab hold of your heart with one hand, and your stomach with the other. Curl into a fetal position and be swept under. Do not turn away when grief knocks upon your heart. With each loss, *You* also die. *You/you* will be unable to return to what was. Certain parts of *You* must wash away. With each flood, your sacred ground is purified.

**Every single thing in your life is an expression of Love and Light. . .
even the hard, painful, and challenging.**

Some moments bring an ocean of tears. All manner of sounds can be experienced. In moments, a crazed banshee can be heard, howling and wailing from deeply within *You/you/YOU*. These cries and heaves are hauntings of trauma and emotional exhaustion. But there are also excruciating moments, where waters run dry. Wails and screams deep within, resounding of hopelessness, helplessness, and despair, will bear no sound. Their energy is jarring, stemming from the weight of visceral pain held through decades. During these experiences, a soundless cry hangs heavy in the air. It seems frozen, as the mouth hangs open for a prolonged time. Aching with a sound of such depth, it is too painful to fathom. Heaves of ancient pain convulse from a bottomless chasm. This anguishing pain is the cry of the living dead, rising from deep within the body's archive. Expressing the intense heartbreak of *Self*-betrayal and heartbreak, this death will be peaceful. These aspects of *Self/self/SELF* have died inside, but they do not rest. They haunt. They carry weapons of self-flagellation: shame, guilt, regret, and remorse.

Others' tears flood forth from a stagnant stew of bacteria-filled waters. These swamps of *being* formed in childhood, holding the condemnations and judgments of others. Over time, these cesspools of toxicity impact *Self*-esteem and *Self*-worth, becoming the green muck of jealousy and the murky depths of bitterness. When esteem and worth are triggered, *You/you* inadvertently return to these boggy places. Use each tear, cry, and flood to clear everything from *You*. Let these sacred waters permeate every part of *You/you/YOU*, pouring out of your eyes, mind, heart, and every cell. Let the flood have its way with *you* and be washed clean.

Once the deluge recedes, feelings of peace shall sprinkle over *You*. Once tears subside, *You* will feel stranded, lying exhausted on the shores of longing. *You* and your body will feel weary. However, succumb to rest for a while. This pause is the kindness your body has been aching for. Open your sacred portals of precipitation.

The windows of the soul need washing now and then.

Tears are especially important for transitioning through experiences of attachment. With attachment, tears drip with need and codependence. With self-absorption, the shadow *Self/self* wallows in the swamp of enmeshment. Even if the dark night feels long, the years have been building an escrow of equivalent light. Know that light will don a new beginning on the other side. Life will bring highs, lows, and distortions. Love and accept them all.

As inner connection and authentic expression grow, it will not matter whether tears express happiness or sadness. Tears associated with detachment offer communion with inner humanity, as a sacred baptism of mind, body, and soul. These moments sweet and tender, rich with vulnerability and intimacy. With detachment, transformation occurs inside and out. Let tears of renewal soften *You*, expanding your ability to access greater love, compassion, and sacredness. Make room, so that holiness has space to flood in. Creativity abounds from your tears. Inspiration will create rich overflow. Embrace the beauty of your nature! All emotions are Go(o)d emotions! The extraordinary is present; right here. . . right now. *You/you/YOU* need only be present to it.

While *You* have a body—*You/you/YOU* are not the body. Your body is a vehicle. Mankind is supported through the cleansing and release of backlogged multidimensional memory. Physical sensations are pointers. Ancient garbled sounds of history surround us. The face of pain and trauma is visible all around us. After facing your grief and pain, *You* will feel the intense ache and pull of pain sitting low and deep within others. *You* will feel the dead weight of those who have passed on. Open to the generational pain that has backed up. The tears *You* shed belong to your mother, grandmothers, and great-grandmothers as far back as time. Your tears release the pain of your father, grandfathers, and great-grandfathers. There are many ways to serve. Channel and absorb the unfelt grief of the ancients, unresolved ancestral trauma, and long-held collective pain.

Imagine the grief of men that are wounded, not allowed to cry, sent to war, and those who became hardened. Consider the grief of women, who lost children, have been battered, and are abused. Allowing these energies to pass through *You* engages sacred activism and soulful service. As a conduit for collective grief, *You* are used in an incredibly sacred manner. In becoming a vessel for release, the burden on future generations clears. Your body can be a conduit for moving unresolved energy. It is not easy work, but it does create ripples of impact. What *You/you/YOU* do for another, *You* do for yourself, and generations to come.

Do not fear feeling your treasure trove of *Being/being*;
swim in your *sea/see* of *Knowing/knowing/KNOWING*.
The pure heart is hidden by
grievances, judgments, and criticism.
Wash these places with holy water.
Let the *I/i/eye*s be cleansed of what was seen.
Grief is a secret passageway to infinite love.
Wade in this holy water. . . it runs deep.
Do not rush the journey or something becomes lost. . .
***You/you/YOU*.**
To truly know love, loving, and what it means to be loved. . .
be swept away by your river of tears.
Let the current carry *You*
to the shores. . . of longing and belonging.
Behold the *SELF*. . .
Behold the *Self*. . .
Get hold of your *self*.
Flood each dimension with *LOVE*.

knowing.
How do I not get lost in the flood?
i/eye can drown; but i/eye won't die.

Knowing.
My tears are sacred; they are holy waters.

. . .

AURA OF THE LIGHT BODY

What does it look like?

Keep burning. . .
Keep letting go. . .
Keep dissolving. . .
Keep evaporating. . .
Keep disappearing. . .
Within nothingness. . . is everything.
Your life requires only that *You*
do more nothing. . .
and BE. . .
more everything.

Most people assume they express humanity, when in truth it is buried, repressed, quashed, and locked away. The kiss of heartbreak reawakens presence to it. Immersing within heartbreak reconnects *You* to the tenderness of *Being*. In facing sadness, heartache, and grief. . . a secret doorway opens. This "backdoor" accelerates enlightened awareness. Grief invites a pause. It gives time for presence to court your humanity, by sinking into the stagnancy inside your body. Through grief, *You* meet an identity whose time has come to die. Trust, a new flowering of *You,* will birth. Dawning of aliveness rests inside your humanity. This awakening showers light through your auric field.

Blocked energy is freed from cells with awareness, breakthroughs, and presence. The dark night of the soul is a cauldron of alchemical transformation. Listen to the sensations of your body. Feel each twinge, pain, and ache. Breathe through them. By doing so, stuck energies move. The body will tell *You* when it is no longer tired, heavy, and burdened.

Lack of *KNOWING* exists because Spirit became disembodied through the weight of wounding and conditioning. Spirit never left your body; *You* did. With increased alignment and inner authority, the body becomes less dense. Your Light Body expands by absorbing all that weighs *you* down: repressed darkness and dense energy. Owning your secrets, lies, and betrayals illuminates the body and *Being/being/BEING*. The Light Body is amplified through the descension process. Light cannot be seen in Light. There, it disappears and becomes sameness. Light is seen in the dark, where it shines brightly. Telling the truth, to yourself and others, lightens *You* up.

Absorb your darkness; release your light.
Illumination rises and radiates with this integration.

When dark times come, particularly *dark-night-of-the-soul* moments, consciousness can rest in the same place for weeks, months, or even years. In becoming present to your unconscious nature of *being*, and its dense thoughts, energy, and emotions... begin dissolving and disintegrating. As these changes occur, your energy, emotions, vibration, and frequency start balancing. Externally, it may appear as if nothing is happening, but subtle and powerful transformations are occurring within the stillness and presence. Deeply feeling profoundly impacts your Light Body.

Powerful experiences are encountered in dark spaces because light shines brightest here. Do not allow life's challenges to take *You/YOU* from center. Let these experiences point *You* to your center of *Being/BEING*. The darkness will cajole *You/you* into a fight. Douse it with *LOVE* and *LIGHT*. Let your *Love/LOVE* shine *Light/LIGHT* into the discordant places of *Self/self*. As a disciple of the darkness and Light, become a powerful receptacle for divine *Being/BEING*. Devotedly and with discipline... Master your mind. Master your emotions. Master your physical body. Master your energy.

Reflect the energy of water to expand the aura of your Light Body.
In raising your vibration, the global reflection of climate change also shifts.

The Light body is fueled by *LOVE*. Let no knowledge of hate, division, or separation remain. Amplify your frequency through *Self/self/SELF*-love, forgiveness, and compassion. The body is not *You*; it is a container for Essence to have form. However, for Essence to rise, the body must be upgraded from *Being/being* a human animal to *BEING* a Divine Temple of *LIGHT*. Align to your Essence. Enlightening of consciousness is a full-bodied experience. Each degree of embodiment increases the amount of Light *You/YOU* are capable of holding. Light is the most vital source available to *You*. It is freely available and abundant.

When consciously filling the body with Light, *You* initiate activations that recalibrate *You/you/YOU* to your original Light Body code. As cells metabolize higher light codes, your body vibrates at higher frequencies. This recoding energetically connects *You* with Source. The sun's rays, nature, nutrition, meditation, and glandular activation further support your absorption of Light. Resonance aligns mental, emotional, physical, and etheric bodies. These multidimensional aspects work in tandem to create the balance of your masculine and feminine poles. The aura of the Light Body appears when living with higher alignment.

Integrate your density, by embodying your humanity.
This is true service to the world.

Life will continually bring *You/you/YOU* to the mystery... willingly or unwillingly. Control is its antithesis. Do not get caught up in your human story. Merely let it guide your steps for transformation and transcendence. Personal growth, *Self/self/SELF*-care, and *Self/self/SELF*-reflection recharge the Light of our world. Embracing your humanity serves the greater whole. As we each embrace more humanity, the whole world is lightened. Illumination comes when individuals are grounded in right condition.

May the sun reveal the warmth of your radiance. May the moon convey your power of Light within darkness. May the stars illustrate your ability to shine. Stay grounded in all that ebbs, flows, and wanes. Once embodied, the aura of your Light Body will beam within the darkest of times and shine on the brightest of days. Your Light Body is the illumination of Mastery.

It is not necessary to know how your Light makes the world brighter; it simply does. *You/you/YOU* are composed of sacred geometry and multidimensional energy forms. The Light Body is a cosmic grid of creation, and your vehicle of transcendence. Light is a natural occurrence of Divine order. *You* are Light.

Do not forget to leave the light on. . .
as *You* move in and out of dark places.
From the absorption, emptiness,
and nothingness that darkness avails,
***You* can uncover the fullness of the void**
and birth many creations.
Find your fulfillment. . .
it lay hidden within every thing,
dark and light.
Embrace all that *IS*. . .
discover *wholeness/holiness*. . .
and see your true face.

knowing.
Where is the light in me?
i/eye can find light in my darkness.

Knowing.
I see the light in me.

KNOWING.
I AM Light.

. . .

FRAGRANCE-EMITTING UNION

What does it smell like?

Open the inner eye for heightened vision.
Open the inner ear for holy listening.
Open higher mind for receptivity of wisdom.

Open the body for higher activation of energy.
Give your raw animal senses over. . .
and be laid bare.
Become naked. . .
undressed from what is illusory.
Let devotion be your perfume. . .
and awaken the scent
of Divine union.

The glandular system is a bridge between the human animal and spiritual awakening. These hormonal and glandular secretions emit a scent or fragrance that is distinctive. In spiritual transcendence, glands create activations that awaken access to higher consciousness. Utilize your animal nature to awaken the mystery of your glandular system. Let instinct guide your masculine and feminine energies, not conditioning. When life smells funky and repelling, it is because *You/you* stand within the sewer of the *Mind/mind*. The stink of the world comes from hunger, ambition, competition, and lust. Any belief in separateness—as caste, creed, religion, personhood, species, object, etc.—is simply that: a belief. Slip through your illusion of multiplicity.

People secrete specific hormones as a means of communication. This is another way for consciousness and creativity to express. Your animal *scent/sense* is an intimate experience of internal *being*ness. Glandular secretions from animals, such as deer musk, present a similar fragrance to what humans emit when they relax into deeply feeling. Musk enhances and activates clairsentience. When fragrant and inviting, the sacred *heart/hearth* within your secret garden visibly expresses in the world.

What *You* do not have. . . give to yourself. What *You* do not understand. . . inquire within for understanding. Whom *You* have not known. . . discover that part of *You/you/YOU*. Meet in the middle of all experiences, expressions, and emotions. Then, *You* will be able to serve without agenda, codependence, or the stench of *Self/self/SELF*-absorption. Bring the fragrance of inner union to all that is externally separate. Let that aliveness waft upon all that *You* encounter.

You are a chemical factory; vibration, alignment, and action determine whether your scent is funky or fragrant.

The pineal gland is the meeting point between physical-body earth and intuitive-etheric heaven. The pineal is a small gland in the center of the brain. Considered the body's clock, it sets many internal rhythms. Becoming active at night and peaking at midnight, the pineal gland loses all nerve connections, except for a few to the eyes, shortly after birth. It matures by age five and calcifies around puberty. The health of the spinal gland is directly related to the adrenal system.

The pituitary gland acts as a thermostat for the lower endocrine glands by secreting hormones that stimulate them. It maintains balance and expresses the mind's tendency toward the crude or the subtle, by enhancing the lower or upper glands. The right and left lobes of this gland control body/mind functions and higher mental/spiritual functions, respectively. Balanced development is spiritually advantageous in this master controlling gland, as it harnesses lower glands and maintains balance.

The thyroid and parathyroid regulate insulin and energy. The thyroid is a butterfly-like gland in the throat. The parathyroids are small peas behind each wingtip of the thyroid and work with calcium and phosphate to maintain bone thickness and strength. These glands affect one's sense of self-worth, and too-little secretion leads to the need to bolster one's ego. Overproduction leads to scattered, unstable thought, while underproduction yields apathy and depression. The proper balance of this gland is important for the mind as well as the body.

Finally, there are the thymus, adrenals, and gonads. The thymus gland is the main definer of *Self* on the biological level. The gonads relate to hormones in the testes or ovaries. The adrenal glands, composed of the adrenal medulla and the adrenal cortex, are related to water balance, sex hormone production, and cortisol. The adrenals also connect synapses for the sympathetic nervous system and hormones related to the fight- or-flight response.

**Through growth as emotional mastery, awaken to the union within,
as *You* dissolve the black hole of lust.**

You/you/YOU are a blend of masculine and feminine, here to discover the equilibration of doing and being. *You/you/YOU* have likely been overgiving and underreceiving. This creates an imbalance of energy that results in taking, pushing, and pulling. *You/you/YOU* are wilting and dying because of this. Whenever *You* move in opposition to the soul's highest desires, a slow death ensues as shadows takeo ver. The higher expression and balance of allowing and receptivity will counteract these shadow expressions. Experience your supreme state of *BEING* where desires are magnetized. Instead of leaning forward into things, recline and allow them to flow in. This divine mastery will envelope every manifestation with your pure fragrance of *BEING*.

To move from imbalance to balance, it is necessary to experience your opposite. To balance your shadow masculine side. . . stop. . . rest. . . and be still. *You/you/YOU* must learn to receive and flow. To balance your feminine side, *You/you/YOU* must fully feel and express. Slip into your dark womb space; wail. . . moan. . . and beat her drum of discord. Express all the sounds, words, and sensations that are suppressed. The shadow feminine side has been manipulative and in hiding, causing her wisdom, listening, and capacity to draw in and become diminished. Let the feminine feel so deeply as to inspire the masculine into creation.

Holy basil emits a fragrance that represents union. This highly regarded herb possesses a wide range of health and psycho-spiritual benefits. Known as *the Elixir of Life* and *Mother Medicine of Nature,* holy basil restores balance and harmony to the mind, body, and spirit, with pronounced effects on the nervous system. Also known as tulsi, it restores and balances the subtle electromagnetic fields generated by the mind and body. It is both fragrant and harmonizing, unifying different layers of the body.

**_You/you/YOU_ cannot be in love, with love, of love, or as love
until anchoring the fragrance and feeling of being loved.**

Open to the flirtatious longings that dance amid your energetics. Give them space to be raw and natural. Be present to your makings of love through creation. The greatest love story of all time exists within the courtship of your two halves. In the shadows and within Light, together *You* have woven many expressions of *Love/love/LOVE*. These energies intertwine as twin flames, combusting life until *You* find balance, reverence, and respect with them. The dance of masculine and feminine energies provides a vast palette of experience. Bring them back to the garden of eden and ground them in the earthen truth of their nature. These two aspects of *You* are the father and mother of all creation, whose union creates the full gamut of life. Ground within your woodsy musk scent, which is naturally rooted inside your earthen soil.

This cosmic love affair is a romance of the deepest integration. Your energies are sacred and birth creation when these two come together. This fragrance of love is yours to experience. This union is for *You* to inhale. Every note holds aspects of *You/you/YOU;* to have and to hold, for better or worse, for richer or poorer, in sickness and in health till death do *You* part. *You* are larger than what *you* see. Until knowing your full spectrum of emotions, *You/you/YOU* are not whole; nor have *You/YOU* known complete humanity. *YOU* are yin, and *YOU* are yang. *YOU* are the darkness within light, and the light within darkness. This is the sacred matrimony of *Self/self/SELF*.

Experience life as a holy vow and fragrant union, with all dimensions of *Self*, awakening to love in each moment. . . and the next. . . and the next. Love created *YOU* like itself. Let nothing hinder that perfection. Receive your fragrance, allowing that whole expression to bless the world. *ONE*ness exists regardless of the situation at hand, because there is only *ONE* of *You/Me/Us/Them*. . . *ONE* heart—*ONE* path—*ONE* door—*ONE* key—*ONE* love—*ONE* peaceful harmony. Let the unified expression of *YOU* exude the fragrant union of your highest expression.

Be still. . . Let the day retire. . . Release what has passed. . .
It is no more. . . nor is it *YOU*. Breathe in today. . .
Be free of the future. . . it is not here. . . nor shall it ever be.
Open your hands for what may be received.
Open to rhythmic movements that serve all.
Open your body to what awakens *You/you/YOU*.
Open your life to the intimacy of *BEING*.
Let the scent of Spirit. . . emit your divine fragrance into the world.

knowing.
Why do i/eye feel disconnected?
i/eye am noticing my individual parts.

Knowing.
I can create inner and outer connection.

KNOWING.
I AM divine union.

FLAVOR OF TENDERNESS

What does it taste like?

Be still. . . Breathe in this moment. . .
It is complete. . .
It is whole. . . It is Now.
It is breath. . . and in-sight.
I am *You/you/YOU*. . .
***You* are *Me/me/ME*.**
In the eternal now,
we always meet.

There is a place past *who I am* and *who am I*. It ventures beyond yesterdays and tomorrows. It rises above thoughts and fears. It has no ambition, nor does it seek recognition. This place is the sinkhole of tenderness. There is no separation here. There is no death; there is no life. There is no attachment, only tenderness for each experience. Everything is present by way of pure thought and feeling. This level of tenderness holds pain and joy with the grace of detachment, fully seeing, feeling, and acknowledging. . . without the need to interfere with or change anything. This sacred presence is a high vibration where there is no animal, human, or God. . . only immersive experience bearing holy witness to the present moment.

When pain comes, the soft human animal removes its hard shell. It feels tender and easily bruises from sharp edges that appear at every turn. Life seems distant and cold. People appear apathetic and aloof. *Mind/mind* projects blame, shame, injustice, and betrayal upon every experience. Much has calcified around your heart, keeping *You/you/ YOU* guarded and turned away. When *you* stumble upon this foreign landscape, tenderly awaken. It is easy to disregard the effect of loss, until intimately knowing loss. It is normal to dismiss grief, until grief is limp in your arms. *You* are arriving at a place of *knowing*. *You* may feel alone, but this is false. *You* are never alone.

Moving quickly through life forms heart walls. Pushing forward is distraction. Go inside. Fully enter the heart space. Get lost within it. Purely felt grief provides a powerful gateway for rebirth. Intimacy with your emotions becomes your solvent that washes away pain. Spiritual power comes through expansion of the heart. To reach your zenith, the heart must break. *You/you/YOU* will awaken through the same doors that brought slumber. Moments of heartbreak squeeze old energies, feelings, and memories out of *You/you/ YOU*. Experiences of grief beckon timelessness. When opening this sacred door—even a crack—a whisper arises, *"Won't you come inside? Find comfort, and a soft place of rest."* The heart needs time to heal, but doing so requires timelessness and tenderness.

As *You* endeavor upon truth in grounding, restore tenderness to life
through the key of tenderness to *Self/self/SELF*.

Humanity is not easy to hold. It is unbearable at times. Respites must be taken. Activities that free the heart from feeling for short periods become necessary. However, to also access subconscious knowledge supports bridging multidimensional layers of *Self*. Creativity expands awareness immensely. "Paint" has the word "pain" within it. Painting provides an integrative, intuitive activity for transmuting pain, while loss brings forth subconscious messages that offer insight and healing. Art stewards the subconscious mind and intuitive nature through fragile moments, by bringing meaning to the meaningless in color, images, and expression.

When there are no words—or where too many can be unnecessarily spoken—imagery, color, texture, and hue offer solace and silence. A canvas can channel wisdom from another dimension, time, or space. When experiencing intense emotion, pick up a paintbrush, crayon, marker, or collage paper. Let these tools speak for *you*. Do not create anything specific; it does not need to look like anything. No one has to see it. Experience a meditative respite from deeply feeling. The soul heals through creative expression. Spirit speaks through art.

Your range of emotional intelligence—through reactivity and response ability—holds an expansive palette of colorful expression. Emotion is the paint with which *You/you/YOU* color relationships, experiences, and expression. Play with your full crayon box. Doing so will awaken an expanding experience of emotional maturity.

**Tenderness is a lamb's compassion for the wolf that stalks it;
the lamb feels the wolf's hunger, pain, and suffering as a common experience.**

Personal experiences with pain cultivate greater authentic presence and empathy with others. Taste the sweetness of *Self/self/SELF*-acceptance. Timeless presence salvages the tenderness of original *Being/BEING*. A tender touch shifts a moment's tone, tenor, and timing in a deeply compassionate way. There is no greater superpower than a tender heart. Through an open ear, understanding heart, and loving hand. . . healing happens. Find yourself in every other. Be the tenderness in humanity's shared experiences. Commonality sits within the fractures of our collective pain. When your wound is held with vulnerability, the ability to remain open to the world's heartbreak blooms. Give yourself the love, safety, caring, and compassion required. Then, unconditionally give that to everyone and everything.

**May *You/you/YOU* be reminded of innocence. . .
the awe of little things. . .
find joy in the ordinary. . .
and beauty with familiar strangers.
May *You/you/YOU* see every other as
untainted, unspoiled, and untrained. . .
expressions of love,
waiting to be loved.
May the silence be filled with peals of laughter. . .
endless declarations of unconditional love
and ooze with celebration.**

knowing.
Why is life harsh; why are people harsh?
i/eye tend to my wounds.

Knowing.
I am tender.

KNOWING.
I AM the expression of divine tenderness.

. . .

MELODY THROUGH BALANCE—APPRECIATION

What does it sound like?

People go up and down. . .
bobbing like waves;
shaken and stirred.
Do not pay attention to other's actions;
this will distract *You*.
Hold your mind. . . your emotions. . . and your body. . . steady. . .
at attention. . . with intention. . . and in focused direction.
Life is a play of comedy and tragedy.
Balance this tightrope. . .
Do not look down;
do not look back,
or behind.
Be present to where *You* are.
Remain in your lane.

The human experience involves building spiritual balance and life balance. These are as intertwined as DNA. One cannot exist without the other, and they take practice. Life is not only the material world, nor is it an ethereal world. It is the integrated experience of inspired spiritual experience through the expression of form. *You* incarnated for the ability to harmonize energies and create matter. *You/you/YOU* are the fluctuation of balance and imbalance; a wave within waves. Your expression is the ebb and flow of light and shadow. Balancing emotions will balance your life. Create a state of balance that lets *You/YOU* feel and know this center point moment by moment. Let the melody of balance form a new foundation.

There exists a melody specific to *YOU*.
***You/you/YOU* are in the process of being tuned.**

You/YOU cannot move past any emotion until it is balanced and neutral. Burden, stress, and pain tease of imbalance. Boulder-like experiences beckon recalibration. Until life hurts bad enough, *You* will not change your behaviors or lifestyle. Do not fit spirituality into your life. This is a setup for imbalance. Fit life into your spirituality.

Balanced living takes place when giving appropriate presence to people and things that matter. Create experiences and relationships that provide greater meaning and fulfillment. Discover hobbies and play. Discern your true desires. As *You* deepen into the power of space and timelessness, your movements will be slower and choices more clearly discerned. Every breath will more deeply embody life. Time is of the Essence; cherishing time allows *You* to discover that doing less actually creates more.

Wisdom through expression shifts *Being* egoist to *BEING* humanitarian; utilize the melody of balance through appreciation, as an act of grace.

Appreciation is a simple prayer, a balm that soothes discordant states of mind. Appreciation grounds greater self-confidence, self-respect, and self-worth. Acknowledge how each person and experience is benefiting *You,* either by growing *You* or affirming your expression. Hold appreciation for everything that comes your way; large and small. . . conflicting and contrasting. . . beautiful and uplifting. Express this appreciation verbally. Let it be felt internally. Write it down. Hum it all day long. Intentionally express appreciation for what *You* have. This creates more. The practice of appreciation changes the lens *You* look through, revealing a life that always unfolds in your favor.

Quit your hustle and bustle; stop your busyness. Finding time to care for yourself, and creating balance each day, cultivates experiences of fulfillment. Internal satisfaction increases. This feeling amplifies what *You/YOU* are able to attract as higher-octave experiences, which cultivates more appreciation. As *You/YOU* ground in unwavering confidence and creativity, greater contentment becomes more embodied. Life is not asking anything of *You/you/YOU*. It is here for *You/you/YOU*. People are not demanding anything of *You/you/YOU*. They always act on your behalf. With conscious presence, the waves of imbalance subside. Your melody of balance orchestrates a masterful soul song.

Let the harmony of your spirit
pulse as electronica.
Let your darkest nights and brightest days
attune to the melody of balance.
Each person *You* meet
is a note
in your grand symphony
of life. . .
liberation. . .
and pursuit
of *SELF*-realization.

knowing.
How do i/eye balance my life?
i/eye take one small step at a time.

Knowing.
I ebb and flow with life.

KNOWING.
I AM divine rhythm.

. . .

VISCERAL WEIGHT

What may be absorbed?

In open space, anything can enter. . .
Be it healing, the answer, the awareness, the idea,
or all of creation. . .
Space is not physical;
it is no where, no time, no thing,
no one, and no mind. . .
This is your nobility. . .
Be emptied.
Find the real *You/you/YOU*
in the emptiness. . . the weightlessness. . . and the freedom of space.

You/you/YOU carry the weight of the world upon your shoulders, holding the burden of time, wounds, and ancestry. Your body is a trunk of old wares and antiques, filled to the brim with memory, belief, and feeling. *You* experience heaviness. Tiredness hangs from your body, although *You* shrug this off, dismissing it as a byproduct of working too much, or not enough sleep. However, your tiredness persists, even with days off and getting enough sleep. Your unconscious choices and subsequent actions are exhausting. Saying "*yes*" when meaning "*no*" is wearing *You* out. The visceral weight of frustration hangs. . . as a dark rain cloud, plump and full.

Sink into all the beautiful layers within *You/you/YOU*. Uncover the sediment. Feel the dis-ease. . . the frustration. . . the density. . . the restlessness. . . and the overwhelm. Feel how much *You* have taken on. Feel the weight of *being. . . Being*. Your perceptions reveal how deeply weighted in muck, mire, and illusion *You/you/YOU* are. Behold the gravity of your consciousness. Do not deny your negativity, judgment, or projection. Allow the weight, of what is within *You/you/YOU*, to sit upon *You*. That is its purpose. When *You/you/YOU* feel tired enough, the weight can be put down and dissolved. Be with your life. Behold the unanswered questions. Be with the unwanted answers, which breed new questions.

**Cultivate appreciation as *You* invite unification with the child aspect;
deep presence accesses your visceral weight of frustration.**

An array of false selves control your existence. Each has an aim and agenda. Bountiful with fears and insecurities, presumptions and perspectives, your personality and characteristics have arisen out of false constructs and weighty burdens. Your body has carried unconscious weight for so long that *You* do not even realize its existence. Your sinus issues and allergies are connected to the frustration of carrying so much. This clutter creates congestion and irritation.

Frustration is cumulative, building from the stress, anger, and depression that has gone unacknowledged and unheard. It stems from wasted time, energy, resources, and gifts. Ultimately, all frustration boils down to frustration with *Self*. But distraction keeps this awareness at bay. Frustration is not a condition of life; it is a response to it. However, it takes presence and awareness to realize that intentions driven by frustration will only create more frustration. As visceral weight compounds, stories collide, creating ongoing sagas of drama and trauma. Despite your unconscious tendencies, all creations are excellent materials for alchemy.

**Life expresses within a safety net of *Living*,
in order to experience your inner net of *being/Being*,
all while being held in your cosmic *not/knot* of *knowing/Knowing*.**

When the world feels heavy, do not look outside for the cause. Look within the weight *You/you/YOU* carry. Find the baggage *You/you/YOU* stuffed into dark corners of your *Being/being*. The weight of unconscious manipulation, deception, and corruption condemns this world into becoming a dumping ground of personal debris. The emotional, mental, and energetic garbage *You* collect piles up, creating the heavy conditions plaguing our planet. It is not just *You*; this is *you/me/us/them*.

The visceral weight of frustration is the rub of our individual and collective victim consciousness. An enormous opportunity for discovery is present. As each individual lightens their load, the full spectrum of consciousness experiences greater resolution. In timelessness, a new narrative unites *You/Me/Us/Them* in *ONENESS* as *ONE-SELF*.

**When all sound becomes no sound,
all things become no thing,
and all that is heavy is brought to light. . .
time will stand in stillness. . .
life will become weightless. . .
and visceral weight will dissolve
into an expression of sensational aliveness.**

knowing.
How do i/eye release weight?
i/eye can lighten up.

Knowing.
I pause when aware of frustration.

KNOWING.
I AM illumination.

. . .

ALCHEMY OF BODY

What can be transmuted?

**Become free of the old self
that became trapped within all *You/you* hell'd.
By drowning in your misery, muck, and mire,
transmutation occurs by all being felt.
You breathe light.
You no longer hold your breath. . .
Emotions have free reign
and the body finds sovereignty.**

There will come moments when *You* feel tired and weary. The smile of *"I'm fine"* trembles as your face betrays the pressure building behind it. The dam *You/you/YOU* have built against your endless ocean of tears will barely hold. *You* are on the verge of falling apart. The fire inside smolders, threatening to dissolve the remnants of another identity. An inner quake shakes and rumbles. Others whisper, and the number of backs that turn away is doubled by ears deafened to your cries. It is a moment of awakening, although it seems deadening. Hope is a barren pot; yet, *Knowing* stirs within it. The body *KNOW*s your truth, despite the *Mind/mind*'s insistence of the illusion. Let the body do what the body does. It has ancient wisdom.

**Receive thyself with the gifts of creativity, imagination, and talent;
these allow tranquility to arise.**

Shock and awe will arrive like waves upon a shore, lapping at your feet and pulling *You/you* into the undertow when not present. Deeply immerse when this happens. *You/you/YOU* are being pulled under for a reason. There are things buried within your sea of emotion. Drown within each wave of transformation, then surrender to what is asked of *You*. The way to surface and breathe is in letting go. Struggling, fighting the "current," only casts *You* further into the depths and darkness of your *em-ocean*.

Sink into your hazy underworld. Let it swirl. Trust it. Let tension sieve golden truth from visceral imprints time has laid upon your body. In this abyss, what was imagined as real shall crumble and be seen as the illusions they were. *You Know* this through feelings that arise. Allow the sensations of time and space to dissolve. While dis-integration occurs, do not try to understand. Do not waste energy processing, analyzing, reasoning, or attaching story. Feel. Only feel. Your physical body holds everything, to remind *You* of *KNOWING*. That truth is buried under many layers, wounds, scars, and fascia tightened by fear and illusion.

Conscious presence brings this murkiness to the fore, unearthing new ways of seeing. Within the fluidity of your primal substance, the raw, animal, and instinctual rests. Feel hunger and restlessness driving and forcing their way. The body remembers this deception from times past. It knows of fight and flight. Your animal has been on heightened alert for a long time. It *knows* hierarchy of shadow consciousness. The body is an ancient *being*, intelligent and intuitively aware.

Let the life *You* lead be a testimony of the soul, not the ego or the animal.

In moments, *You/you/YOU* can feel the animal writhing beneath your flesh. From time to time, the sharp twinge of being tied down will rise to awareness. The heat lingers, and the burn is painful. It throbs, burns, and smolders beneath the skin of *Being/being*. When the heat subsides, the smell. . . feel. . . and touch leave a cold hunger. *You/you/YOU* buck these sensations and fight feeling trapped. Ride the waves of anxiety, as *you* surf the waves surging within. Slip into the depressions threatening to take hold. Be pierced by the jagged tendrils of phantom fear. Be overtaken by the icy breath of craving, aversion, hunger, and lust. *You* will not die from fully feeling; only the ego will. Temper the frenzy of your ego through pure presence. Tenderly caress and soothe your wounded animal. Care for *him/her/it*. Love *him/ her/it* to death, and *You* into renewed aliveness. Tightness releases with each breath. Tension softens with each touch. Through *Self/self*-love, a natural state of relaxation can return.

The wreckage, aloneness, and barrenness *You/you/YOU* find amid life's challenges is the debris of separateness. Be with what has been denied and deeply repressed. Soak within the tears of suffering that rise up. Let these quench the thirst that the unknown *KNOW*s. As your life burns away, recognize what your body is saying. With disciplined presence, alchemy naturally rises from your wreckage. As the mind undergoes calcination, a process of purification occurs. Everything solid (or known) feels liquid and malleable. What is real, and what is not, can seem unclear. Do not let this create confusion, doubt, and further questioning of *Self*. Stay present, breathe, and feel. The body is the lock, and *You* are the key. Your body is defined by what has been digested, believed, and held ont o. Tiredness is part of the healing experience. Exhaustion is your body's message of *emergency/immerge-and-see*.

To *KNOW* your true aliveness, all that was must die.

Do not condemn the body for communicating with *You*. Do not be disgusted by pain or discomfort; it is a signal. Do not judge emotions for expressing; your inner guidance system is operating correctly. Instead, appreciate the moment for its offering of devotion to *You*. The body is a highly sophisticated piece of equipment that requires mastery. Caring for and strengthening your relationship with the body provides access to a sacred storehouse of *Knowing/KNOWING*.

You inhabit holy earthen soil, molded by the musings of celestial dreaming. *You* were not breathed into a clay pot but were delicately placed inside a sacred vessel. Be with it devotionally, prayerfully, and humbly. You are sacred essence that was placed *in/on* earth. Let this sacred ground be tilled for patience and trust. Sink into infinite nothingness, where the velvety blackness of creation twinkles with starlight. Allow creation's dark, molten womb to retool *You/you/YOU* into an alchemical force of nature. Let the dark night slip away as *You/you/YOU* reconnect with clear lucidity.

There is one true destination, and it is far greater than anything material. *You* are the Universe; not the one projected millions of miles into the heavens, but a vast network of galactivity that is sparked by the consciousness of *mind/Mind/MIND*. A Divine Light on the front of your spine connects *this* heaven to the sacred ground your *Spirit* inhabits. Place what *You/you/YOU* most desire upon your divine line. Kneel before this altar, daily. Breathe this lightning rod of illumination with *Holy Presence*. Focus upon vertically aligning with Source. Actively transmute your base *metal/mettle* into gold. Soul and *Highest SELF* reside in your body and *BEING*. Be *Golden/GOLDEN*; for that *IS* who *YOU* are... what *YOU* are... why *YOU* are, for all eternity.

Through each alchemical shift,
regain your sense of *BEING* eternal.
***You/you/YOU* are life in magnificence;**
a divine blueprint never to be replicated or repeated...
always renewed and rebirthed.
Within every dark night
is a new dawn...
sacred ground to be traversed and built upon...
traveled and divinely held.
With the embrace of Essence...
what blocks your path dissolves.
With truth...
all illusion dissipates.
With space...
discordance disintegrates.
Each souljourn requires
one breath at a time...
one step after another...
one life to be lived...
as if each day is the last.
The promise of death
is always new life.
The fulfillment of life
is an eternity
of aliveness.

knowing.
How do i/eye take better care of myself?
i/eye remember to breathe.

Knowing.
I create daily self-care.

KNOWING.
I AM sacred ground.

...

ESSENCE AS TRANQUILITY

What may be embodied?

There are never multiple lifetimes.
There is only *ONE*.
There are never many individuals.
There is only *ONE*.
There are never many realities.
There is only *ONE*.
There are never many souls.
There is only *ONE*.
There are never many Gods.
There is only *ONE*.
The dis-illusion of many
has been the illusion of *One*,
and the psychosis of another *one*.
Beyond these two
is *ONE* truth.
YOU* are the infinite space of the *ONE
who created all of it.

Do not seek tranquility outside *You,* in outer space or from the material world. Become tranquil within, despite your circumstances and conditions. Imagine the center of *BEING*. Anchor there and smile. Let this smile spread throughout your body, and into every cell. Access the smile of *BEING* that lives inside each cell of your body. Live from that place of *Knowing/KNOWING*. Tranquility has been present all along; conditioning keeps *You* from accessing it.

Remove what blocks your ability to access, see, feel, and *KNOW* it. Grievances and judgments hide the light of *YOU* from *You/you*. Step away from thoughts and actions of the moment. Let your senses have a time-out. Experience windows of timelessness, in which to become tranquil. Close all sense doors and experience this. *You* have permission to return to duality any time, should *You* choose.

Practices of virtue, meditation, and wisdom cultivate the remembrance of innate tranquility. Invoking your Light body, by seeing and feeling every cell illuminated with joy, loving kindness, and love, catalyzes this sense of calm. Allow the fresh breeze of nothingness to enter. Let your mind, body, and soul experience respite. Visit your internal island in the sun. Beyond the vision of tranquil waters lie an energetic manifestation of new life *Being/BEING* created. Tap into the patience of th*IS* eternal power. Recline into the release of control. Be held by the contemplation of your boundlessness. When *You* release the smallness of *you,* expansiveness dawns. Tranquil vastness will be wherever *You* are.

What is in front of *You/YOU* came out of the conditioning behind *You/you/YOU*. Let tranquility equilibrate *You/you* to the frequency of Essence alive within *YOU*.

EYE/I in the center of *BEING* is tranquil, unconditional, and neutral. This is not "the neutral" of complacency. That state assumes satisfaction from disempowered resolve, which keeps *You* from trying your best. In complacency, *You* are ignorant to what is happening, or the dangers present. Remaining blind to opportunities and possibilities, there is no active participation. This maintains an image of deception, where *You* appear unattached while hiding attachment. Complacency is a passive, shadow expression of neutrality.

Tranquility is a state of calm neutrality, which exists amid fluctuations. It is not dependent upon the external. This space is free of worry, tension, and distraction. It is held through deliberate intention. Despite any conditions, struggles, darkness, or challenge... tranquility is a devotional commitment to *NOW*, where *You* remain present and focused to the eternal truth of *NOW*. This is far beyond *Now,* which entails staying present to the moment *You* are in. *NOW* is presence to *Truth/TRUTH* of *Essence/ESSENCE*. There can be no ill, or disturbance, with this *Knowing/KNOWING*. *Being/BEING* "neutral" from higher awareness creates an inner foundation of well-*Being/BEING*, regardless of what rises.

**Forgive your attachments;
this creates the wisdom for giving detachment to *Self.***

Connect, moment by moment, to higher *Self/SELF*. Keep inquiring as to what is beyond each experience *Self/self/SELF* encounters. Be *One/ONE* that is strengthened by *Knowing/KNOWING* Spirit as ever present and guiding. Stand back, look at your life, and ask... *Who am I witnessing?* Then ask... *Who is the One/ONE witnessing me, as the witness?* Then proceed... *Who sees the One/ONE watching the witness?* How far inside *Self/self/SELF* can *You* go before *mind/Mind/MIND* sees no *one/One/ONE*?

As long as a witness is present, identity exists and story remains. Can *You* continue until there is no longer a witness to behold? Until there is no longer a *mind/Mind/MIND*? Until there are no "I's" with which to see? Until there is no longer a *you*? A *You*? A *You/you/YOU*? A *YOU*? Or a "me"? In that space, there shall be no question... no inquiry... no contemplation... nor answer. There will be silence; only ... TRANQUILITY.

If *You/you* break my heart,
I will thank *You/you*.
If *You/you* take from me,
I will bless *You/you*.
If *You/you* disregard me,
I will hold space for *You/you*.
If *You/you* hate me,
I will love *You/you*.
You/you are me,
and I am *You/you*;
to see, hear, and acknowledge...

for giving, receiving, and growing.
Anything other than that
is how *You/you* and *eye/i* play
a game of pretend.
Until we let go
and discover,
we were never really here.
Nothing ever was.

knowing.
How do i/eye feel something; or anything?
It is enough to realize that i/eye am numb.

Knowing.
I Am on a ladder of vibrations, always moving higher.

KNOWING.
I AM tranquility.

. . .

FORGIVING ATTACHMENT—FOR GIVING DETACHMENT

I forgive life's experience of loss, abandonment, and suffering.
I forgive this earthen dimension for being painful.
I forgive sticky webs of codependence and agenda.
I forgive echoes of wounds and wounding.
I forgive myself for creating a world of duality.
I am for giving healthy connection.
I am for giving emotional intelligence.
I am for giving experiences of love, care, and compassion.
I am for giving pure and sacred witnessing.
I am for giving attention to appreciation and gratitude.
I give presence to the emotions of each moment.
I give way to respectful interactions.
I give in to genuine connection.
I give communion.
I give my human *Self* the grace of detachment.
I alchemize my world with the aura of light.
I alchemize my relationships with the fragrance of union.

I alchemize my connections with the flavor of tenderness.
I alchemize my interactions with the melody of balance.
I alchemize my emotional reactivity with the Essence of tranquility.
I am *ONE* with the *DIVINE PRESENCE*;
I transform and transmute attachment through the grace of detachment. . .
I open to the absorption of all visceral weight and residual frustration.
May *DIVINE ALCHEMY* wash through my form and purify the lustful *self*.
May I adorn the swan's wings
to bridge the illusion of the physical plane with the reality of the spirit world.
I glide with faith, toward a heavenly embodiment.
I am for giving the swan's gifts of purity and peace,
devotion and elegance. . . divination and balance.
May these gifts of *KNOWING* be granted by *DIVINE GRACE*.
I am the light of *GOD*.
I AM the unity of *GOD*.
I AM the tenderness of *GOD*.
I AM the sacred balance of *GOD*.
I AM the *MIND* of *GOD*.
I am the tranquility of *GOD*.
I AM.

. . .

UP-LEVEL CONNECTION

INTIMACY shifts your POINT OF ATTRACTION

self ——-> *Self* ——-> *SELF*

Be present. Gradually, shift into higher octaves of presence, awareness, and perception.
Move up the vibrational ladder. Feel your way and ascend to a new reality.
The second human expression of grace establishes a new paradigm in which to engage relationship. This requires empathy; discerning there is no *You* or other. To create a healthier bond, *You/you/YOU* must become vulnerable. When the heart space is ready, existing walls will crumble away. Kiss the past. Bless it, so that your present is graced. Free your enemy and receive freedom. *You/you/YOU* hold the key to changing your world.

Up-level connection—through intimacy—with the truth of who *YOU* are. As *You* more deeply anchor within *SELF*—and specifically the *GOD* within *YOU*—your ability to create a life of deep connection and community unfolds. *You* are an ever-expanding, energetic expression of creative capacity. Awaken *Knowing*. . . *KNOWING*. Give life something to respond to.

living.

————————————————

acknowledgment
(slow down and feel.)

————————————————————

eye/i do not like contrast. eye/i want things to change. eye/i want life to feel easier. eye/i keep getting the opposite of what eye/i intend. eye/i don't like people. eye/i want to like people. eye/i want what they have. eye/i want the good life. eye/i don't want to do this anymore. eye/i keep doing the work and nothing changes. eye/I want to like myself. eye/i want to love my life. eye/i want to feel like eye/i figured this all out.

being.

————————————————

acceptance
(bring attention to your breath.)

————————————————————

eye/i feel frustrated. eye/i feel stressed. eye/i crave what eye/i don't have. eye/i feel averse to what eye/i do have. eye/i feel shame for the secrets eye/i keep. eye/i feel guilt for the lies eye/i tell. eye/i feel embarrassed about how eye/i deceive myself. eye/i feel tense. eye/i feel challenged by people, places, and things around me. eye/i feel like crying. . . and like screaming.

knowing.

————————————————

anticipation
(breathe slowly, deepen into your body.)

————————————————————

eye/i can heal my childhood wounds. This challenge is bringing growth. eye/i can tell myself and others the truth. eye/i see this as part of a larger picture. eye/i know this experience is teaching me about me. This challenge is asking me to be creative. eye/i can use my imagination. eye/i can ask, "What's possible?" eye/i can discover gifts, skills, and talents through this challenge.

Living.

————————————————

appreciation
(pause and be present to what the moment is asking.)

————————————————————

I am grateful the tears come when they need to. I am grateful for the relief I feel after shedding what I have held onto . I appreciate how water soothes me. I appreciate oceans and waterfalls, babbling brooks and streams. I appreciate my ability to ground, as I learn mastery. I appreciate that I feel, especially in a world that seems numb and indifferent. I appreciate my humanity. I appreciate being a humanitarian. I appreciate myself for being the change I wish to see.

Being.

————————————————

satisfaction
(connect mind to heart to gut to ground.)

————————————————————————————

I feel satisfied that I am opening to all of my emotions more each day. I am satisfied that I judged myself less today than yesterday. I am satisfied that I am accepting more and more of myself. I feel satisfied with the choices I am making. I feel satisfied that I am becoming more conscious. I feel the satisfaction of being fluid. I feel satisfaction when I experience all of myself. I feel satisfied taking care of myself. I feel satisfied when I drink more water, eat well, and exercise. I feel satisfied when engaging in fun and laughter. I find satisfaction with friends and family.

Knowing.

————————————————

adoration
(inhale deeply and absorb what is present.)

————————————————————————————

I love being in the question. I love questioning the status quo. I love life's ability to make me continually question. I love awareness. I love receiving insights. I love reaching answers to my questions. I love how my answers to questions bring more questions. The more I question, the more I know myself. I love the movement of life. I love movement. I love moving my body. I love moving my hips. I love moving my feet. I love a good rhythm. I love dancing. I love a good bold beat. I love moving the energy. I love the melody my life is moving to. I love music.

LIVING.

————————————————

celebration
(rise above and rejoice.)

————————————————————————————

I celebrate emotions ebbing and flowing. I celebrate waking up each day. I celebrate the contrast for expanding me. I celebrate that I am attracting people that mirror my changes. I celebrate creativity and imagination as a way of creating something new. I celebrate my talents and those I have yet to discover. I celebrate giving and receiving throughout life's experiences.

BEING.

————————————————

exaltation
(ground in sacredness, devotion, and equanimity. . . unconditionally Love!)

————————————————————————————

I flow easily. I rain gently. I cleanse daily. I waterfall effervescently. I stream beautifully. I trickle tenderly. I pool. I puddle. I energize. I receive abundantly. I smile radiantly. I regulate. I empathize. I distill. I feel deeply. I purify. I transform. I transmute. I give generously. I speak. I beam brightly. I balance. I unify. I communicate boldly. I strengthen. I inform. I fulfill.

KNOWING.

—————————————————

jubilation
(exhale your newly created vibrational reality and. . . believe!)

——————————————————————————

I AM abundance. I AM appreciation. I AM creative. I AM fluid. I'm a Divine Child.
I Am play. I Am playfulness. I Am the playground. I Am laughter.
I Am giggles. I Am hums and whistles.
I AM perseverance. I AM mercy. I AM restoration. I AM rejuvenation. I AM reverence.
I AM TENDERNESS. I AM UNION. I AM LIGHT.
I AM EXPRESSION. I AM DETACHMENT.
I AM IMAGINATION. I AM SACRED GROUND.
I AM FLOW. I AM TRANQUILITY.
I AM THAT. . . I AM. I AM THAT. . . I AM. I AM THAT. . . I AM.

Always begin exactly where *You/you/YOU* are. Be truthful with how *You/you/YOU* feel. Be authentic in what *You/you/YOU* are thinking. A new human builds from the ashes of your old life. Let your words be catalysts for transformation and transmutation. *You* are the bridge between where *you* are and where *You* want to go. *You* grow into *KNOWING* as *You* ascend the ladder of consciousness. What *You* place into the universal vortex remains in escrow. Belief supports physical presence. *KNOWING* creates change, transformation, and miracles.

NOTES

passion.

What has to dissolve?

You can choose to *be*. . .
raw, reptilian, negative, and shadowed.
You can choose to *Be*. . .
vulnerable, intimate, empathic, and human.
You can choose to *BE*. . .
sacred, divine, aligned, and enlightened.
In each second. . . moment. . . hour. . . day. . . week. . . year. . .
which do *You/you/YOU* choose?
Which experience. . . expression. . . conversation. . . creation. . . construct. . .
will *You* ground within?
Life unconditionally gifts *You* with. . .
choice. . . Choice. . . CHOICE.
Unconditionally embrace the experiences that come from. . .
what *You/you/YOU* are choosing.

The latin root of the word *passion* means *to suffer*. Following your passions inherently implies suffering is part of the path. Does *follow your suffering* have the same appeal as *follow your passion*? If pausing and peering deeply, *You* will discover that your passion is born out of reaction and restlessness. Passions carry seeds of wounding, insecurity, and pain. These seeds create weeds; they will flower but are weeds nonetheless. Although passions create beauty, art, innovation, and service. . . these endeavors create further complexity. Eventually, these weeds choke true aliveness from flowering.

Passions are often born of negative experiences, laced with unconscious beliefs. The ember that sparks a passion holds fears, resentments, and hidden fury from wounding. What *You* believe *you* have gotten past remains alive with your passionate energy. When sitting with the fires of passion, the heat of inadequacy, jealousy, insignificance, and hunger can be subtly felt. Passions project what *You* deny, ignore, push away, or must heal. A person's passion holds within it what they need to learn.

The ego will tease of fantasy, pleasure, and purpose. Convinced that your heart is speaking, that impulse will become your voice, mission, business, and calling. A passion, purpose, and persona births a new identity, keeping *you* bound, determined, and steeped in doing. Such things require an audience, a customer base, or a tribe. Little do you realize, *YOU* have just been abducted by the illusions of evolution, identity, and time.

Passion may sound lofty and exciting. This adventurous path is filled with highs and lows. It can bring recognition, fame, and applause. *You* may have lots of followers on social media, but passion does not promise happiness or fulfillment. Do not be surprised if *You* feel empty in the still, quiet moments, because your outside will never fill your inside. Feeling empty, unimportant, and lost reflects a disconnection with *self.*

Passion has nothing to do with purpose;
it has everything to do with polarity.

Passion is a lower vibration, closely related to hunger. It is driven from wanting and consists of drive, push, ambition, and lust. What pulls at or drives *You* are meanderings of shadow and ego. These aspects, rampant with *self*-need, seek entertainment, significance, and meaning. Following an impulse without addressing what inspires it creates the risk of becoming enslaved by your passion. In some, this is full blown; in others, very subtle. Passions keep *You* locked in your story, identity, and equivalent vibration. Passion controls instead of leads. . . pushes instead of serves. . . takes instead of gives. . . and is *Self/self*-serving rather than *Self/self*less.

Sometimes, passion exists within stagnancy. At an unconscious level, allegiance to victimization, wounding, or seemingly broken aspects of *Self/self/SELF* keeps a low burn going. Intense focus on a problem, or feeling stuck in a situation, exudes a different type of passion, which makes *You* unconsciously loyal to oppression. Fighting the good fight, protesting, holding a grudge, charity, or advocacy for a cause are examples of causes and careers stemming from the unconscious need to save others. This projection of the *self* that feels unseen, unheard, unacknowledged, and unprotected becomes a drug of distraction to overcompensate for what feels lacking. When nothing exists to feed the need "to be seen," withdrawal sets in, revealing holes of boredom, slothfulness, and lust. Passions based on personal obsession hum with bitterness and frustration.

You are conditioned to follow passions. *You* were not taught to temper this externally sparked flame. What *You/you/YOU* follow, and the reasons why, have gone unexplored. *You* believe that purpose, worth, and meaning are dependent upon fulfilling a specific passion. However, passion is conformity that stems from societal pressure. It is an itch. When *you* scratch an itch, it becomes inflamed. Learn how to sit with the itch. Do not deceive yourself into thinking something must be done with it. Go to the source of your irritation.

Instead of following passion, feel into what stokes it. Be drawn, like a moth to this flame. Spend time sitting with its fire. Let it warm *You* to *its* purpose. . . *its* burning need. . . *its* hot emotion. . . so that unconscious drives rise into awareness. See what drives *You*, sets *you* on fire, or lights *You/you* up. Even this language sounds fiery, burning, and hot. Fire is meant to to purify, cleanse, and burn away. The deceptive intelligence is clever. Passion is the ego's trick for conjuring outlets of worthiness, to keep *You* distracted from feelings of unworthiness.

Passion projects will distract *You/you/YOU* from true work.
Should it be chosen,
***You* will evenly be brought back to the work of *Self/self/SELF*.**

Let each impulse that arises. . . each spark of passion that pulls. . . and each explosive idea. . . sit within the cauldron of your belly. Do nothing for a season, as *You* meditate upon the reason it stirs within. This is counterintuitive to what society would have *You* do. However, it will lead *You* further in growth, expansion, and fulfillment. Two paths shift passion into presence.

First, engage activities that maintain neutral presence, something unrelated to the passion pulling at *You/you/YOU*. This activity will flow to *You/YOU*, rather than a passion *You/you* run toward. It will keep your ego busy but will not create distracting rabbit holes for *You* to slip into.

Second, inner work puts out the fires that drive ambition. Let everything cloaked in shadow become the gift that creates alignment. Communion and remaining present to your body do not allow for mental gymnastics. Achieve neutrality, so that passion does not control your mind, time, or perceptual lens. With passion quelled. . . actions, steps, and pursuits are void of wounding and purified of shadow and ego. Inner work provides direction and leads to enhanced soul connection. Your mission is to stay present.

At first, a fire will burn passionately,
but eventually it will go up in smoke and fizzle out.

Your soul desires wholehearted commitment to something larger than *You/you*. Do not let the ego fool *You* into believing worth is outside. Do not become drunk with passion. *Your* greatest service lies in discerning the nature of your authentic, sacred *SELF*. This cannot come from manipulation of *mind/Mind*. Preoccupation with *Mind/mind* steers humanity away from softness and connection. *Mind/mind* is an incredible processor, but be careful; it will turn *You* into a machine. Drop into the heart and listen. Choose what nurtures, fills, and relaxes *You/you/YOU* from the inside. Continually lean into the heart; otherwise, humanity is lost.

There is no one else here. . . there is only *You/you/YOU*. . . and me *as You/you/ YOU*. . . and everyone and everything else. . . reflecting *You/you/YOU*. The seeds *You/ YOU* plant become the mycelia of our world. Deepen into "why" *You* want what *You/ you/YOU* want, and what your real agenda is. Engage experiences of play; true joyful play and ease. Your true work in the world is meant to feel like play. When your soul is truly fulfilled. . . identity, thinking, and time disappear. *You/you/YOU* are swept away; lost, in the best of ways. As you discover the beauty of dispassion, life's ebbs and flows will subside, allowing *You/YOU* to glide upon calmer waters.

Live with reverence and humility
and behold the fullness of your brothers and sisters.
It is with equality that all thrive.
It is with neutrality *You* become alive.
See *all*. . . *All*. . . *ALL*. . .
for the beauty and magnificence of their presence
in whatever way this appears.
Each *one*. . . *One*. . . *ONE*. . .
is a thread that weaves into the cosmic narrative of time.
Only those of the purest intent slip through the *Eye/I* of the needle.

knowing.
How do i/eye find my passion?
i/eye find ways to avoid my pain.

Knowing.
I feel valuable when I engage passion and purpose.

KNOWING.
I AM enough.

the grace of dispassion.

What is the remembering?

Invite the grace of dispassion.
Consciously initiate this.
Let the kiss of snow invoke your aura of the crystalline body.
The fragrance of wisdom reveals truth.
The flavor of kindness expands energy.
Through peace, the visceral fight of remorse dissolves;
Your essence of purity brings forth the alchemy of heart,
taking *You/you* to solid ground.
Receive this gift of human grace.
***KNOW*. . . that your presence is enough.**

Dispassion encompasses an attitude of noninterference and nonemotion. This is not apathy, indifference, or complacency. There is caring and feeling; however, not so much that *You* are pulled in, dragged down, or distracted from your spiritual path. Nor are *You* creating effect. By not getting involved, *You* do not create complexity. When becoming involved, the side effect is karma; shared or traded between individuals. . . rippling through families and lineages. . . compounding into communities, countries, and the world. *You* are the butterfly; flapping your wings can be felt across years, miles, and generations to come. Fly gently; move softly. Flap dispassionately. Nature is dispassionate, following natural cycles and rhythms without interference.

Within the blessing of conflict and the illusion of money,
***You/you/YOU* created passion,**
in order to discover the grace of dispassion, as a way of awakening humanity.

As *You/you/YOU* move through life challenges, losses, and upheavals, the temporal nature of reality becomes more apparent. As trauma and pain are experienced, desire and happiness will wane. During this time, ego and identity are humbled, as your material world shrinks. With life becoming simpler, awareness of inner disgust and exhaustion rises. The deceptions and toxicities of the world trigger a clearer sense of the negativity and dissatisfaction held within *You/you/YOU*. With continued presence, these rumblings become louder.

Within dissatisfaction is a fire-breathing, multiheaded serpent that bitterly spits your deeply held beliefs around money, people, materialism, and consumerism. It is the fiery spray of passion that engulfs *You* when unable to be with *self*. During this part of the purification and transmutation process, what *You/you* will express increases reactivity, passionate rants, and erratic outbursts. The grace of dispassion steadies your course and initiates conscious change. Dispassion arises out of detachment. It can be received only through compassion for *Self/self*. Dispassion is not an intellectual process; it is cultivated through a steady mind and open heart.

The Grace of Dispassion	The Remembering	Knowing
The Illusion—Passion	What has to dissolve?	Aliveness
True Love's Kiss—The Snow	What nature is required?	Creation
Aura of the Chyrstalline Body	What is emerging?	Unification
Fragrance Emitting Wisdom	What is the inhale?	Truth
Flavor of Kindness	What is the exhale?	Energy
Melody Through Peace	What is harmonizing?	Growth
Visceral Flight—Bitterness	What is being absorbed?	Wisdom
Alchemy of Heart	What can be transmuted?	The Void
Essence as Purity	What may be embodied?	Infinite Presence
Forgiving Passion— For Giving Dispassion	What is for giving?	Equanimity

Once removed from the peril of attachments, dispassion offers freedom for the soul. This is a different kind of power, empowerment, and joy. *You* lean toward soulful *Living/LIVING,* as opposed to *ego/gross* entanglements. With dispassion, *You* are no longer tied to, or controlled by, the external world. Out of burgeoning trust and safety, the magnitude of life begins to be felt within. *You/YOU* move beyond material trappings of the world, as *You* begin to notice how everything is connected. *You* also start understanding that all action is interference, thus creating disturbances within life's natural flow. Through detachment and dispassion, *You* open to *Being/BEING* part of life, rather than separate from it. Emptied of everything *You/you/YOU* once possessed... or are possessed by. . . your focus can turn toward embodying peace as personal power and purpose.

**Do not be defined by your dreams, desires, and experiences.
Neutralize passion and your world becomes refined.**

Dispassion requires conscious presence. *You* deeply feel, without falling into fluctuations of emotion, impulse, or distraction. Mind, heart, body, and energy maintain balance, stillness, and neutrality. With detachment, ego is pointed toward good use. These qualities create freedom from bondage and cultivate deepened presence with the world, without *being* of the world. This stage of *Knowing* makes way for acceptance of duality. Here, *You* not only see the river and its direction but choose to follow the current without resistance.

Dispassion is the straight and narrow road of sublime and equanimous living. There are no highs or lows; simply a neutral, grounded, and calm path. There is no passion; yet, there is everyday purposeful *Living/LIVING*. There is likely no fame or applause, but experiences of fulfillment and joy become more available. Dispassion empowers spiritual maturity through equanimity with all things. Emotions are regulated, denoting mastery over the emotional body. Deconditioning strips *You/you/YOU* of what was known, so that the Sacred Unknown may emerge. Essence is remembered through practices of detachment and dispassion. This means everything *You* identify with must be removed. Essence has no identity. The Essence of a thing is always at its core. Find that.

The Universe does not judge your creations;
only *You/you/YOU* do.
Do not minimize your experiences by calling them lessons.
Open yourself to them as grand initiations.
Endeavor upon these as sacred energetic activations.
Step through these powerful portals.
Let these doorways awaken new landscapes.
Stay in the inquiry. . .
Follow each to the end.
Let each new beginning
be a leap toward your Divine end.
Life is but a dream. . .

knowing.
How do i/eye focus on myself?
i/eye am distracted, until i/eye am not.

Knowing.
I soak in everything.

KNOWING.
My presence is enough.

. . .

TRUE LOVE'S KISS—THE SNOW

What nature is required?

Life is always in your favor.
It never leaves *You/you/YOU* hanging.
However, the ego keeps wanting.
Let your winters bring forth
the shelter of *ice-soul-elation*. . .
where the sheer beauty of aloneness
expands the celebration
of your own company.
Perfect your attitude of gratitude,
by letting winter's brisk wind come.
Feel the cold against your skin
and stick out your tongue.
Find your bliss. . .
as snow and ice kiss your lips.

As snow falls, excitement stirs. The gentle whisper of flakes brings the freshness of something new. What was known is covered by a pristine blank canvas. The ecstatic chaos of confetti'd rain dances and flurries, spreading joyful noise. Momentarily, the cold hard ground resting beneath the softly fallen snow is forgotten. It is the past, amid this heavenly present. But as snow falls more heavily, it becomes harder to see. In the quickening, obstacles must be navigated with care. It becomes necessary to move more slowly, and with greater care. With each step, the damp dirt beneath the pure-white surface begins to reveal its dark face. What was pristine and untouched becomes compressed and muddied. A slushy cocktail of ice and mud forms, re-creating contrast from perceived newness. As the wind increases, an oncoming blizzard makes movement nearly impossible. Soon, nothing can be seen, bringing *You* to a standstill.

The current irreconcilable person, place, thing, or situation is your abominable snowman. Feel *him/her/it* grabbing hold of your life. Let *his/her/its* icy hand show *You* when, where, and how *you* move into fight, flight, and freeze. *He/she/it* will point toward your icy stares, cold heart, and sharp movements. Witness the reflection *he/she/it* brings.

Let the kiss of snow reveal your hardened, cold, apathetic, and indifferent places of mind and heart. Let its chill reveal where *You/you/YOU* are frozen. Let it reveal the thick blocks of ice within relationship to lovers, friends, family, money, and *Self/self/SELF*. Let frost reveal the cold hard truth of your insufficiency and greed. Take a polar plunge into *Self*, and encounter your *icyness/i-see-mess*. A cold bucket of ice water is an invigorating experience. It will wake *You/you/YOU* up.

**In engaging the path of visionary, material obsessions abound,
creating softly falling snow and heavy blizzards,
which hide within your earthen ground.**

Hibernation offers time to tune int o sensations of the body. Check in with your body periodically. Be present to where and when *You/you* go cold. When the body, heart, or mind feel cold. . . love is dormant, distant, or absent. Ever notice a chill in the moments *You/you* feel unloved, isolated, abandoned, or lonely? Amid the wintry barrenness of more-challenging life experiences, pause and find your breath. The road less traveled is often a cold, lonely, and bumpy one.

Give yourself permission to rest. Remain in your cave. Sleep. Renew within peace and quiet. Inhale and exhale deeply. Bring your *Self* back to life slowly. This is permission to pause. . . to stop. . . to hibernate. . . to consciously sleep. When *You* have a chill, simply breathe and feel. Witness sensations until they dissolve. Watch experiences shift. Let the body have its way with *You*. In clearing the debris, and weight of subtle sensations, lightness of *Being/BEING* will express through *You*.

There are times when it is necessary to come in from the cold. When the icy chill grips your bones, pause for a moment. Sit still. Lean into the fire. Notice the contrast. Feel the heat of the moment. Movement may appear minimal. However, al ot is occurring. In moments of great silence and stillness, great strides can be made. *You* will know when to kindle the hearth. Let the heart space become a warm cottage. Let the furnace build inside. Amid the heat, discern which flames whip of anger, rage, and *self*-righteousness; or warmth, love, and compassion. Be sparked by the fire of your sacred hearth and be renewed by the kiss of snow. *You* are always guided, held, and protected by the elements.

**Until *You* sleep deeply,
it is challenging to know if *you* have woken up.**

Let aloneness become your wise counsel, healer, and friend during this period. Let silence be the guardian, guide, and angel that supports *You/you* in garnering great insight. Be warmed by your inner voice, Spirit guidance, and heart callings. Build an igloo of understanding. Remain inside for the long haul and be amazed by the benefit *You* reap. The full embrace of an inner winter energizes alchemy within the heart; that which blazes a new revolution. *You/you/YOU* ascend to high places. *You/you/YOU* melt from frozen ice into flowing fresh waters of rebirth. In these times of timelessness, relax your shoulders. Breathe longer, deeper breaths. Soon, breath will flow more easily. Your belly will soften. Let the animal within purr in satisfaction.

In the silence of a cold, dark night, snow creates a clearing, quieting, and quickening. Space is made, while everything covered over becomes still, dormant, and unto itself. Whether a light flurry or cold, hard winter, snow brings play, softening, freshness, and renewal. Even nature knows to go inside. . . to stop. . . rest. . . and nestle in. This arctic vision quest will reunite *You* with multiple levels of *Self/self/SELF*. Let Infinite Spirit softly fall into your awareness. . . dust all over *You/you/YOU*. . . melt what is frozen within and create a blanket of pure *Knowing/KNOWING*. Excavate the divine crystalline design that *IS* unique to *YOU*.

On this sacred day,
bless "the enemy";
hold the "ill" as healed,
the "broken" as whole,
and the "lost" as found.
Love the way *You/you/YOU* want to be loved;
let others live the way *You/you/YOU* desire to live.
Create Oneness of Spirit.
See beauty in everything
and experience each moment in wonder.
Allow the flow.

knowing.
Why does my body feel cold?
i/eye remind myself i/eye am not alone.

Knowing.
In each moment, I look at life with fresh eyes.

KNOWING.
I AM innocent.

. . .

AURA OF THE CRYSTALLINE BODY

What does it look like?

From *ONE*,
there were two,
and that made three. . .
Life is a riddle that looks like you and me.
A breath. . . A stretch. . . A nod. . .
A step. . . A jump. . . A leap. . .
A dive. . . A death. . . A birth. . .
A song. . . A melody. . .
A Life. . . A You. . . A Me. . . A We. . . An Us. . .

Conscious presence impacts your physical world, making it feel lighter and freer. As *You* disengage negativity, fight, and flight. . . an upgrade of DNA light codes integrates the old and new. Dissolving density comes from absorbing separation and wounding. The commitment *You* bring to this absorption of *self/Self,* and the embodiment of *Self/SELF,* strengthens your physical container. This reflects more Light through the body. With this grounding, anchoring and strengthening, Spirit more easily descends into awareness.

**Inside your hard shell is a vast crystalline wonderland. . .
an entire cosmos that exists as *You*.**

Because of life experiences, *You* are like a geode. Brilliance and energetic power reside within these intricate structures. Over time, compounding density builds pressure for heat to initiate a process of crystallization. Life hardened your outer surface, but what lies within is multifaceted, shimmering beauty. As your emotional magma cools through dispassion, *You/ you/YOU* become strengthened. This initiates a quantum upgrade, increasing crystalline light within the cells of your body. Like a diamond. . . heat, force, and pressure are required to bring out your brilliance and perfection. Within *You/you/YOU* is the mystery of life.

You/you/YOU are a multifaceted crystalline form that is able to radiate light and frequency. Access to your crystalline body comes by living from the heart center, rather than the head. This is an expression of inner strength and burgeoning inner authority. As *You* increase vibrational frequency, a gradual emergence of crystalline energy radiates from your body. Each aligned choice expands your field for greater communion with life. This expanded intimacy includes connection to earthen forms, etheric formlessness, and the celestial realms.

You are walking the bridge of disidentification. Whereas reality creation has been an intellectual concept, it is now becoming embodied expression. As more light enters the body, density, disease, and shadow frequencies are burned off. Deep inner work leads to outer transformation and inner transfiguration. This leads to improved health, greater vitality, and antiaging. At this stage, it is increasingly important to hold your energy within yourself. Otherwise, it becomes entangled, infected, dispersed, or weakened once again.

**Reflect the energy of air to expand your aura of the crystalline body.
In raising your vibration, the global reflection of fashion also shifts.**

As *You* shift and change, synchronicities and signs increase because *You/YOU* are more present and aware. Thoughts manifest more rapidly. Déjà vu, lucid dreaming, and intuition will also heighten. Soul gifts such as clairaudience, clairsentience, and clairvoyance may also emerge. Additionally, there is greater capacity to shape-shift, bilocate, or tune int o the thoughts of others. Your body will begin to emit an aura that shines through your eyes and skin. People will experience *You* as lit up, bright, shining, and inspiring. Creation must be grounded within the heart, through healthy, balanced, and feminine and masculine energies. Action must be initiated only when masculine energy has been inspired by the receptivity of feminine energy.

As the human body continues to transform and transfigure through increasing frequencies, a luminous new human will birth upon the planet. When individuals encompass vibrations of high crystalline frequency, they shift toward Godhood awareness. The crystalline body reflects the beginnings of ascension into a new experience of human aliveness. Life asks for complete surrender now. Bend your will toward Divine Will. Do more nothing. Each moment is an opportunity to awaken to a brand-new dream, a uniquely beautiful one. The unified impulse for all creation is *Love*; to be *Love*, experience *Love,* and rise into *LOVE.*

Wormholes will appear and move life forward. These often require going back to original thoughts and creations that pulled *You* down a rabbit hole. That step back, if walked with presence, catapults awakening into truth. Within the illusion of dimensional *Living/living/LIVING*, *You/you/YOU* are the imagination that guides... the experience that experiences... and, most importantly, the expression who expresses. The time has come to begin freeing yourself of all ties that bind... the very ones *you* created.

To move into higher octaves of experience, be in acceptance of where *You/you/YOU* are physically, mentally, emotionally, and vibrationally—seeing, hearing, feeling, and acknowledging levels of *Self/self/SELF*. Now ask, "*What's possible?*" Support *self* in ways *you* feel unsupported by the world by sacredly holding this moment. Empower *Self* through discovering how *You* are capable. Fiercely advocate for *SELF* emerging and actualizing infinite possibilities. Through a triune practice of jubilant praise, focused faith, and grateful receptivity, *You/you/YOU* shall be lifted *On High,* to a heavenly and high place.

You are alchemy;
life is the alchemist.
Transfiguration is the descent of "*god/God*"
meeting animal and demon...
through the embrace of humanity
and the remembrance of truth
as a Divine *GOD BEING*.
Meet *God/god/GOD*'s eyes
by looking into your own.

knowing.
Who am i/eye?
i/eye have many faces.

Knowing.
I Am multifaceted.

KNOWING.
I AM a diamond.

FRAGRANCE-EMITTING WISDOM

What does it smell like?

If passion is present,
then ego, identity, and willfulness are too.
Let dispassion rise. . .
so that Source creates through *You.*
Otherwise, *You/you/YOU* interfere with the Divine plan.
Not to worry;
there are no errors.
Your will adds texture, dimension, and shadow to life's tapestry.
Your pathways and detours will eventually lead back to the High Way.
Life's paths are designed to awaken higher frequencies of energy,
bring forth greater experiences of truth,
and provide infinite expressions of growth
for the fragrance of wisdom to emit through *You.*

Do you remember being on a road trip as a child and continually asking, "*Are we there yet?*" Life can often feel this way, especially when hitting bumps and roadblocks. Notice how *You* have never really stopped asking that question; albeit, sometimes silently within the mind. Every storyli ne holds a bandwidth of dark and light. Every thought is a line in your story. Every word is a prayer within your sacred text. Each breath activates many "sons and daughters of creation," which expand your thoughts and manifestations. Illusions, fantasies, stories, desires, and dreams are always seeding creations that bind *you* with strings and strands of codependency, pressure, and doing. These binding threads tie *You* to a narrative that is not true.

As a child at play, lost in *his/her/their* own creation, *You/you/YOU* twist and twirl. . . leap and fly. . . glide and glissade. Once in a while, a magical experience appears, creating a delightful gasp. Every so often, a villainous creature pops up, sucking the air out of the room. They come for the purposes of healing. Until each *piece/peace* is returned to the void, storyli nes overlap.

It is easy to become bogged down and forget that *You* are here as experience, to experience, and for *Knowing* the wisdom of experience. Do not rush to the finish line, or the experience is missed. And even that is experience. Wherever *You* find yourself, move slowly. Enjoy the scenery. Take in every moment of each experience. Breathe in the fragrance that it brings.

**Through growth and mind mastery, awaken to wisdom,
as *You* dissolve the black hole of greed.**

Wisdom is found in the gentle ecstasy of a silent mind. Your open and fertile landscape is ripe for knowledge when given seeds to bear fruit. This field of consciousness can produce new imaginings and endless possibility through your tending. Here, everything is harvested for nourishment: the weeds, wheat, chaff, and fruit. Each part is useful within the soul biome. Cast nothing away casually, or unconsciously. The soul specifically came for experience, and every nuance within it. By cultivating landscapes *You/you/YOU* have built and crossed, the resulting wisdom not only feeds your soul but also offers rich nourishment for others.

To attain wisdom of the *God/god/GOD*s, fully experience every level below that. If not fully feeling the conditions of your life. . . body. . . and human experience, *You* block the flow of wisdom. Do not fight receiving what is yours. Wisdom is one of love's many forms. Regardless of your choices, more choices shall be offered around each bend. This is the ultimate wisdom of experience.

> **To believe *You/you/YOU* are ever being tested is an error of mind.**
> ***You/you/YOU* are being grown. . . harvested. . . expanded and celebrated.**

Wisdom comes through *Self/self/SELF*-as-soulmate love and listening. It is the golden thread that weaves together all levels, aspects, and expressions of an experience into a rich tapestry. Remember, *You/you/YOU* are the Divine presence in form, unique in expression. . . bold in capacity. . . powerful in a multitude of frequencies. . . and abundant in dimensions of love, light, and shadow. Wisdom is the gold *You* came for. Through integration, it becomes your fragrance.

Witness the heart flutter as *You* are spritzed by your own fragrance. Daringly *Living/living/LIVING* the life you've been given. . . produces your perfume. Your fragrance of wisdom wafts through creative inspirations that rise from your heart. It is spicy, filled with the zest for life. Rich in aroma and tinged with the scent of adventure, your journey is filled with notes of wisdom.

When *You/YOU* behold everything as Divine Perfection, *You* will be astounded by the beauty of life. Multiple dimensions of *Self* and story have been necessary to create your depth and breadth of wisdom. The collaboration among your shadow, humanity, and Divinity. . . amid multiple expressions, lives, births, and deaths. . . throughout moments, experiences, and lifetimes brings forth endless volumes of wisdom. Experience is the Divine unfolding. *You/you/YOU* are as intended, inspired by divine design and through unknown, organic surprise. *You* are magyck, the magician, and the spark.

> **When consciously choosing the dark night,**
> ***You* will find all that *You/you* fear. . .**
> **but, in facing those fears, *You/you/YOU* shall be set free.**

You will know—without doubt—when reaching the end of an experience; otherwise it is not the end. And what of the beginning? That is often overlooked, until the ending. In the final moment of an experience, *You* truly behold the original seeds planted. Your original intention, initiating action, and the energetics are often deeper than *You/you/*

YOU knew. What set life in motion reveals when wise enough to behold that point of view. *Knowing/KNOWING* your point of attraction simultaneously reveals the beginning and the end. You are eternity in the making. Wisdom is your guiding staff.

Let each day be a colorful work of art; each moment, an intentional stroke upon your canvas of life and *Living/living/LIVING*. May each heartbreak support *You/you/YOU* in loving better. . . every challenge make *You/you/YOU* stronger. . . each obstacle inspire greater compassion. . . and all pain transform into ever-increasing experiences of joy. May your Light shine brighter each day. . . may every second echo the expansion of your dreams. . . each moment bring greater adventure. . . and every hour illuminate your golden *SELF*. May each day present a clear and sacred path. . . and through every step, may *You/you/YOU* celebrate the whispers, the wonders, and the wounded for the precious wisdom they bring into collective consciousness. There is much hidden in the treasure of *You/Me/Us/Them*. Bring forth your spicy fragrance; such elixirs are rare and priceless.

Embrace the wisdom of experience. . .
but also. . .
let it slip through your fingers.
***Know/know/KNOW* everything;**
cling to no thing.
Embody this Divine understanding.
This is *KNOWING*.

knowing.
How did i/eye get here?
My best thinking got me here.

Knowing.
I am a student of experience.

KNOWING.
I AM wise.

. . .

FLAVOR OF KINDNESS

What does it taste like?

You **were born into a body**
filled with Spirit,
but your mind pulled away.

You ascended
as *you/YOU* went undercover.
With no wings to fly,
You chose to nest.
They were tucked away. . .
while stopping to rest.

There come moments when *You* have no idea who *You/you/YOU* are. . . why *You/you/YOU* are. . . or where *You/you/YOU* are. These are times of contraction. The skin of your life is *being* torn away because it no longer serves. Yet, it feels as if *You/you/YOU* are plunged deeper into conflict. There is no need to control, defend, or fight anything. Transformation happens by rooting where *You* are. Accept what is happening. Be neutral in your approach but feel into each second with care. A barren field can become a beautiful harvest. *You* can grow corn in the desert. *You* came to discover that love, beauty, and vitality are alive and well, even within the marsh. What is outside is not required to change, although it will. What is inside must change.

Let the noise of the world be so deafening that *You* seek a quiet place. There is no greater kindness to give *Self/self/SELF* than space for listening. Listen for your ocean of insight. When *You/you/YOU* receive this, your capacity to give listening to the world expands. *You* are every piece, and part, of the world speaking back to *You/you/YOU,* about *You/you/YOU. You* are not your sister's keeper, *You/you/YOU* are your sister. *You* are not your brother's keeper, *You/you/YOU* are your brother. *You* are not the keeper of your mother, father, son, or daughter, *You/you/YOU* are your mother. . . your father. . . your son. . . and your daughter. This is the essence of kindness. Listening—seeing and acknowledging them—is the greatest kindness that exists.

You have greater power in your cells than your mind can imagine.
To listen from this depth is to offer the ears of *God/GOD*.

We are one family. . . one body. . . one *BEING*. In seeing one another's beauty and tragedy, we reconcile all separated parts and return to wholeness and oneness. Dismiss no one, because everyone is *YOU* with another face. Honor them. Love them. Celebrate each one. Condemn no one. But do what is yours to do with deep compassion, kindness, and strength. The kindest thing *You/you* can do for our world is not have an agenda. When you need others for something, *You/you* cast into consciousness the conditions they are required to be in to achieve your end. Begin to look at what *You/you* do and ask yourself, What's my agenda in this. . . conversation? Activity? Action? Work? Free yourself of agenda and *You/you* free others of your lasso. The flavor of your kindness midwifes renewal. Open to and expand the loving kindness of your humanity.

Each time you take a bath, it is a cleansing of *Self/self*.
Bathing in the essence of *SELF* is a baptism of Spirit.

Baths heal, nourish, and renew. Emotions are easier to express, whether grief or love. Transformation occurs. Inflammation decreases and the body is soothed with a good soak. Water combined with intention creates a ritualistic atmosphere for clearing negativity from situations.

Spiritual baths cleanse the aura and revitalize the subtle senses. They clear the mind, balancing energy and connecting with soul. They offer release. Spiritual baths create a greater sense of inner peace. This devotional practice brings in the sacred, especially when combined with elements that enliven your senses. Diffuse essential oils and light candles, soak in salts, or burn incense. By connecting with the *scent-ual/sensual*, *You* subconsciously carry fragrance in your actions. How *You* treat *Self* reflects in how *You* treat others. This is one way of seeing the sacred, being with the sacred, and *Knowing* the sacred.

**As *You* endeavor upon truth in Essence,
restore kindness through the key of trust.**

Loving kindness is a byproduct of wisdom. When *You/you/YOU* block this expression, *You* block love. Encompassing generosity and unconditional giving. . . kindness builds bridges, fosters hope, and creates gratitude. The flavor of kindness is a sacred offering of presence and time; not only of your human *Self*, but also your holy *SELF*. It is the willing sacrifice of your shadow *self* toward something greater than its needs. The energy of kindness heals relationships and transforms lives.

To be kind is to be of good use. *Self/self/SELF* obsession or *Self/self* absorption cannot exist if the flavor of kindness is present in *You*. The need to play small is released. Within *You/you/YOU* lie unlimited power, potential, and infinite possibility. Kindness is *Self/self*-less. Small acts of kindness are the foundation for grounding true humanity within the world. The way to begin creating this higher frequency comes with unconditional loving kindness to *Self/self/SELF*. Then, this overflows onto others.

Be kind to your body. Be kind to your heart. Be kind to your shadow nature. Be kind to time. Be kind to your schedule. Let the flavor of kindness season your thoughts. . . tenderize your words. . . garnish your actions. . . and marinate within your intentions. Make yourself whole through small acts of kindness.

**Sit with me.
Hold me.
Love me.
Laugh with me.
Dance with me.
Sing your song to me.
Cherish me.
Be with me.
Beloved One,
be kind.**

knowing.
When will i/eye fit in?
Maybe i/eye am not supposed to fit in.

Knowing.
I am open to diversity;
mine and others.

KNOWING.
I AM a unique piece of the Divine Puzzle
and the Divine Plan.

. . .

MELODY THROUGH PEACE—SATISFACTION

What does it sound like?

Never base your visions and dreams on others. . .
not on critics or those *You/you/YOU* love and admire.
Do not give them a piece of *You*,
or you feed their shadow.
Do not give them your peace;
they must hold their own.
Each person has their own path,
unique to their wounds, inadequacies, and codependencies. . .
gifts, skills, and talents.
Trust the melody.
Remain calm.
Temper *Self/self/SELF*;
peace be with *You*.

What is in a name, condition, or experience? Nothing and everything. Name and identity are subtle castings of judgment, which is always in opposition to peace. When naming anything, the meaning assigned must unfold. Naming is a form of subtle prayer. Each hidden, denied, and cast-aside named piece of *You/you/YOU* must be held with love and brought home to the heart. This return frees *Self/self/SELF* from past prisons. Suffering and struggle are compost for enriching aspirations of peace and enlightenment. Peace awakens when admitting to and embracing your deepest inequities and fears. In loosing the threads of skepticism, lack, and negativity, the focus within Essence expands. *You* will find peace outside when discovering peace inside.

**Wisdom through witnessing shifts *Being* businessman to *BEING* philanthropist;
utilize the melody of peace through satisfaction, as an act of grace.**

Life presents waves as a function for mastering inner peace. The ego and identity—adorned with accoutrements of distraction—always seek to change, fix, heal, or numb discomfort. The *One/ONE* dressed in peace does not need anything external to change. They live in the land of satisfaction. These individuals have grounded within deep inner comfort. They consciously choose to find the places of satisfaction within their lives, rather than focusing upon the appearance of otherwise. Real and lasting peace is attained when experience is bathed in this continual embrace.

Keep tuning to the melody of peace through experiences where *You/you/YOU* feel satisfied. Be filled. Align creations and expressions with Divine Will, instead of your personal will's manipulative hand. With more satisfaction felt in present circumstances, more joy will build, and more satisfaction will be experienced. With more satisfaction, the rhythm of satisfaction will be created, allowing satisfaction, attraction, and receiving to become a constant. By focusing on what works instead of what does not, the ability to attract what is truly desired enters your life.

You/you/YOU are the experience of the Universe in motion. Harmonic melody is designed to come through *You*, and yours is a peace-filled *ONE*. No passion is ever more important than peace. Expect one Blessing after another; that's all there is.

Peace is a choice. . . a sane, conscious, enlightened one.

Do not hold back from experiencing the contrasts, constructs, and structures that exist. Living and *Being* in the world must be held with a loose tether. Life is a temporal construct. A Master of peace willingly walks through life, accepting what comes. There is no preoccupation with time or identity. Through nondoing, an aura of equality with all people, places, and things is cultivated. The Master knows the present moment requires nothing. Spirituality is having connection to all that is *You/you/YOU*, and honoring this relationship as sacred. This brings peace within and without.

Peace is the consciousness of pure acceptance. In this state of nonresistance, possibilities for *what is* expand. Through this holy rite of mastery. . . the vulnerable, curious, and tumultuous steps of being human are lifted into the arms of divine grace. Grounding in detachment and dispassion equilibrates life's play of energies. This means trusting the cycles and rhythms of nature, and life's ability to balance all things. Peace is available to everyone, and most accessible to those who do not require it.

**Never underestimate pain's power for alchemizing change.
This is your *mettle* turning to gold;
the rich alchemical process of transformation and transmutation lie within.**

The homesickness *You/you/YOU* feel is the *Knowing* of a space beyond here, beyond any place; a *ONEness* beyond any-*One/one/ONE*. The serenity of *Home/HOME* holds *Love/LOVE* that is boundless. A melody of peace can be found within the timeless. . . natural. . . expansive. . . union and reunion with Spirit. Life, as it unfolds, is your soul song. Spirit dances through *You/you/YOU*. How *You/you/YOU* harmonize amid your soul's meanderings determines your melody of peace.

Spirituality is not so much about the cosmic as it is about illuminating the ordinary. Spirituality enables people to see more within the world and within others, which leads to a greater sense of connection. Grounded spirituality in *Self* creates greater satisfaction, which consists of ordinary experiences that feel satiating. Spirituality, in its purest form, is not an escape from the world but a richer engagement with it. The root of spirituality is the Latin *spiritualis,* "pertaining to breath, breathing, wind, or air." To truly create peace in one's life, endeavor upon what creates satisfaction and brings forward a deeper state of relaxation for life as it is.

Rest in peace. . .
as the imagination plays.
Duality. Separation. Oneness.
Be at peace.
Love. Fear. Indifference.
Remembrance.
Hater. Lover. Beloved.
Peace be with *You/you/YOU*.
Shadow. Darkness. Light.
Accept all with peace.
This is a game
of hide-and-seek.
A Divine child's playground
of the strong and the meek.
Let the wisdom of expression unite
all of your lost pieces
and any missing peace.

knowing.
Why do i/eye feel anxious?
If I did not get caught inside of my head, I would feel greater peace.

Knowing.
I can calm my mind

KNOWING.
I AM peace.

. . .

VISCERAL FIGHT

What may be absorbed?

Insanity begins in the mind.
When justified by others,
it becomes hysteria.
Ultimately, each position. . .
instigator, victim, or villain,
reflects a part of *You/you/YOU*.
Collectively, victim, villain, saint, and hero
create the body of *God/god/GOD*.
There is truly only. . . *ONE*.
Whatever you see, hear, face, fight, and love. . .
regardless of face or form,
it is the *ONE*.
The only one in the room is
***You* and *God*.**

You will encounter conflict. These moments are instigated by your inner conflicts. Sometimes that connection is clear; other times, not at all. The external fight feels real and may have to play out. However, the resolution is not where *You* think. Stand your ground within the subconscious *Mind/mind*. This is your true battlefield. The enemy is within *You*. The *One/one/ONE* outside is simply an angel in disguise. This person or experience is designed to point *You* back to your *Self/self/SELF*. Irritation is meant to provoke pondering. There are subtle rumblings deep inside. This is the drumming of visceral fight.

Although there are legitimate threats in life, much of your fight response is memory. This may be real, imagined, or perceived. Some threats *You/you/YOU* were made to believe. If not present to your layers and depths, the fight beneath the surface will sabotage oncoming experiences. The subtle energies of bitterness and resentment build within unresolved conflict. These energies accumulate when not speaking your truth, asking for your desires, or expressing feelings. *Self/SELF*-betrayal always creates inner conflict. Visceral fight is the physical memory of long-held arguments, bitterness, and contempt. Fight creates discordance in the body. Unconsciously ruminating over how wronged or victimized *You/you/YOU* are prolongs emotional pain, undermines health, and distorts perspective. This state of vengeful bondage erodes well-being.

Most fight is physiological, beginning before *You/you/YOU* had emotional or intellectual capacity. This keeps the body tense. Energies lodged within your physiology result in sensations, aches, and physical discomfort. Anxiety and stress create a hypervigilant state and guarded stance. Words are spoken quickly and restlessly. Irregular heartbeats and high blood pressure display signs of unconscious antagonism. Shallow breathing displays how a body experiences tension. Energy is frenzied. The energy of fight is inside your cells. Jaws are tight. Teeth are clenched. Fists are curled up. Shoulders are high.

The neck is taut. Ultimately, illness and dis-ease erupt as *You* fight yourself. Bitterness becomes the body's prison when held for a long time; for some, it becomes a death sentence. In truth, the only *One/one/ONE You* ever truly fight with is. . . *You/you/YOU*. The persistence of memory—from between utero and age seven—reincarnates unresolved inner conflict, for the purposes of healing.

Cultivate connection as *You* invite unification with the Creative Aspect;
deep presence is required to access your visceral fight of bitterness.

All fight stems from fear: fear of loss. . . fear of grief. . . fear of sadness. . . and fear of pain. . . fear of not being loved and accepted. Although there are legitimate threats throughout life, much of your fight stems from unaddressed visceral memory. *You* are a drop in the great ocean of consciousness; your fight is in the undertow. Do not get sucked under by your own force. The false *self* judges, condemns, and fights. This lower frequency contributes to the global experience of conflict and oppression. Then, *You* fight, they fight; we all fight.

Bitterness is the undertow in the emotional body. This grating hum, once triggered, rises like a sleeping tiger. Once poked, it will have *You/you/YOU* twisting and turning, moaning and groaning, hemming and hawing. *You* victimize yourself with bitterness. Anger and resentment ferment into bitterness, especially through continual *Self/self/SELF*-betrayal. Ultimately, what leaves a bitter taste is the result of imbalanced exchanges of time, space, relationship, and energy. Bitterness builds from beliefs in life's unfairness. Retelling the story compounds the original trauma.

The ego clamors, making up stories, conditions, and causes so that *You/you/YOU* remain active and distracted. It loves to fight. That is the ego's gauntlet, sword, and shield. The need to fight becomes your psychological culture. Being right becomes the cross to carry. To resist *what is* only creates more resistance. To fight *what is* brings more wounding and bruising. Pushing against conditions, or the body, is futile. Salvation lies in surrender. Once this friction is reconciled and absorbed, external triggers will no longer wound or create resistance. Be still. Be present. Be kind. What if *You* let go?

To antagonize. . . to hate. . . to judge and condemn. . . to criticize and conform. . .
buries peace among the dead and keeps conflict raging.

You may be fighting an illusion, and most often *You/you/YOU* are. *Mind/mind/MIND* does not know the difference between something real or imagined. Fight can become a way of life, a pattern, a behavior, and a sporting attitude that is often celebrated. But this is the energy of force. Whether *You* fight for something, or push against it, does not matter. The mere act of fighting creates duality; winning and losing. Early messaging taught *you* that fighting is the way of this world. *You* were shown that aggression, subtle or strong, achieves things. History taught *You/you/YOU* to fight for what *You* need. . . for your beliefs. . . your voice. . . your individuality. . . and your rights. *You* fight conditions. *You* take on the world. This energy brings more fight. However, *You* are not here to kill off *Mind/mind* or win at anything. Instead, master each moment. Master your *Mind/mind/MIND*. The deeply subtle archive of visceral fight weighs down intuition, sacred power, and Divine *Knowing/KNOWING*.

You pray, beg, and plead for relief. But when it arrives, *You/you/YOU* cling to the old, creating further suffering. Do not make life harder than it needs to be. Nor should *You* make life's experiences more than they are. Life is teaching *You* to let go of these material passions; your stories, arguments, rightness, and identity. *YOU* came and then became... to forget and then remember. This is the soul contract, which requires the release of everything collected along the way.

You pulled the wool over your eyes. Contractions exist within emotional experiences. Breathe into each discordant thought until it dissolves. Contractions become more frequent with pressure and limitation. Breathe through the tightness until it expands. Contractions intensify when *One* sees two, and those two are separating... individuating... and parting. Breathe... to ease the pain of new birth. Fight always leads to rebirth, but it also requires a death. Breathe... to allow the integration of what has come to pass. With each breath and awareness, *You/you* dissolve and *YOU* form.

Instead of looking at all that is wrong,
look at what is right.
Instead of seeing how people used *You/you/YOU*,
see how they empowered *You/you/YOU*.
Instead of perceiving lack and scarcity,
look at the abundance of experience that is present.
Instead of feeling betrayed,
notice how *You* have been invited to participate.
***You/you/YOU* paint the world with perception.**
***You/you/YOU* color it with thought.**
***You/you/YOU* draw pictures with the mind...**
to remember what *You/you/YOU* forgot.

knowing.
Why does everything feel like a fight?
i/eye can stop fighting life.

Knowing.
I surrender to the moment.

KNOWING.
I AM satisfied.

ALCHEMY OF HEART

What can be transmuted?

The shadow led
and *You/you/YOU* followed.
It gave *You* gifts today,
for *You* to experience gratitude tomorrow.
It held *You/you/YOU,*
even in your fall.
Your humanity lifted *You/you/YOU*
to stand grand and tall.
Ego gave *You/you/YOU* wings
so *You/you/YOU* could fly.
It created a perfect pathway,
an experience, in which to die.
Shadow always put *You* first,
so that *YOU* could experience powerful rebirth.
Higher *SELF* observed,
as sacred witness, advocate, and life steward.

Deep in the valley, *You* have slipped into feeling and seeing the underworld. Blazing hot with fire, while drowning within the fluidity of impending rebirth, is a heart-wrenching place. *You* are on life support; inside the dark womb, once again. This is the womb of death and rebirth. There is no tangible *mother* here, only the darkness of creation's void. This is the *MOTHER* of all *Mother*s; the unconditional, eternal, and everlasting. Not even your biological mother can steward *You/you/YOU* through this. What must break down belongs to her. . . your father. . . and many generations before them. *You* are layered with the ancestral residues of withholding, secrets, lies, and unknown traumas. Your soul knows things that mind and body are disconnected from. These rest in your energetic, emotional, and cellular memory.

Although breathing, *You/you/YOU* are deeply present to how *You* do not fully breathe. Intuitively there exists *Knowing* that *You* are connected, yet *you* feel separate from everything. *You* are seemingly alone but are not. *You/you/YOU* find yourself feeling alone within your body, disconnected from flesh, blood, and bone. Your spirit writhes within a skin suit that no longer feels like it fits. In moments, it is loose and baggy and hangs off. *You/you/YOU* feel small, inept, and inadequate within it. More often, it seems tight and clingy, suffocating and strangling. *You/you/YOU* want out, but that is terrifying. *You* want to connect—in a way that *you* sense—but have long forgotten. *You/you/YOU* want to go home but feel homeless. *You/you/YOU* feel utterly alone, and apart from the world. *You/you/YOU* isolate.

Heal thyself with the gifts of light, love and compassion;
these blessings allow purity to rise.

Only one activity can lift *You/you* to your next best step, being alone with yourself. Not simply a day or a weekend, but a stretch of time. Life requires pauses and full stops; otherwise nothing real can be remembered. Most people will not understand your pause, unless they have done so for themselves. This deeply loving step is one of courage, boldness, and fierce advocacy. This act of true love will lift *You* into higher consciousness, to a vantage point far above where most perceive.

When *You/you/YOU* move away from distraction and make the inner world more important than the outer, *You/you/YOU* receive all that the world offers. Moving through dis-integration can be an extremely lonely process. But to be focused and effective, time alone must occur. Loneliness points toward what is real and infinitely more extraordinary. Walking through this darkened narrow passageway leads to *Being/BEING* empowered through your aloneness. Loneliness brings the best of *You/you/YOU* to relationship, because *You* learn how to be alone with your *Self.* Through the sheer beauty of aloneness comes the pleasure of your own company. *You* get to know yourself in a way that outer relationships never can. Allow time for sacred intimacy.

True communion is found inside aloneness. Be willing to be with the most important one on Earth. . . *YOU.* The most important relationship *You* can ever have is with *Self/self/SELF.* Sacred aloneness reveals what *You/you/YOU* are truly made of. . . in thought, word, and deed. *Know/know/KNOW* thyself. Sacred aloneness is a treasure trove of insight and riches. Let the harmony inside bring forth the movement of your body and soul.

Sacred aloneness strengthens your ability to be kind. With greater peace and wisdom under your belt, a more stable stance exists. Build your crystalline grids of creation and bathe in satisfaction of the heart's path to awakening. *You* are becoming increasingly present. Each deliberate and intentional step supports solid ground in building. What your life is built upon from this point forward shall be more secure. New energetic structures are *Being/BEING* created within *You,* preparing the way for sovereign dominion.

Fall in love with your aloneness. Discover how to be with yourself, without the trappings of the world. Begin to give yourself all the love, gifts, and service *You* have been doting on others. When yearning for another, give yourself what *You/you/YOU* seek from them. When *You/you/YOU* no longer codependently need another, the correct *One/ONE* will appear. This new experience of love and loving will be whole, complete, and interdependent. That experience will blossom into true spiritual partnership, as long as *You/YOU* remain in your highest expression. Two coming together as *ONE* is possible when two interdependent beings are grounded in the higher nature of their whole and unique, creative expression.

Solemnly vow. . . to YOU.
to have and to hold, in sickness and in health, for richer or poorer,
till death do *You* part. . . for as long as *You/you/YOU* live.

Do not rush to be supernatural. Your richness rests in awakening to the natural. Do not hastily leave the land of the familiar. The makings of true heart alchemy rest where *You/you/YOU* are. When *You* know true love, losing everything or gaining anything is of no consequence. It becomes background music. Your pain will cure *You/you/YOU*. Humanity is buried beneath your rubble. Sink low and deep to find it.

Alchemy of the heart occurs through deeply feeling. Experience everything, every sensation to the deepest degree. In this way, *You* are born again. While gaining the ability to see how your condition came to be, *You* activate the loving mother and compassionate father within. The tender, whole heart *KNOW*s how to parent and nurture your multiple facets, dimensions, and fragments of *self. . . Self. . . and SELF*.

When *You* are enamored and amused by your own existence, alchemy occurs. The heart experiences an opening. Ground in the delight of your shadow *self* playing with the child *self/Self*. Sacred communion will deepen through the child *self/Self* leaping into the embrace of your human *Self*. This triad of *Self/self/SELF* creates the ecstatic devotion for your human *Self* to ascend to the *Higher Self/SELF*. *Higher Self/SELF* bows in sacred service to your *Divine and Holy SELF* with the ecstatic rhapsody of *Knowing/KNOWING*. Life shall sprinkle with inspiration as Essence begets its own golden awareness.

Diving into the dark. . .
rising amid the Light.
Deepening into the heart. . .
awakening to fright, fight, and flight.
Feeling the creamy center of a spirit broken
for the sacred heart's discovery of longing and belonging.
In love, *You/you/YOU*. . .
the child, the shadow, and humanity. . .
unite with one another.
The realization dawns
of *Being/being/BEING*
every child, brother, sister, father, and mother.

knowing.
Why did my heart have to break?
There is a blessing in this, even if i/eye don't see it right now.

Knowing.
I remain grounded in my heart space.

KNOWING.
I AM solid ground.

. . .

ESSENCE AS PURITY

What may be embodied?

Every sunrise has a sunset;
every beginning, an end.
Every night has a new day.
In due time, *You/you/YOU* always win.
Be peaceful in heart and mind.
Be grounded in love and compassion.
Be rooted in empathy.
Let purity be your graceful fashion.

Vanity is the experience of falling in love with your story, your identity, and all associated trappings. Vanity is also entitlement, expressed when attempting to control, manage, dictate, or project personal will onto life's divine design. It is the projection of your human *Self/self, overshadowing* your *GOD/SELF.* This creates very diverse and dense expressions within the human experience, which creates the need for causes and cures. Man's passions, causes, and creations are vain projections of false humility.

The path of Light is not to be taken lightly. The higher path of soulful expression involves tremendous sacrifice and surrender. Letting go of your vain projections of the small *Self/self* is worth their sacrifice. Trust. Hand everything over to *Spirit/SPIRIT* and surrender to higher expression. Sacrifice means giving up what is lower, to receive of what is higher. Rather than acting out lower-density vices, embody and express your keys of higher virtue. Honor the real, not illusion and delusion. *God/god/GOD* is the only thing between us, and also what connects us. The question is whether we will fill the space with the meanderings of a lower *God/god* or a High *GOD.* Purity is falling in love with Essence shining through *You.* It is giving the glory to Divine Will, sacrificing personal will. *Source/GOD/Universe/LOVE* smiles through *You/you/YOU.*

Purity holds the energy of catharsis. It is the space for clearing, cleansing, and purification. Purity brings on transformation. It is foretold by shedding old skins and releasing old patterns. When purity is experienced internally, an external transformation is sure to quickly follow. When unwilling to shed the friction and drives that stem from within the mind and body, accessing purity is not possible. This keeps *You* from receiving your purity of Essence and purity of compassion. It also has You withhold your pure presence, love, beauty, and power.

Forgiving passion creates the inspiration for giving dispassion to *Self.*

Dissatisfaction will be your great nemesis. It robs *You* of peace and purity. Born out of expectation and control, dissatisfaction is like a slow-growing mold that blankets your ability to see the good in life. It creates habits of negative thinking, stewing, venting, and complaining, eventually leading to deeply held bitterness. Dissatisfaction is impatience with others, life, and *Self.* What is yours is meant for *You;* otherwise it cannot be your experience. *You* have no idea of what is in motion, or how that relates to your destiny.

The Universe flows through every action and choice. The eternal as no agenda. There is no rush. Nothing can be lost, missed, or forsaken.

Let patience always be your guide. Life will teach *You* this. Healing journeys and spiritual walks call for presence, perseverance, and patient devotion. These are necessary for overcoming emotion, dis-ease, and discordant thinking. Difficulties and challenges will always appear. The ego wants to rush through, fix, and finish with situations that feel uncomfortable. But this only creates more obstacles. Each life experience will ask for your patience. That could mean a few hours, a few days, a few weeks, months, or longer. Eventually the awareness, gift, or expansion shall appear. Accept each experience for what it holds. *You* do not have to figure things out.

Patience is an aspect of spiritual maturity. It is active presence while trusting life's wisdom and intelligence. Trust is foundational. Faith and trust allow things in their own time. These are strengthened through your relationship with *Source/GOD/Universe/ LOVE*. Faith in *Source/GOD/Universe/LOVE* creates the sustenance needed for persevering through dark times. Have faith and trust that everything occurring is the will of *God/god/ GOD*. Discern the *God/god/GOD* with which *You* are willing. When the virtue of patience is present, wisdom of experience is gained. Patience is silent, relaxed, yet active presence. Patience grounds soul dharma. Patience rests in *KNOWING*.

YOU... embody a unique "piece/peace" of a Divine puzzle... for life's Divine Plan.
Through *You/you/YOU*... life experiences...
Allness... Everythingness... Expansiveness... Nothingness... *ISness*.

The journey of *You* is on the inner planes. Let Essence create everything there, in the purity of holy vision. Aliveness, dreams, and truth are there. Once anchored in the pure essence of these, reflect the world *YOU* desire. Let there be no interference. Dreams and desires require wholehearted commitment... not just consideration. The body is not *You/ you/YOU*. It is a container for *Essence* to have form.

You are the Universe in all of its splendor... human in your doing, *God/GOD* in your *Being/BEING*. Extend your arms and connect that which is human to that which is Holy. There is no separation; there never has been. The sacredness within *You/you/YOU* waits patiently. Source never pushes, rushes, or demands anything of *You/you/YOU*. The universe has immeasurable patience for *You/you/YOU*; anchor into the purity of your patience. Have patience with your *Self/self/SELF*.

Allow for silence; return to center. Create time for entering the temple. Bow down. Sit with *presence/Presence/PRESENCE*. Sacred stillness is the fountain that *You/you/YOU* have been longing for... and dreaming of. Dip into this pool of pure patience. Be anointed by immersing within it. Patience is the only true action; all else is control. With pure patience, there is no past or future; only Divine Presence. There is no story; only creation. There will be no witness, doing, or protocol for *BEING*. This quiet purity... *IS*... The Essence... of *YOU. IS*ness *IS* pure Divine Awareness.

You/you/YOU are a crystalline form.
The essential oil.
The incense.

You/you/YOU are the ember.
The flame.
The light.
The lighter.
You/you/YOU are the Sacred Space.
The prayer
The altar.
The Divine One.
You/you/YOU.
YES...
You/you/YOU.
Always...
You/you/YOU.

knowing.
Why don't i/eye feel "good enough"?
i/eye can accept who i/eye am right now.

Knowing.
I Am enough.

KNOWING.
I AM pure essence.

. . .

FORGIVING PASSION—FOR GIVING DISPASSION

What can be transmuted?

I forgive life's experience of illusion.
I forgive this earthen dimension for contrast and volatility.
I forgive herd mentality.
I forgive hunger.
I forgive drive, ambition, and passion.
I am for giving space.
I am for giving rest.
I am for giving relaxation.
I am for giving ease.
I am for giving equality.
I give presence to *Self/self/SELF*-love.
I give way to natural being.

I give in to organic living.
I give of grace-filled *Knowing/KNOWING*.
I give my human *Self* the grace of dispassion.
I alchemize my perception with the aura of the crystalline body.
I alchemize reflection with the fragrance of wisdom.
I alchemize my faith with the flavor of tenderness.
I alchemize witnessing through the melody of peace.
I alchemize my imaginings with the Essence of purity.
I am *ONE* with the *DIVINE PRESENCE*;
I transform and transmute all passion through the grace of dispassion...
I open to the absorption of all visceral fight and residual bitterness.
May *DIVINE ALCHEMY* sieve through my ambition and calm the greedy, driven *self*.
May I adorn the peacock's plumes
so to bridge the illusion of the material plane with the reality of the spiritual world.
I step with trust toward a heavenly embodiment.
I am for giving the peacock's gifts of vision and guidance,
integrity, and *SELF*-expression... protection and watchfulness.
May these gifts of *KNOWING* be granted by *DIVINE GRACE*.
I am the crystalized body of *GOD*.
I AM the wisdom of *GOD*.
I AM the kindness of *GOD*.
I AM the peace of *GOD*.
I AM the purity of *GOD*.
I AM the form of *GOD*.
I AM.

. . .

UP-LEVEL PERSONAL POWER

GROUNDING shifts your POINT OF ATTRACTION

self ——-> *Self* ——-> *SELF*

Be present. Gradually shift into higher octaves of presence, awareness, and perception.
Move up the vibrational ladder. Feel your way and ascend to a new reality.
The third human expression of grace establishes a new foundation from which to radiate
your central sun. It requires anchoring solidly into the ground. Raise your face to the sun
and remember golden radiance. Become a generator of warmth and light. Just as the sun
supports seasons of change, be the ever-present celestial body that the entire universe is
powered by. Awaken early. Lift your hands to the sky. Kiss the sun's rays and bless them,
so that your actions and words are graceful beams of light.
   Up-level personal power—through presence—to the truth of who *YOU* are.

Move gradually into fulfillment, purpose, and personal power through focus, vibration, and grounding as your point of attraction. As *You* more deeply anchor within yourself—and specifically the *GOD* within *YOU*—your ability to create a life of personal power and purpose unfolds. *You* are an ever-expanding, energetic expression of creative capacity. Awaken your *knowing. . . Knowing. . . KNOWING*. Give life something to respond to.

living.
— — — — — — — — — — — —

acknowledgment
(slow down and feel.)
— —

eye/i never seem to have enough. eye/i work and work and work. eye/i didn't get the breaks they got. eye/i keep getting more and more bills. eye/i want to make more money. eye/i want to buy nice things. eye/i never get a lucky break. eye/i will never get there. eye/i just can't get ahead. eye/i don't have enough. eye/i am not enough. eye/i am not worthy. eye/i can't catch a break.

being.
— — — — — — — — — — — —

acceptance
(bring attention to your breath.)
— —

eye/i feel. . . stretched beyond my comfort zone. eye/i am hungry; eye/i want more. eye/i feel bitter about life. eye/i feel negatively about certain people. eye/i feel poor. eye/i feel like an animal. eye/i feel angry and competitive. eye/i feel petty and abrasive. eye/i feel gnarly and mean. eye/i manipulate, so that eye/i get my needs met. eye/i am codependent in my relationships. eye/i feel the low growl of an animal inside of me.

knowing.
— — — — — — — — — — — —

anticipation
(breathe slowly; deepen into your body.)
— —

eye/i sometimes feel eye/i have nothing to offer the world. But Source created me; that makes me worthy. eye/i am triggered by others, but this shows me where to look within. eye/i react at times, but that helps me see that a wound still exists. eye/i can explore my creative side. eye/i can't wait to see what eye/i create. eye/i am learning how to feel and express authentically. Within the contrast, eye/i feel what no longer serves me. eye/i am seeing more of me each day.

Living.
— — — — — — — — — — — —

appreciation
(pause and be present to what the moment is asking.)
— —

Whether or not my wallet is with me, I appreciate feeling rich within. I appreciate my innocence. I am grateful to be able to give. I find appreciation in holding the presence of peace. I appreciate the purity of each moment. I appreciate transformation. I am grateful that I am unique. I appreciate the visions I receive. I appreciate my intuition. I am grateful that I am learning to trust myself. I appreciate learning to trust the world. I am grateful to deepen trust with Source.

Being.

----

satisfaction
(connect mind to heart to gut to ground.)

I feel satisfied when I focus on my personal growth. It's satisfying to receive messages when I need them. It is satisfying to see things in a positive light. I feel satisfied with how far I have come. Deep breaths are satisfying. An inhale is always a satisfying experience. Exhaling with sound is incredibly satisfying. I feel satisfied each time my mindset is upgraded. I find satisfaction in strengthening my mind. I am satisfied that I will continue growing more and more.

Knowing.

----

adoration
(inhale deeply and absorb what is present.)

I love essence. I love God. I love Source, I love the Universe. I love all things cosmic. I love the stars. I love that I am part of the universe. I love that I am connected to Source. I love that I am filled with Essence. I love that I get to remember Essence. I love that remembering is what I came for. I love that opposites attract. I love that my opposite helps me align to Essence. I love that possibilities exist. I love that my life holds infinite possibility. I love that I am infinite.

LIVING.

----

celebration
(rise above and rejoice.)

I celebrate my insights. I celebrate my visions. I celebrate forward movement. I celebrate being visionary. I celebrate individuals who trigger me into expansion. I celebrate circumstances that constrict me into breaking through. I celebrate that I get to continually increase my frequency of light. I celebrate that I continually expand my ability to love. I celebrate that life is giving me everything required to be soulfully compassionate. I celebrate that I am connected… that I create connection… and I am connecting to myself on many different levels.

BEING.

----

exaltation
(ground in sacredness, devotion, and equanimity. . . unconditionally Love!)

I learn. I initiate. I question. I ponder. I mind. I mine. I engineer. I remind. I inquire. I process.
I understand. I think. I comprehend. I multiply. I add. I divide. I compartmentalize. I define.
I realize. I unknow. I awaken. I open. I close. I disconnect. I quiet. I breathe. I inhale. I exhale.
I align. I deepen. I immerse. I fill. I fuel. I free. I evaporate. I envelop. I internalize. I eternalize.

KNOWING.

———————————————

jubilation
(exhale your newly created vibrational reality and. . . believe!)

————————————————————————————————

I AM visionary. I AM witness. I AM satisfied. I AM kind. I AM dispassion. I AM possibility.
I AM wonder. I AM crystalline. I AM multifaceted. I AM multidimensional.
I AM unique. I AM whole. I AM fabulous. I AM fertile ground. I AM sunshine.
I AM acceptance. I AM purpose.
I AM PEACE. I AM LIGHT. I AM LOVE.
I AM COMPASSION. I AM CONNECTION.
I AM PURITY. I AM PRESENCE. I AM HEART.
I AM LOVING KINDNESS. I AM WISDOM.
I AM THAT. . . I AM. I AM THAT. . . IAM. I AM THAT. . . IAM.

Always begin exactly where *You/you/YOU* are. Be truthful with how *You/you/YOU* feel. Be authentic in what *You/you/YOU* are thinking. A new human builds from the ashes of your old life. Let your words be catalysts for transformation and transmutation. *You* are the bridge between where *you* are and where *You* want to go. *You* grow into *KNOWING* as *You* ascend the ladder of consciousness. What *You* place into the universal vortex remains in escrow. Belief supports physical presence. *KNOWING* creates change, transformation, and miracles.

NOTES

resistance.

What do you have to dissolve?

**Life appears to be reality,
but it is illusion.
Life is a dream that feels real
but fades in mind.
Life becomes what *You* believe
until truth be known.
Aliveness is eternal;
no birth or life exists. . .
only ISness.**

Each circumstance that exists is a convergence point for balancing collective energies and time. Everything serves. Every thing serves the greater good. Each thing labeled "good" or "bad" serves a picture larger than your own. Life even uses your resistance. Discovering how, what, and why *You* resist is integral to experiencing freedom. Resistance is an invisible wall that stands between your aspirations and *SELF*-actualization. This invisible barrier stands guard on behalf of your ego, false selves, and masks. Let *unknowing* free *You/you/ YOU*. Meet your resistance as a stranger, but let it leave as a friend.

**Resistance will rise; get to *know* it and face it.
Break down that barrier and experience a breakthrough.**

Resistance is the ego's attempt at hiding insecurity, fear, inability, or wrongness. It expresses in many ways: procrastination, confusion, and indecision. . . passive aggressive tendencies. . . anxiety and cynicism. . . unconscious deafness. . . hardened identities. . . narrowly focused stands.

Regardless of how resistance shows up, it is *Self/self/SELF*-sabotage. These can be conscious, unconscious, psychological, or energetic; felt in the body as withholding, gripping, or stiffening. Due to the highly unconscious nature of resistance, feeling dazed, disoriented, or confused is how the ego clings and hides. Resistance shows up most often when letting go, taking action, or experiencing change. Resistance appears in scary and powerful experiences, feeling like stubbornness, heart-pounding, mental anxiety, or panic attacks.

The urge to leave, run, escape, or be done with something appears during times of resistance. *You/you/YOU* might respond in a variety of ways, such as stampeding through or submitting to behaviors that dishonor *Self*. However, these methods of distraction do not provide what is necessary to be released from resistance's spindly fingers and bony claws. Resistance and avoidance are signs to come present to the moment, the body, and your feelings. Something is not energetically, psychologically, or emotionally complete. There exists pain, attachment, wounding, and upset that must be resolved. Fears must be faced. Sit in your resistance. Hunker down and feel into what your resistance is truly about.

Resistance forms an inner barrier. Stubbornness comes from resistance. Psychological defenses rise. The wall of resistance is encountered when something rubs against the edges of identity. With resistance, *You/you/YOU* don't want to *know* what *You* don't *know*. However, what *You/you* push against will push back. In pushing against life, life pushes back. When pushing against someone, they will push back. It always takes two hands to clap.

The world holds nothing from *You*.
You/you/YOU withhold the world from yourself.

Resistance is futile. Release the tension of resistance by meeting it as a student. *You* are *Being/being* called to stretch beyond what is known. Resistance speaks most loudly in your unwillingness to take action. When *You/you/YOU* feel recoil and resistance... retrace your steps. Go back; find common ground. Be open to starting anew. Sometimes, it is necessary to go back... in order to go forward. Direction and discernment go hand in hand. Deepen beyond the resistance... mind... feeling... body... and moment... for the heart's whisper to be heard. The heart *Know/KNOW*s. Continue meeting your resistance until able to feel the safety and security of heart-based *Knowing/KNOWING*. Recalibration is integral in aligning to Divine Time. Life is intended to be a wholehearted excursion. Leave nothing behind *You/you/YOU*. Grab each golden nugget and treasured feeling.

Even now, *You* may wonder why grief, pain, and suffering still remain part of this conversation long after so much inner work has been done. It is because layers upon layers of experience are archived and hidden within your body. Much has been collected over time. It is necessary to crack apart and dissolve all that has hardened *You/you/YOU*. Breaking through resistance, pain, and suffering is the portal for higher awakening. Resistance creates an arduous and lengthy process out of grief and pain.

Heartbreak is difficult to endure, yet it offers a crack through which light can enter again. You are tender to the touch, words, and actions of a world in trauma. Yet, this trauma-filled world serves in bringing forth exactly what will shatter the hardened heart. Each challenging life experience arises in advocacy to *break down / break through* aspects of *You/you* and your life that no longer can serve. *YOU* are the *eye/i/I* of the needle; the thread of life slips through *You*.

Trust higher good to bring greater possibilities than *You/you* can imagine.

Part of *You/you/YOU* wants to stay safe, small, and the same. This means taking no risks. This is complacency; holding ont o the familiar and habitual. Another part of *You/you/YOU* desires to grow and transform. Make space by doing more nothing. Resistance is doing something; it is passive action. Doing more nothing is neutral action that allows space for revelation. Space opportunity for a shift in perception, belief, behavior, or the course of your life. Soften into your *Self/self/SELF*. In doing so, *You* soften resistance.

Your ultimate resistance is internal. The greatest nemesis of resistance and fear is holy innocence. When *You/you* drop resistance to the sacred power within, miscreation shall transform into new creation. Your greatest place of resistance regards your true nature and divine inheritance. *You/you/YOU* are afraid of your immense power and divinity. *You* resist your sacredness. *You* resist your sovereignty. *You/you/YOU* resist your *TRUTH*. *You* resist *KNOWING*. You resist personal power, purpose, and peace yet deeply crave these things. *You/you* resist *KNOWING* and embodying the *GOD* that *IS YOU*.

**Each *One/one/ONE* has experiences that
expand or limit,
are beautiful or painful,
and are tragic or blissful.
Open your mind.
Lighten your heart.
See each person and experience
as human and Divine. . .
There is no good or bad,
right or wrong,
past or future. . .
only the unfolding opportunity
for *ONE*ness.
You are not defined by your experiences,
but how *You/you/YOU* respond to them.
Offer your resistance
the gift of acceptance.**

knowing.
Why is the world against me?
Maybe i/eye am against the world.

Knowing.
The world is safe.
(breathe)

KNOWING.
I AM lovable.

the grace of forgiveness.

What is the remembering?

**Invite the grace of forgiveness. Consciously initiate this.
Let the kiss of drought invoke your aura of the rainbow body.
The fragrance in reunion reveals truth.
The flavor of groundedness expands your energy.
Through service, the visceral smoke of jealousy dissolves;
the essence of generosity brings forth your alchemy of spirit, taking *You/you* to
fertile ground. Receive this gift of human grace.
KNOW... your presence is enough.**

You have to swim through it, not over it; not around it, or past it. This moment is asking *You/you/YOU* to swim through each illusion created. Breathe in forgiveness and *self*-love and breathe out honesty and radical acceptance. Stop lying about who *You/you/YOU* have been, what *You/you/YOU* have or have not done, and who *YOU* really are. When *You/you/YOU* burn away every judgment, criticism, doubt, and deficiency, *You/YOU* build a Rainbow Body of Light. Until then, embrace each experience of fire as a gift of purification, toward the grace of forgiveness.

**Within the blessing of chaos and the illusion of hierarchy,
You/you/YOU created resistance
in order to discover the grace of forgiveness, as a way of awakening humanity.**

By loving into what *You/you/YOU* do not, *You* awaken to more *Self/self/SELF*. Within resistance is a wounded, orphaned child in need of loving care. As the inner child receives, they guide the powerful expression *You* were born to experience. Your powerful *SELF* has always been present. No wound could ever truly damage the real *You/YOU*. Forgiveness appears as if it is for the other, but it is for *You/you/YOU*. Forgive those *you* believe caused wounds and pain. Forgive yourself for what *You* believe was done or not done. Forgiveness is a healing elixir.

Forgive. Forgive each and every person, place, and thing. Forgive each experience, expression, and creation. Forgive everything and be free. Forgive the institutions and the process. Forgive the government, healthcare system, legal system... forgive all the systems and structures for how *You/you* believe they work and do not work. With forgiveness, free *Self/self/SELF*. Free your life. Free your body. Free your mind. Free your soul. Pray in peace and harmony to imprint upon the soul. Pray to have love for all men and women. Forgive them. Forgive *Self/self/SELF*. Forgiveness is for giving them. Forgiveness is for giving *You/you/YOU*.

The Grace of Forgiveness	The Remembering	Knowing
The Illusion—Resistance	What has to dissolve?	Aliveness
True Love's Kiss—The Drought	What nature is required?	Creation
Aura of the Rainbow Body	What is emerging?	Unification
Fragrance Emitting Reunion	What is the inhale?	Truth
Flavor of Groundedness	What is the exhale?	Energy
Melody Through Service	What is harmonizing?	Growth
Visceral Smoke—Jealousy	What is being absorbed?	Wisdom
Alchemy of Earth	What can be transmuted?	The Void
Essence as Generosity	What may be embodied?	Infinite Presence
Forgiving Resistance—For Giving Acceptance	What is for giving?	Peace

Now more than ever, hold a vision of others in their highest Essence, especially those *You/you/YOU* name as "enemy." The world needs *you/me/us/them* to check our beliefs about others, safety, and reality. What *you/i/we/they* see is a result of collective belief. Do not mask the moment with positive thinking. Now, more than ever, go deep. Focus. Forgive. Out of your sheer will and desire to change circumstances, *You* will mine your *Mind/mind* for what needs to be forgiven. This devotional endeavor will exhaust *You* to a point of surrender. Ultimately that surrender will exhaust personal will so that *You* finally begin opening to Divine Will.

Forgiveness brings many gifts, beginning with freedom. Transformation also occurs through this powerful spiritual understanding. Change happens with the embodiment of gratitude from forgiveness and understanding. When taking radical responsibility, *You* become ruler of your kingdom. Until then, *You* are *subject* to all that *is/was* created by unconscious decree. *You* will *soldier* many experiences of conflict. Be the *head of your state;* your spirit will be enlightened through the power reclaimed.

Love everyone. . . Forgive everything.

As *You* practice "doing" forgiveness, it will naturally shift into an experience of "*Being.*" In truth, *You* can never "do" forgiveness. It is not an action or activity. Acceptance will organically begin flowing for everyone and everything. *You* will forgive every person, place, and thing from your past. As this occurs, life balance will be restored. In a sudden insight of innocence, an embodied *Knowing* will arise. *There is actually nothing to forgive. There never has been.* This will be the "sit down, tell the truth" moment of your life. *You* were innocent. They were innocent. Every action stems from innocence.

Innocently, every individual has responded through conditioning that they took on. Innocently, *You/you/YOU* created it all—every circumstance, situation, and experience. *You/you/YOU* created every interaction, interchange, and conflict. *You* initiated each obstacle, challenge, and moment of chaos. *You* are the inciter of endless births and deaths. The instigator of your entire life experience is *You*. This will have your *Mind/mind* spinning with a need to rampage forgiveness upon *Self*. However, this distraction is the ego's tomfoolery. Even this forgiveness is unnecessary. There is nothing to forgive your *Self/self/SELF* for.

True forgiveness flowers. Forgiveness is an awareness of Essence that flowers from within. Give your *Self* time… patience… and loving kindness. Forgiveness is and always has been for giving *You/you/YOU* back to *YOU*.

Hold a steady vision for the highest in all.

As *You* look into your eyes… as *You* embrace *You/you/YOU*… as *You* take time to witness your *Self/self/SELF*… experience Namaste. As *You* speak to your heart… as *You* listen to your soul… recognize that *You* and *eye/i/I* are *God/god/GOD*. Our faces are different, but *We/we/WE are* the same. In a space of true beholding, see the Divinity that rests within *One/one/ONE* and *ALL*. In the spaces between *Us/us* is the forgiveness that reconnects *US*.

May your nights be filled with sweetness… your dreams dance in joy, and your body be held in love's gentle grasp. May your mind be cradled in truth, your heart marinate in Essence, and your Spirit fly wild and free. May *You* awaken into that reality… moment by moment… day by day… for all of eternity.

When *You/you/YOU* let go of needing to know why,
You/you/YOU are present to what is.
When *You/you/YOU* let go of needing to know what,
You/you/YOU are present to creativity.
When *You/you/YOU* let go of needing to know whom,
You/you/YOU embrace what's bigger than *You/you*.
When *You/you/YOU* let go of needing to know when,
You/you/YOU live in the now and zen.
Forget it… Forget them… Receive the present.
YOU are the gift. *You* have been waiting for.

knowing.
Why is everyone against me?
i/eye can change how i/eye see others.

Knowing.
I can trust others.

KNOWING.
I AM loved.

...

TRUE LOVE'S KISS—THE DROUGHT

What nature is required?

You are not a doorway to somewhere else.
You are not a container to be filled.
You are not a window to be seen out of.
You are not an ambition to be willed.

You/you/YOU have been carrying on with such courage. *You/you/YOU* have been trudging through life, one experience after another, never fully feeling the ocean inside. Feelings and emotions that were unfelt for too long created a desert within. *You* want to have faith, but when conditions do not change, *You* question if there is anything to truly believe in. The separation between *You* and Source is the desert to be crossed. Drought occurs with complacency, apathy, and indifference. Hopelessness builds. Drought might last for days, months, or years, until fully present with it. *SELF*-denial creates periods of pressure and heat that worsen the human condition. This substantially impacts *your/my/our/their* psycho-emotional-energetic ecosystem.

The kiss of drought is an unconscious communion with *Self/self*-hate. This is at the very bottom of your well; everyone's well. Most would never admit to this dis-ease, because it is deeply unconscious. *Self*-hate is a scary concept. It will be horrifying to face. However, this is a result of the lies *You* told your *Self*, and the many ways *Self/self/SELF* betrayal has been enacted. It is the result of repetitively dishonoring, disobeying, and ignoring your needs. *Self/self*-hate affirms that the pain and suffering experienced were deserved. It means that every core wound and belief—not good enough, stupid, not worthy, unlovable, not important—was true. *Self*-hate is the lie of all lies. It is the cancer of humanity. Until willing to acknowledge this, *You* unknowingly project hate onto yourself and your world in small and large ways. It appears as gossip, criticism, condemnation, rage, anger, and abuse. The hate *You/you* see in the world is *your/my/our/their Self*-hate collectively rearing its head. Let love heal your hate.

In engaging the path of humanitarian, personal obsessions abound,
creating drought, which has hidden within your earthen ground.

You have a choice in how *You/you/YOU* respond. The only question *You* need ask is... "What response is the most loving in this moment?" Then, follow that response. Sometimes this means being more present. At times, it means stepping away. Your mission is to create a space of love where the highest good is served. In truly seeing one another, each person can bow their heads in grace for the other's suffering, and in reverence for the other's miracles. With each step, the animal *self/Self* waits at the altar of your humanity. When *You* fully love this *one*, then love will become the answer to every question. Selfless means beyond *self*.

Love is strong enough to hold everything. To do anything other creates a mirage that is unlike love. *You know* the solution is love, but only giving this out results in depletion. Another solution is to feel "loved," but that also has an inherent flaw. It turns apathetic from too much receiving and nothing being given. The real answer is "to love and be loved" in equal measure. Loving means engaging with, and receiving, each other in an experience of balanced reciprocity.

Express your love. Express your essence.
Let your waterfalls heal the desert of its dryness.

Doubt and drought appear so that *You/you/YOU* dig deep within the well. *You* must feel the parched earthen experience your thoughts, actions, and will created. Life has been a struggle due to your karma, and the buildup of generational karma. This is not punishment. It is purely cause and effect, mostly from what is held in your subconscious. Drought lets the cracked, hard ground be seen for what it is, and where it needs to be fertilized for renewal. There is a barren, dry desert inside. It is your final place of discovery. Before the death of what-no-longer-serves can occur, the initial seed of the human condition must be found. Never rush the journey, or something becomes lost along the way. . . and it might be *YOU.*

Know that who *You* are inside and how *you* think, act, and believe always shows itself. Celebrate all of your reflections. Fully embrace the large and small nuances within *Self/self/SELF*. Freedom lies in the truth-telling of your human experience. Time is a sacred rite of passage that reveals that *You* have always carried love, courage, and commitment. Those virtues come through experiences and expressions *You/you/YOU* overcome. The *eye/i/I* is the most important part of *You*. . . it sees. . . visions. . . knows. . . interprets. . . receives. . . and creates. Be the pupil. Discovery is imminent. . . *You/you* are not on a journey. . . *You/you/YOU* ARE THE JOURNEY. When in service, *You* move into receivership of the greater go(o)d. . . and a greater *GOD*. To know your *SELF*, step outside who *You/you/YOU* are. *You* cannot do that in your normal environment. . . amid regular activities. . . or with the current state of mind. Find a place that does not know *You/you/YOU.* A quiet place.

You are many experiences, with room to wander.
You are endless dreams to be pondered.
You are creations gifts to be garnered.
You are the physicality of God to be honored.

knowing.
How would I/eye love myself if i/eye knew i/eye were sacred?
i/eye can shift from scared to sacred in any instant.

Knowing.
I love many things about myself.

KNOWING.
I AM sacred.

. . .

AURA OF THE RAINBOW BODY

What does it look like?

Red is for root. . . orange for relation. . . and yellow, for creation.
Green is for love. . . blue for expression. . . and violet, for vision from above.
You are the rainbow, and golden hue.
You shine within the darkness and appear powerfully in light too.

A rainbow high-way lies within all beings. *You/you/YOU* are a ray of light, sound, and color that is here to play. *You* are a matrix, moving through veils of your own darkness, shadows, and masks of light and density. Here, *You/you/YOU* get to wiggle your toes in the mud and lift your face to the sun. Every experience is part of that "essence-tial" play. Tag! *You/you/YOU* are it! *You/you/YOU* are *THE ONE*!

You/YOU are a new day dawning; the first kiss of morning air. *You* are the experience of breath; inhalation and exhalation. *You* are the Light; the essence of illumination. As Light, *You* spread the glow of goodness, happiness, and gentleness in every place, to every person. *You* are brilliant, beautiful radiance which burns with increasing intensity, reaching far beyond your physical encasement.

You are the Light that infinitely spreads across your home, city, state, and world. *You* boldly beam Light upon this planet. As your Divine flame blazes, discordant and inharmonious energies and patterns embedded within earthen forms are cleansed and purified into *BEING*.

Reflect the energy of earth to expand your aura of the rainbow body.
In raising your vibration, the global reflection of human rights also shifts.

You are the red, warm womb that holds humanity's dreams and aspirations. *You* are the orange body of healing what no longer serves. *You* are the golden radiance of strength, triumph, and love that empowers. *You* are the emerald heart that transforms what was-lost into the wholeness of *BEING* found. As indigo blue, *You* are the voice of truth, wisdom, and oneness that transmutes lies, ignorance, and division. *You* are the violet flame of purification that brings forth your pure Divine nature. *You* are the white light that crowns the Essence of Spirit.

Through this body of light, sound, and radiant color. . . *You/you/YOU* raise consciousness and connection for a whole universe. *You* are strong. . . *You* have always been. *YOU* ripple as a rainbow that unites others. *You* have a rainbow body. This rainbow comes from the colors of the elemental: white (space), red/orange (fire), blue (water), green (wind or air), yellow (earth), violet (ether), and black (void). This light brings universal order and structure with it. Your universe is based on alignment. The choices *You* make align vertically or horizontally. Your reality is created by perspective and position. Many realities can exist within a singular one, based on your perception. What *You/you/YOU* see is true. . . for *You*.

Your universe is an experience of ripples and repetitions; echoes of time, space, and form. This consistency is the flowering of life. It is a diversity of parts. However, the whole is more than the sum of these parts. The universe stems from a creation of threes, which has within it masculine, feminine, and masculine/feminine balance. This trinity exists within all things. Each manifestation has this foundation that expresses through stillness, movement, and the bridge between them. All things ultimately must come into balance. Life is the unfolding dance of balance and equilibration. Duality is the swinging of polarities, where balance *is* and *IS* not present.

Multiplicity is the expansion into allies that is eternal balance. Oneness is the integration of this balance. Space is the *between*; between breath. . . between creation and manifestation. . . between tension and intention. . . between rest and relaxation. Space is the open quality of infinite possibility. Everything is energy, vibration, and frequency where like attracts like. With like attracts like, duality becomes more distinct. Even within this world of duality, *You/I/We/They* are and have always been, one likeness.

Celebrate the ordinary, extraordinary, and everything in between.

With all of this magnificence, don't *You* see you are of immense creative capacity? If the elements can create the beauty of rainbows, *You* can too. *You* are creative Essence. Create wildly. . . lovingly. . . and endlessly. Become your own muse. Across a blanket of velvet sky shimmers a star brighter than *You/you/YOU* have ever known. It sparkles at *You,* beckoning, calling, and inviting *You* to blaze. *You/I/We/They* are of the same body. . . the same Spirit. . . the same Source. *You* are Spirit that can't be broken. You are Light, the most Divine kind. Own it. The rainbow body is a bridge to the realm of pure light where *BEING* resides.

Deep insights. . . creative delight.
Rich communion. . . intuitive insight.
A spirit of fun. . . each song well sung.
Deliciousness. . . and lightness of touch.
An adventurous spirit. . . with crescendos of grace and love.

knowing.
How would i/eye treat myself if nothing was wrong?
i/eye only see what i/eye want to see.

Knowing.
There is no thing/nothing wrong.

KNOWING.
All is well; I AM well.

...

FRAGRANCE-EMITTING REUNION

What does it smell like?

Body—Mind—Spirit.
Father—Son—Holy Ghost.
Mother—Father—Child.
These are symbolic representations
of the triune that is *YOU*.
Light—Shadow—Form.
Human—Devil—God.
self—Self—SELF
These are that triune too.
There is *ONE* power
that exists in all.

You/you/YOU bought into a lie of separation. One lie always leads to another, and another, and another. Soon, there are so many lies that *Truth/TRUTH* becomes lost. Are *You* believing the lies? Are *You* living a lie? They begin early in life, becoming tapes that recycle beneath the surface of your *Mind/mind*. Old tapes play within your head, creating the lens through which *You* see life. Your lies are the basis of separation, wounding, and pain. Erase these tapes and clear your lens. Listen for *Truth/TRUTH*. Reunion is found in remembrance.

The subtle or strong homesickness *You/you/YOU* feel is a *Knowing/knowing* of space beyond any place... oneness beyond anyone... and love that knows no bounds. Find this fragrance within the timeless... natural... expansive... union of reunion.

Through growth as physical mastery, awaken to reunion,
as *You* dissolve the black hole of envy.

During this stage of dis-integration, *You* find yourself having crossed the bridge. The old world is moving behind *You*, and the new one can be seen in the distance. Waiting on the edge, prepared to step into a brand-new world, pause. Let excitement fill *You* as anticipation builds. Appreciate each moment that *You* have overcome. Sit in deep satisfaction for how far *You* have traveled. Build the energy so that *You* overflow. Become deliberate in your creations. Let the foundation *You* have created be consciously seeded for new life. *You* have been preparing the soil, cultivating *Higher Ground... Sacred Ground... Solid Ground*. Give yourself a moment to imagine and hold a fertile vision. Become pregnant with possibility.

Fresh new ground lies before *You*, waiting for the taste of reunion. Coming home seems strange and foreign. Yet, there is something familiar. *You/YOU* sense *remembering*, even though it is no where in sight. *You* also feel like a stranger in this foreign land. Thiss is normal. Moving slowly will support conscious choices and deliberate steps.

Moving too quickly makes it too easy to slip back into slumber. In haste, *You/you* can fall back into unconscious patterns, behaviors, and routines. Explore your new world, and *Self*, with conscious curiosity.

In the next step forward, *You* will meet *Self/SELF* like a stranger. Initially, a soulmate connection will be experienced, as if *You* knew this *Self/SELF* at another time, in some other place. *You* may shyly flutter with love from time to time, when catching glimpses in the mirror. Locking eyes creates a swell of joyful remembering. In other moments, *You* will feel awkward. *You* are a stranger to yourself. Who *You/you/YOU* were is fading away. There is much to learn about the new; likes, dislikes, desires, dreams, hopes, aspirations. A reunion is occurring within *You*, even though new behaviors and activities are forming. Get to know *You* inside; then, bring that out. Revel in the courtship with *Self/SELF*. Meet the renewed *You/YOU*; become friends. Engage in conversation with the re*MIND*ed *YOU*. Find new interests and outlets. Play with *Self/SELF*. Laugh with *Self/SELF*. Fall in love with *Self/SELF*. Have a reunion with your highest, best, most sacred *Self/SELF*.

You/you/YOU and *eye/i/I* may appear separate, existing as single points of Light. However, *You/I/We/They* are Source. *We* are measurements of this unfathomable, luminous, infinite power. When honoring the lower *Self/self* as the giver, and the Higher *Self/SELF* as the receiver, the two merge as One/*ONE,* creating the sacred Merkabah. As above, so below; what *You* give from your heavenly consciousness manifests upon earth. Build creations, not miscreations.

Being/BEING—in the world but not of it—arises out of the full embodiment of *Self, self,* and *SELF.* The golden thread of *ONE*ness wraps this triune with energy, truth, growth, and wisdom. This no other can give *You;* it comes with reunion. As *self* moves into the tender embrace of *Self,* and *Self* leans into devotion to *SELF,* a sacred triangle of *Truth* is formed. This trinity is the sacred geometry of connection and communion. This flowers with the fragrance of reunion. *Self/self/SELF* love will be your sustenance. Celebrate yourself as the Divine walking, immersing in all manner of expressions. Hold steady the sacred love that *You/I/We/They* are.

Walking clears the mind. Love cleanses the heart. Prayer clarifies the soul.

The fragrance of reunion is pungent; a sharp, woodsy nutmeg scent. Its fragrance is otherworldly, depicting the path of peace and transformation. The *Yew/You* tree is an evergreen that offers the perfect symbolism for the eternal cycle of life, death, transformation, regeneration, and rebirth. Yews signify peaceful rest until ready to rejoin life. Their serene and timeless energy calms and soothes the fluctuations and contrast of life. Yews are said to nurture the soul, while also grounding space for new incarnations within one's life. The fragrance of reunion is one that has notes that remind of what has been, what is changing, and what is birthing. A combination that will be loved by some and seem repelling to others, depending on one's openness to newness and change. . . this is *Yew/You*.

I Am. . . You Are. . . We Are the Yew tree. In moments of completion, *You* will look back and notice the thread of magic, mystery, and miracles. These are woven within the strands of your DNA. There is no greater embodiment than of your natural Divine Power. When *You/YOU* realize humility, life reflects that quiet power. At your core is Divine

Infinite Space. Stretch out and stay a while. Upon this human plane, *You/you/YOU* are endowed with an inner GPS... *Guiding Power Source*. Your inner GPS is always leading *You* home. Stay connected. The time is now. Close your eyes and be still. The present is... for receiving; *You/you/YOU* are for-giving. The gift of both lie within.

Charity begins at home;
***You/you/YOU* are always your most important, service project.**

You discover personal magic when willing to recognize and celebrate others. Whether or not others celebrate, approve, or recognize *You/you/YOU* does not matter. *You/YOU* hold knowing of the other's Divine heart, even if it is not expressed in the moment. Hold *Them/them/THEM* that way. See *THEM* in *THEIR* Essence. If *You/YOU* know who *They/THEY* are, do not forget this with your words and actions. If *You/YOU* recognize *Their/THEIR* soul as your own, be present with that version of *THEM*. *You/YOU* do not need to remind them of *Their/THEIR* truth; *You/you/YOU* must be reminded of your own. How *You/YOU* show up has everything to do with how *They/THEY* change. How *You/YOU* see them impacts *Their/THEIR* ability to become. *You* are that powerful.

Be the vision, voice, and presence of Essence in the way *You* love, serve, and embody oneness. Your home is inside *Them/them/THEM*, and *Their/THEIR* home is inside *YOU*. The place where *YOU/I/WE/THEY* meet is more same than different. In that safety and sacredness, *YOU/I/WE/THEY* begin to know *ONE* as another. This reuniting of selves is the fragrance of holy belonging. *BE* holy-hearted in your *Loving/LOVING*... holy-bodied in *Living/LIVING*... holy-minded in *Knowing/KNOWING*... and holy-integrated in *Being/BEING*. *BE* w(h)oly Divine.

Humans are not to create division, or hate, or war;
small minds know of these small things
because the lower *Mind/mind* holds big fears.
Divine humans embody inclusion, love, compassion, and possibility...
these are of the Higher *Mind/MIND*, of collective faith.
Separation is the lie...
Union has always been;
a reunion of *Mind/mind* with *Mind/MIND*,
must be grounded within.

knowing.
How do I/eye belong in this world?
Maybe, this world was made for me.

Knowing.
I connect openly with the world around me.

KNOWING.
I AM belonging.

...

FLAVOR OF GROUNDEDNESS

What does it taste like?

**I am free.
I am free to participate in life.
I am free to choose my next best step.
I am free to make mistakes and learn from them.
I am free to succeed.
I am free to live an abundant life.
I am free spirited.
I Am free. . .
I AM free.**

The dark forest invites the seeker to be guided by love, becoming a love catalyst within their own experience. These archetypes are the keepers of the keys. The flavor of groundedness is likened to a seven-course meal; sit and savor every portion. The longer *You* stay, the more *You/you/YOU* relax into it. With each flavor of grounding, *You/you/YOU* become filled and full. Revere every rising wave into the body for absorption and integration. This creates strength of *Being/BEINGness* and a secure feeling of groundedness.

Without a daily practice of sitting, listening, and coming home to *Self/self/SELF*, *You/you/YOU* become disconnected. For duality to cease, *You/you/YOU* must practice reuniting with *Self, self,* and *SELF* daily. These three must meet in the dark forest of the *Mind/mind/MIND* to root and ground. Meet each new sunrise as ONE, in alignment.

Groundedness intertwines the devotion of an ascetic, and the aspiration of the visionary. This can appear like ecstatic dance, where vast creativity rises but *You* need not rush into anything. This will require the rooted discipline of the mystic, and the lighthearted adventure of a rebel humanitarian.

**As *You* endeavor upon truth in stillness, restore groundedness
through the key of balance.**

Compassionate presence grounded in *Self/self/SELF* awakens gifts. Whatever *You* are feeling, and wherever *You* stand. . . rise above that by grounding deeply within. Feelings and stances are based on what *You/you/YOU* were taught, shown, and modeled. It is conditioned identity, resulting from the perceptions of others. In truth, *You/you/YOU* do not know what is real, or what is not real. *You* were given hand-me-downs that continue to be passed on, until thrown away. Weeds build between the layers of these hand-me-downs, which uproot your foundation. When this occurs, all that maintained groundedness falls away.

Each, as a son or daughter of creation, manifests uniquely different circumstances. We all encounter the characteristics of experience, including dis-ease, shadow, pain, loss... light, love, abundance, and joy. We are *Self/self/SELF*-absorbed illustrations of *Self/self/SELF*-obsession, who desire to see ourselves in every creation. These qualities express within every unconscious step, thought, action, and achievement. Additionally, they steward the creations of obstacles, crisis, defeat, and betrayal. These miscreations are... mine, yours, his, hers, theirs... all of ours. *Self/self/SELF*-obsession has no measure of success, or failure. It is dis-ease.

The full polarity of emotions and the growth of emotional intelligence are vital to health and well-being. *You* were not taught how to express gentleness, tenderness, or kindness to *Self*. These were based on conditional love that was modeled by others. Current definitions and expressions are intellectual constructs, backed by shadow expressions of insecurity and insignificance... people pleasing and obligation. Most acts of kindness seek something in return. They reek with codependency, since actions are laced with "needing a reason to feel good" or "requiring action to create a sense of worth."

> **Groundedness releases attachment, rooting into**
> **something larger than the *Self/self/SELF*.**
> **This does not mean *You* must let go of everything, but *You/you/YOU* must be willing.**

Rise above identity, race, creed, color, religion, economic status, political party, and any other identifier *You/you/YOU* cling to. See yourself as part of a human family... a global community of friends and lovers... the soul collective... a Divine Kaleidoscope. See yourself as *One/one/ONE*, knowing there is no stranger among *You;* all people want good blessings... more love... more joy... more pleasure... more happiness... more fulfillment and purpose. Ground within that consciousness, uniting *One/one/ONE* and all alike. For change to be rooted... it must begin inside the ground, your groundedness. These roots must grow deep and spread wide, becoming a strong, vital root cause of higher love, kindness, consciousness, and compassion. Each person contributes to whether or not the world is grounded. Each and what is *Being/being/BEING* grounded in.

> **Absorb what was placed within your holy space.**
> **Be filled; be emptied. Then, ground into *soulfulfillment*.**

All that happens is draped in blessing and swathed in good. Eliminate blocks to hearing by grounding in inner listening. Remove control and the need to know by rooting into the cycles and rhythms of Earth. Wrap yourself in a blanket of trust and lie upon a matted ground of surrender. Be held in the loving embrace of Mother Nature and call all of the world your kin. This is a time for grounding and rooting within your earthen home; to know yourself as one with the great mother. Touch the earth. Embrace the sky. Whisper to the wind.

Slow down and experience the little things... the great loves... the beautiful in everything. Stop chasing the future. Instead, look around and discover what *You* have always wanted. Only the *Ego/ego/EGO*, with its insecurity, clamors for more and more. That uprootedness keeps *You/you/YOU* sleepwalking. Your life, just as it appears, is where *You/you/YOU* are to plant your *Self/self/SELF*. If this were not true, *You/you/YOU* would not be there. Life reveals only perfection. Receive it in that way; ground in the perfection given, and receive your complete design. How much love can you stand? Until accepting your own, *You/you/YOU* cannot know.

Live your truth, fully devoted to what your soul came for.
In the eyes of the Divine, an ant is as important and sacred as a herd of buffalo.

Heights... success... goals... dreams... visions will never fill the inner well unless grounded in humility, *Self/self/SELF*-acceptance, and love. The illusion of what looks good has value only if it feels good. Discern reality from illusion, and heart from mind. The moment *You/you/YOU* take the scary-exciting-unknown into your heart, magic is initiated.

Grounding energetically draws resonance. *You/you/YOU* do not have to know *who, how, what,* or even *when. You/you/YOU* need only root in *KNOWING... it is done.* Sit; let that seed guide and grow the tree of knowledge. Each time you sit, *You/you/YOU* will be given more. Your roots will grow, and so will *You/you/YOU.* True love begins with *Self/self/SELF.*

To ground is to become calm. It is the stable foundation upon which anything can be built. The soil has been tilled, carefully shuffled back and forth many times. With each leveling, strength and solidity anchor. Life is a dance, one in which your steps vary in rhythm and staccato. Get used to dancing. Make it part of your practice. Learn to dance through every experience, intimately knowing the soil beneath your feet.

You/you/YOU are free.
You/you/YOU are free to extend a hand.
You/you/YOU are the freedom that knows no bounds.
You/you/YOU are free to create your destiny.
You/you/YOU are free to be an example.
You/you/YOU are free to be inspired.
You/you/YOU are the freedom that walks in creativity and expression.
You/you/YOU are free to live fully, laugh intensely, love deeply,
create incessantly, and experience abundantly.
You/you/YOU are the gift...
Be grounded in freedom.

knowing.
Why don't I/eye feel worthy?
i/eye am not yet able to grasp my own worth; but, i/eye am working on it.

Knowing.
I was born worthy; I ground into that more and more each day.

KNOWING.
I AM worthy.

. . .

MELODY THROUGH SERVICE—ADORATION
What does it sound like?

Let the *i* serve the *eye*. . . the *eye* serve the *I* and the *I* serve the *WE*. . .
Let the *WE* serve the *ALL*. . . the *ALL* serve the *I AM*.
In an instant, discover there was none to serve;
Every *One/one/ONE* was *You* all along.
Herein is infinity, and the interplay of reality and illusion;
the joyful intimacy of the *ONE I AM*.

You are an example, whether or not *You* choose to be. The manner in which *You* move through life is the teaching; the modeling and example. Live as a continual explorer, actively engaging inner work, reflection, and integration. Life is your teacher, guru, and guide. Spiritual growth reveals greater appreciation for the little things in life. The desires of the ego slip into the background as the fulfillment of the soul begins to take precedence.

There is no ugliness that requires your focus. That is a means of distraction. Higher Power is bigger than anything *You/you* are facing. Don't mistakenly make people, things, and experiences larger than that. Trust; all things serve, and a greater use of *You* is at hand. A Divine hand. Everything *You* touch, create, and steward must be grounded in the power of love. Then, love expands. The test is simply illusion. Only love exists; only love is real. Focus on the beauty that *IS*. . . your beauty. . . the beauty of what *You/you* can create. . . the beauty of compassion, forgiveness, love, and celebration. Be a source of inspiration. Remain centered in the heart, hearing its melody of love and service.

**Wisdom through listening shifts *Being* politician to *BEING* servant leader;
utilize the melody of service through adoration, as an act of grace.**

There is nothing *You/you/YOU* cannot do, no one *You/you/YOU* cannot be, and no place *You/you/YOU* cannot go. *You/you/YOU* are not only creative, or simply the creative spark, but the creative faculty of Divine Mind. As this creative faculty, *You* create lessons, work, extracurricular activities, and special projects for the higher education of mastery. But this keeps *You/you/YOU* running, exhausted, and distracted. *You* make others more important than yourself. This is not serving *You/you/YOU* or any other. It amplifies personal and collective issues. True service is performed on the inside. The augmented version of *You* is of service when cultivating a sacred inner world. Devotion and discipline are vital to service in the world.

Serve your eternal Divine *SELF* rather than the fickle, temporary whims of the human *Self/self*. Sacredness encompasses both, but the former peers through the lens of conscious response, whereas the latter restlessly, unconsciously reacts. *YOU* are bigger than *You/you*. Discover the larger unknown *YOU* that lives beyond drive, ambition, greed, and hunger. Life is not about your outer achievements, who *You* become, or what is accumulated.

There is nothing wrong with external accoutrements when engaged with unconditional, pure pleasure of expression. Wealth versus poverty, or success versus failure, is not the destination. Neutrality, equanimity, and humility amid these things are the true gain.

When *You/you/YOU* move from *"What's in it for me?"* to *"What part of me is in this?,"* not only do *You/you/YOU* discover your motives, world paradigms shift! If *You/you/YOU* are creating from the state of me, me, *me/my/mine,* my, my... based on what *You/you/YOU* can get, the small *self* is merely throwing a tantrum. When in a state of *WE/We/WE,* actions ground in a state of service, which ultimately serves *You* too.

Do not let yesterday design today or tomorrow.
Awaken to each day with fresh eyes, a clear mind, and an open heart.
Let the day show you where to go.

Personal prayer and adoration help discern what Spirit wants for *You.* This opportunity for reflection in the prayerful space deepens the communal space between human being and spiritual essence. It is important to make time to sit in divine presence and listen. Ask Source to speak to your mind and heart and give the graces and guidance needed. Dedicate time to sit with Spirit, ignoring any distracting thoughts that might be on your mind. Listen, just listen. The graces from adoration might not be noticed right away, but the relationship created while getting there is of incredible value.

Service is the natural devotional aspect of *LOVE.* Aspire to align, attune, and commune with *LOVE* as Essence. *You/I/We/They* are all pure of heart. When serving *ALL* through the purification of *Self, You/you/YOU* expand the power of Love's Essence within the world. As an activator of collective awakening, *You/you/YOU* become a vehicle for higher expressions of creation. The small mind cannot comprehend how each individual is used to fulfill a larger saga. It is more than *You/you/YOU* can fathom. Do not *think* your way through life; feel your way. Let Spirit use *You.*

Let the winds of change teach *You* to soar above the clouds.
Trust completely in all of life's movements.
This is true freedom and Divine flight.
Love is unconditional.
Love is your right.
Worry no more.
Experience the wealth of the *SELF*.
Anchor deeply in Essence.
Source is your wealth.

knowing.
How can i/eye be of greater service?

Knowing.
In taking care of myself, I can more powerfully serve others.

KNOWING.
I AM a living sanctuary.

...

VISCERAL SMOKE

What may be absorbed?

You are the breath of spirit.
Smoke is the smoldering of shadow.
Life is your mirror of form.
You are a reflection of all that is holy.
You are everything.
You are nothing.
You are illusion.
YOU are real.
Your awareness. . .
is the gold of awakening.

As long as *You/you/YOU* hold division, separation, judgment, and criticism. . . that is all that *You/you/YOU* will see. If you want true change to happen, then it must occur within *You/you/YOU*; otherwise *You/you/YOU* are part of the problem. This is not saying turn a blind eye to what is; however, do not turn a blind eye or deaf ear to your part in creating what *Is/is/IS*. Perhaps the only change required is in who, what, and how *You/you/YOU* judge, criticize, and condemn. Mastery occurs when *You/you/YOU* temper your speech, not another's. Mastery is when *You/you/YOU* choose to see a world of love instead of one filled with division and hate.

Nonforgiveness creates dis-ease in the body. . . your body. . . and the collective body. If *You* are in the midst of sadness, anger, anxiety, depression, or guilt. . . *You/you/YOU* are somewhere other than here. *You/you/YOU* are not "now." Your "now" is where *You/you/YOU* may witness, experience, and express change. Focusing elsewhere fragments *You* into a future that does not exist, or into a past that is not forgiven, forgotten, or real. Realign "now."

Cultivate conversation as *You* invite unification with the feminine aspect;
deep presence is required to access your visceral smoke of jealousy.

Releasing wounding is the most unconditionally loving act *You* can give *Self/self/SELF* and other. Doing so allows each new moment to be faced with fresh eyes, a more open heart, and a clearer mind. Memory creates veils. These veils are not on the outside; they exist within your psychology and physiology. These release, dissipating slowly. Visceral smoke rises when *You* become triggered. It reveals subtle and unconscious jealousy.

Jealousy is a normal feeling. It becomes unconscious background noise as the ego and identity grow. It is a universal human emotion, existing as a shadow expression of love. Jealousy is born out of a perceived imbalance of power. It is an outgrowth of hierarchy and plays upon insecurity and issues of self-esteem. Jealousy can rumble with rage or be weepy with depression. It does not want what is present. It is, in a sense, triggered by self-abandonment because there is no acceptance for oneself, or the life created. Instead, the grass appears greener elsewhere. Although jealousy appears to be about desire, it has more to do with lost opportunities and missteps. Jealousy can be a painful emotion that you are aware of. However, it lives within most people in a very subtle way. It is unconscious brooding that can be triggered by a cocktail of emotions such as self-doubt, insecurity, rage, shame, and embarrassment.

Do not become this misalignment. Do not let lies pull *You* into their shadowy places. Nothing real can be taken. The dark night is the spell unknowingly cast. These moments beckon the Light of truth from within. This karma is the blessing to take you deeper. Each experience occurs to hone and deepen your communication, empathy, and intuition. Life is an exercise in choosing what feels loving to *Self*, kind to others, and generous of *Spirit*. For visceral smoke to dissipate, you must ask yourself about jealousy. Stop fanning the flames that reignite the wound. Stop telling the story. Instead, remain in the fire and experience the smoke that rises.

The degree to which you have suppressed jealousies may be beyond comprehension, but this pain operates as a backseat driver in your life. This wounding can be felt when situations heat up. By dropping below rage, feel the smoke that rises. Imagine that every thing, every one, every circumstance, and every situation was specifically created to bring remembrance of your complete sacredness. The illusionist hides in the darkness. Jealousy is that phantom menace. Truth is transparent.

Love comes in many shades of gray. Light does as well. Even black is a degree of light; the densest degree. Move toward the highest frequency of light and love *You* can express. And see the highest frequency of light and love in others. It is the only way to create this within our world. If you envision darkness… then *You* will see that play out. If *You* envision light… it will become so bright it could be blinding.

In the pain, find your power.
In the enemy, find your mirror;
In the stranger, see your real family.
In the uncommon is a common bond.
In the unknown, discover what can be known.
In the small is the immense and eternal.
In the dark, discover real light.

knowing.
Why do i/eye feel jealous?
i/eye am projecting onto them.

Knowing.
I dissolve all feelings that inhibit my success.

KNOWING.
I AM capable.

ALCHEMY OF EARTH

What can be transmuted?

Your heart holds great treasure, while life holds your endless possibility.
A bountiful body of wonder, a garden in which to grow.
A landscape to tend to and seeds that must be sown.
For gratitude and reverence to rise amid each of life's blessings
a cornucopia of plenty. . . amid flowers, rainbows, and fireflies.

Conditions of health and well-being begin the instant you become a thought form. From that moment of conception as Divine thought, a visceral identity emerges from within the field. Thoughts layer, forming energetic structures as veils. These build with each impression, suppression, repression, depression, and oppression. Each layer creates greater mental, emotional, energetic, and physical substance within earthen matter. These raw materials of alchemy are imbued with the elements of transformation. With earth, air, water, wind, fire, and ether. . . the process of alchemy is always available.

Know thyself with the gifts of communication, empathy, and intuition;
these blessings allow generosity to rise.

Underpinning every thought, word, and deed is the visceral that directly connects to your nervous system. A subtle ingrained arrhythmia courses through. It feels weighty, which will have you become listless, apathetic, slothful, or bored at times. Or it will be so heavy that *You* move restlessly and reactively, catapulting *You* into outward action and distraction. This is the visceral smoke carried from experience to experience. It appears as tiredness, sluggishness, and lethargy. It is evident in yawns, slumped shoulders, and dull eyes.

As *You* let down your guard and break down the defenses of the false self, chiseled monuments of identity and personality are more clearly recognized. As these hardened structures are torn down, dissolution can begin. There will be less and less identification with the false selves that have built up. *You* will not cling to identity as strongly. *You* will free yourself from holes of pride, ego, and doubt. At first, *You* will experience exhaustion from laying down all of the associated stress, responsibility, and tension of each identity. With rest, *You* begin to feel lighter and more natural.

From this vantage point, *You* gain a genuine assessment of your positives and negatives. It is as if *You* see yourself clearly for the first time, albeit complete with flaws and foibles, misdirection and missteps, tensions and intensity. *You* will feel tender in a way that is beyond skin deep. Yet, *You* are also privy to gifts and talents, beauty and benevolence, possibility and higher potential not fully seen before. *You* will be able to own your impact on people and places, viscerally aware of good and bad deeds, ill and negative thinking, and the actions put in motion to create the life *You* currently experience.

Every moment of your life is to bring *You* to a place of nothingness. It is to break away the framework *You* believed necessary. When *You* completely break apart, nothingness becomes your expansion into everything. *You* are not the body, the identity, the ego, your job, your role, your personality. That is the house of cards. Let it crumble. This is life's alchemical process at work.

When *You* embrace a name, *You* step into a container with edges.
When *You* release your name. . . *You* become the unknown.

You are in fermentation. This is the rebirth process. It is transformation, such as the caterpillar into the butterfly, the grape into wine, or scrap metal into a work of art. Here, *You* are able to access a more refined self. Fermentation involves putrefaction and spiritization. In putrefaction, inner death occurs. Old elements rot and decompose. This is the decomposition of the conscious and unconscious *Self/self*. *You* may experience this as the dark night of the soul. In scientific terms, it can be experienced as depression; the sinkhole of all that was held down from birth. Our world is experiencing more issues of mental illness because people have not been taught to hold their feelings of depression. Depression is natural and must be allowed to surface and be felt. It is the only way that facades can be torn down.

As the old decays, *You* begin to see the world in new ways. Looking through a different lens, spiritization unfolds a new, lighter perspective. This stage involves letting go of the aspects of *Self/self* that no longer serve. *You* realize what no longer contributes to spiritual growth. Begin letting go of the face that has been shown to the world for too long. Let the strong veneer fall and the vulnerable face be a model of humanity. In doing so, experience moments of stillness, inner peace, and joy.

This is the alchemy of earth taking place within your body. *You* are fertile ground. Through innocence, vulnerability, and openness. . . light begins to warm the soil of your Being. Emotion keeps this fertile ground moist and replenished with vital nutrients for humanity to flower into powerful forms of creativity. Each passing day, your roots grow stronger as *You* open to a more authentic *Self*.

To touch life is to be blessed.
Knowing the sweet invitation of tomorrow and the rich passing of yesterday's goodbye quenches the soul's thirst for experience.
The juiciness of each moment fills every day with life's infinite mystery.
Reclaim your precious earth as a holy miracle;
each and every day is opportunity for another.

knowing.
Why do i/eye feel separate?
i/eye can take a moment to ground each day.

Knowing.
I place my feet in the ground, allowing mother earth to nourish me.

KNOWING.
I AM fertile ground.

ESSENCE AS GENEROSITY

What may be embodied?

**Coming together
with one another,
beautiful hearts and treasured souls.
Unconditionally loving sisters and brothers. . .
this was our role.
Being present
and holding focus and vision.
Giving and receiving. . .
love and communication.
A simple space. . .
where wisdom and gratitude flow.**

When experiences of life take all from *You/you/YOU*, step in and give even more. If they take your gold, give them your silver too. Your Divine power is greater. Give of *SELF*; such giving cultivates greater experiences of Spirit. The true spirit of generosity rises through, wholeheartedly sharing your gifts, skills, and talents. Give, give, give, give. . . and give more. Overflow with joy, bliss, passion, creativity, and purpose fullness. *You* are an endless container of life, love, and experience. *You* are a sacred vessel; beautiful and divine. . . rare and unique. . . a treasure of wisdom and thought. *You* are a pitcher, continuously filled and outpouring; the *I AM* presence of pure, clear, fluid, liquid Light.

Forgiving resistance creates the inspiration for giving acceptance to *Self*.

Sit in a space of openness. Do not think, plan, control, or contemplate. Just allow what comes. Be an empty vessel; one that fills and empties regularly. . . rhythmically. . . continuously. This experience of giving and receiving is an emergence of universal generosity through *You*. Witness with no attachment to touching, influencing, impacting, or triggering another. Do not let your ego attach or manipulate this witnessing. Become the vessel of Spirit and allow things to flow. . . generously. Be this with *Self*. Be this with others. Be generous with *Being/BEING*, and flowing.

Pull your energy in, hold it close. . . send your Love out. . . spread it wide. You are the bridge between worlds; the conduit of heaven and Earth experiencing itself as human and divine. Deepen into the ache. . . open to curiosity. . . and a path will appear. Be that embodiment of connection, communication, and cooperation. Transformation is not singular; it is interconnected. In *Being/BEING* so, *You* shall find life bountiful with all *You/you/YOU* have given.

In order to fan this beautiful flame. . . release *self*. . . release identity. Embrace every wave. Immerse within remembering. Ride the *current*. It does not matter how many paths *You/you/YOU* take or the number of processes *You/you/YOU* undergo. *You/you/YOU* can play with every technique and protocol, but play with understanding. Keep reminding *Self* that there is nowhere to go. . . there is nothing to do. . . and no one *You* must become. *You* need only be present to your absolute *SELF*. With this intention. . . play all the day long. . . and deep into the night. Through this level of deliberate creation, there can be only Light. *You* glide on the wings of *Spirit*, so to cast our own. Greater intimacy opens the way for experiencing Allness. Your example awakens others to celebrating and sharing in authentic ways. Then, illusion morphs into new realities.

It will be easy at this point to fall back into old impulses and patterns. The mind and ego will tell You of all the reasons that time is being wasted. *You* will project your discomfort on to the world, creating a desire to go create something that fixes that broken world. This is all smoke and mirrors. Right now, the generosity of Spirit would have *You/you* rest; truly rest. *You* have no idea how weary your soul is. The path *You* have taken is not one of the world. It is against everything the ego stands for. This path is not celebrated by those who have not done this work. Little do they realize how generously *You* give of yourself by staying exactly where *You* are. The world of illusion appears real. But it is illusion. *You* are going for truth. *You* are going for gold.

If *You* were to realize nothing means anything,
You would live to feel the present moment.
Things have meaning only because _You_ assigned this;
in truth, the mask of identity and ego assign, need, and look for meaning.

After stepping back from the world for a bit, *You* will begin to see how busy everyone is. *You* also will become aware of how unconscious most actions are. The words being espoused sound odd. *You* begin discerning how pointedly people are always speaking. However, they project the work they are in need of. . . onto others. *You* will notice the deep cravings of people to be seen and heard. *You* will see that an entire world is screaming at the top of their lungs, and no one is really listening. It can be a challenging moment because there is nothing to do about it except to witness. All of a sudden, *You* will realize that it truly does not matter what *You* do with this life. Ultimately, *You* must do what fulfills *You*.

Gain clarity on what is real for you. . . on the true desires of your soul, not the impulses of the conditioned mind. That vision will flow easily. Release the cloak of conditioning, the hood of homogenization, and the mask of make-believe. The true *YOU* is beneath all of those layers. Let your touch be gentle upon everyone *You* meet. . . Let your voice softly speak. . . Let your eyes land within the eyes of all *You* see. . . Let your Being express who the soul intended *You* to BE.

May angels soothe your soul. . . and blessings sprinkle upon your choices. . . May Grace kiss each experience. . . and generosity wrap every encounter. . . May love hold all steps. . . and awareness abound in discovery of all that is. May *Knowing/KNOWING* be in each breath. . . wisdom be the way. . . and love resound in each heart. May humans rise to new heights where the heart and mind of greatest good prevail. . . May Mother Earth hear the laughter of children across many landscapes. . . gentle footsteps of animals grazing her kingdom. . . and the flourishing and flowering of nature. . .

Diving into the dark. . .
Rising amid the Light. . .
Deepening into the heart. . .
that is ready to take flight.
Pay your respects. . .
soothe your soul.
Give generously of your nature. . .
and then *You* will know
the love that *You* are,
all that *You* bless. . .
and the unbroken chain
that humanity is.

knowing.
Why do i/eye feel so alone?
i/eye realize how i/eye isolate.

Knowing.
I befriend myself first.

KNOWING.
I AM the generosity of Spirit.

. . .

FORGIVING RESISTANCE—
FOR GIVING ACCEPTANCE

I forgive life's experience of friction.
I forgive this earthen dimension for divisiveness.
I forgive hierarchy.
I forgive blame and shame.
I forgive judgment and opinion.
I am for giving neutrality.
I am for giving calm.
I am for giving balance.
I am for giving acceptance.
I am for giving celebration.
I give presence to humanity.
I give way to healthy feminine energy.
I give in to healthy masculine energy.

I give of the joyful inner child.
I give my human *Self* the grace of forgiveness.
I alchemize my humanity with the aura of the rainbow body.
I alchemize listening with the fragrance of reunion.
I alchemize stillness with the flavor of groundedness.
I alchemize movement through the melody of service.
I alchemize leadership with the Essence of generosity.
I am *ONE* with *DIVINE PRESENCE*;
I transform and transmute resistance through the grace of forgiveness. . .
I open to the absorption of all visceral smoke and residual jealousy.
May *DIVINE ALCHEMY* emerge through my consciousness and burn away the
envious *Self/self*.
May I embody the phoenix rising,
so to bridge the earth plane with the spirit world.
I take flight toward a heavenly embodiment.
I am for giving the phoenix's gifts of transformation and rebirth,
strength and renewal. . . solitude and regeneration. . . eternity and foreverness.
May these gifts of *KNOWING* be granted by *DIVINE GRACE*.
I am the rising of *GOD*.
I AM the presence of *GOD*.
I AM the abundance of *GOD*.
I AM the power of *GOD*.
I AM the prosperity of *GOD*.
I AM the light of *GOD*.

. . .

UP-LEVEL LOVE

LOVING shifts your POINT OF ATTRACTION

self ——-> *Self* ——-> *SELF*

Be present. Gradually shift into higher octaves of presence, awareness, and perception.
Move up the vibrational ladder. Feel your way and ascend to a new reality.
The fourth human expression of grace establishes a new energy from which to give and
receive. It requires anchoring solidly into loving and being loved. Close your eyes and
begin with romancing *Self/self/SELF*. The love *You* hold inside is your greatest wealth;
this is the richness *YOU* are to share. Share it with one, or with many, but give all of your
heart. Love and be Loved.

Up-level Love—through being Loved—by the fullness of who *YOU* are. Move gradually
into essence, angelic presence, and sacredness through focus, vibration, and loving as your

point of attraction. As *You* more deeply anchor within the *Love* that *YOU* are—and specifically the DIVINE LOVE within *YOU*—your ability to create a life of beautiful and rich encounters unfolds. *You* are an ever-expanding, energetic expression of creative capacity. Awaken your *knowing. . . Knowing. . . KNOWING*. Give others something new to respond to.

living.
—————————————————

acknowledgment
(slow down and feel.)
—————————————————————

eye/i can never get ahead. eye/i am always last. eye/i don't know how to make them see me. eye/i have to work twice as hard to get where they are. eye/i am just as good as they are, but life is not fair. eye/i don't look like them. eye/i am not smart enough. eye/i never win anything. eye/i try but its never enough. eye/i am busting my butt and still getting nowhere. eye/i give up.

being.
—————————————————

acceptance
(bring attention to your breath.)
—————————————————————

eye/i feel. . . envious of others. eye/i feel as if eye/i am invisible and unworthy. eye/i feel low on the totem pole. eye/i feel unimportant. eye/i feel unseen, unheard, and unacknowledged. eye/i feel like they don't deserve what they have. eye/i feel eye/i don't deserve my desires. eye/i feel eye/i won't make it. eye/i feel tired of always having to climb. eye/i feel pain; eye/i want pleasure.

knowing.
—————————————————

anticipation
(breathe slowly, deepen into your body.)
—————————————————————

eye/i can embrace my wounds and heal. eye/i can find power in my pain. eye/i can embrace the chaos for how it breaks apart what is not working in my life. eye/i can peer into the chaos as a mirror for what is changing. eye/i can become the calm in the chaos. The chaos drops me into my womb space. eye/i am given the opportunity to balance my sacral energy of relationships and connection when chaos arises. eye/i meet my feminine faces within the struggle.

Living.
—————————————————

appreciation
(pause and be present to what the moment is asking.)
—————————————————————

I appreciate hope. I appreciate my gratitude journal. I am appreciative for the prayers that have been answered. I am grateful for the gifts of Spirit. I appreciate being given the opportunity to lead. Servant leadership fills me with gratitude. I appreciate my inner authority. I am grateful for my voice. I am grateful for every courageous step I have made. I appreciate how chaos is leading me to a rainbow. I appreciate the ways I am creating more balance in my life. I appreciate me.

Being.

– – – – – – – – – – – – – – – – –

satisfaction
(connect mind to heart to gut to ground.)

– –

I feel satisfied when I eat healthful, nourishing food. I feel satisfied when I care for my body. Water satisfies my thirst. I may not always like to exercise, but when I do I feel deeply satisfied. I feel satisfied learning how to master my physical world. There is great satisfaction in achieving balance. Offering service is satisfying. I find satisfaction with inner work as servant leadership. I take great satisfaction in connecting with Mother Earth. I feel satisfied when I place my feet in the dirt. Grounding is satisfying. I feel satisfied when I place my back against a tree.

Knowing.

– – – – – – – – – – – – – –

adoration
(inhale deeply and absorb what is present.)

– –

I love how chaos gets me still. I love how chaos makes me find my center. I love stillness. I love centering. I love the quiet. I love how noise helps me appreciate silence. I love how silence and stillness ground me. I love how silence and stillness bring me to service. I love serving. I love to serve others. I am learning to serve myself. I love gentle acts of service. I especially love to serve animals and children. I love how true service is giving and receiving. I love learning I don't have to create chaos to have stillness, silence, and solace.

LIVING.

– – – – – – – – – – – – – –

celebration
(rise above and rejoice.)

– –

I celebrate humanity. I celebrate feeling and knowing myself. I celebrate the beauty and richness of my humanity. I celebrate being a humanitarian through the authentic expression of my whole self. I celebrate empathy and emotional intelligence. I celebrate conversation in how it awakens, inspires, and expands. I celebrate conversing with myself and others. I celebrate how communication becomes a bridge to understanding, connection, and communion. I celebrate how chaos allows for the deep immersion and discovery of clear communication and conversation. I love how feeling all of my emotions supports intuition. I love getting intuitive hits.

BEING.

————————————————

exaltation
(ground in sacredness, devotion, and equanimity. . . unconditionally Love!)

————————————————————————

I ground. I bow. I stand. I root. I bud. I blossom. I flower. I shed. I release.
I hibernate. I silence. I act. I unfurl. I unfold. I seed. I plant. I till. I toil.
I plow. I harvest. I hug. I kiss. I make love.
I procreate. I massage. I cry. I tear. I giggle. I laugh. I rejoice. I inspire.
I pray. I praise. I intend.

KNOWING.

————————————————

jubilation
(exhale your newly created vibrational reality and. . . believe!)

————————————————————————————————

I AM wise. I AM resilient. I AM worthy. I AM valuable.
I AM strong. I AM courageous.
I AM streams. I AM valleys. I AM mountains. I AM earth.
I AM rain. I AM stars. I AM heaven.
I AM CREATIVITY. I AM REUNION. I AM ADORATION.
I AM BALANCE. I AM MASTERY.
I AM AWESOME. I AM RECEPTIVE. I AM VIBRANT.
I AM ENERGY. I AM AWARE.
I AM EXPANSION. I AM EXPERIENCE. I AM PATIENCE.
I AM LIBERATION. I AM FREE.
I AM THAT. . . I AM. I AM THAT. . . I AM. I AM THAT. . . I AM.

Always begin exactly where *You/you/YOU* are. Be truthful with how *You/you/YOU* feel. Be authentic in what *You/you/YOU* are thinking. A new human builds from the ashes of your old life. Let your words be catalysts for transformation and transmutation. *You* are the bridge between where *you* are and where *You* want to go. *You* grow into *KNOWING* as *You* ascend the ladder of consciousness. What *You* place into the universal vortex remains in escrow. Belief supports physical presence. *KNOWING* creates change, transformation, and miracles.

ego's fight.

What has to dissolve?

I AM of two worlds.
One feels real
but is illusion.
The other appears as illusion
but is real.
One seems like life
but is a dream.
The other feels like endless death
but is eternal awakening into true aliveness.
The challenge is discerning which is which,
but real power lies where *eye/i* least expect.

You move into different expressions of *Self/self/SELF* through iterations of birth, life, death, and rebirth. Incremental vibrations are expressed through the awareness of how *you* fight, whom *You/you* surrender to, whom *You* let go of, and whom *YOU* remember. Story is the spiraling of many selves within this cyclical wave of experience experiencing itself. *You/you/he/she/they* are of the old story. At some point, transitions raise *You/you/he/she/they* into a new story. Transitions of *Self* come through the continual transcendence of ego's fight. Life's various rites of passage steward the sacrifice of your lower *Self/self* for a higher experience and expression of *You/YOU*.

The old *You/you/he/she/they* did nothing wrong. In fact, *You/you/he/she/they* did everything right. Integration contributes to your balance of energy, relationship, experience, and expression. Each time ego's fight wanes and an ego death occurs, spiritual awareness expands your ability to manifest higher levels of creation. This is how growth and greater ascension of *mind/body/spirit/oneness* are achieved.

Ego's fight and ego death
have been here before and will be again and again,
until *You* cease to exist. Yet, it is possible for the body to remain.

Your point of view, story, and set of correlating experiences form the concept of *You*, but that is only a character. Once *You* realize this, the choice to shift lenses will occur. *You/you* have been living in an enclosed, darkened room, with no idea what light really is. Once *you* step into light, there is no way to go back into your prior mode of sleep. Once *You* know something new, it cannot be forgotten. Thus, the process of letting go begins. Step by step, continually choosing to step into light, leaves the darkness behind. *Self/SELF*-actualization requires moving through many versions of ego. Between those that exist and those that birth after others dissolve, *You* will discover that the ego is deceptively intelligent at finding ways to sneak back in. The ego will keep fighting to stay alive.

Awakening moments offer the experience of expansiveness. Touching the beauty and bigness of *Self/SELF* creates a worldview that did not exist prior. But beware, the ego will slip in and take hold again, at its earliest opportunity. Your ego will point *You/you* toward denial, fear thoughts, and shut down. It creates panic attacks, confusion, emotional spikes, or full-on freakout mode. Using the mind, ego explains, justifies, conceptualizes, and resists the present moment. Witness. Watching the ego, without reacting or responding, helps burn away old ways of *Being/being*. Rather than following ego down a rabbit hole, do the inner work that anchors a new truth.

Attached to everything, especially image, the ego believes the world revolves around it. The lies it perpetuates affect your *Self/self*-image, *Self/self*-identity, and level of *Self/self*-esteem. The ego is secure in its hold over your life through the complexity of attachments it creates, the passions it spurs, and the resistance it builds within *You/you*. These conditions keep your world spinning and the ego alive and well.

Loosening any of the aforementioned cogs initiates spiritual awakening and lights a fire under the ego. This heat will have the ego fighting and reactive because it does not like to be tested or questioned. Dissolving the ego requires vigilance, discipline, and radical honesty.

Today is a good day to die.
The real does not die; the illusion does.

Ego's fight creates sleepless nights, as thoughts cycle endlessly in *Mind/mind*. Attempting to push these away will only tighten their hold. Let thoughts course through, while focusing on deeply breathing. Concentrate on your breath, inhaling slowly to your toes and exhaling up the body. This will keep *You/you* from hooking any emotions to thoughts. Fight, flight, pushing, toiling, or moving against the ego will only create tiredness, weakness, apathy, and exhaustion. *You* might feel overwhelmed or burned out. This is the ego's trick. Its focus is to wear *You/you* down and maintain control. Instead, be present with it and give the ego space to wear itself out. Trick the ego by becoming aware of it.

Ego death can be smooth or painful, depending on the willingness to release what *You/you/YOU* are attached to. The more identified *You* are with ego determines the difficulty of your ego death experience. *You/you* will likely feel fear. Phantom pains may arise within the body, as a way for the ego to create distraction. In truth, the fear *You* feel is the ego fearing its own demise. It does not want *You/YOU* in authentic power. It will go, kicking and screaming every step of the way. The ego believes in worst-case scenarios, making *You* feel as if *you*, your life, and your image are disappearing. Do not despair. The ego can die, but *You* and your body will remain alive. Do not focus on the drama of the ego, but watch how it creates. Do nothing. Simply witness your own drama. Continue breathing in awareness. Keep letting go.

Ego deaths can be excruciating. *You* might even cry out your willingness to die. This is the ego's melodrama. In truth, *You* will not die. This death, this experience, will not kill *You*. However, the ego will; an identity will. It will feel as if your heart is being ripped out of your chest. The ego's needs, rants, cravings, and clamoring are temporary. These illusions are what become dust and ashes, long after Soul Essence departs. Do not become swept away by the temporary feeling that *You* miss the real. This passage requires your patience, resilience, energy, and love. It takes courage. Let this loved one pass, so that it may rest in peace. Allow *what is* to die.

The ego was formed as a means of protection for the young child.
You are no longer in need of protection;
believing *You/you/YOU* do is the ego's lie.

Identity death is akin to ego death. As the ego dies, it takes with it the personas, roles, and identities that are part of its gang. Allow space for grieving these passages. These ephemeral moments are for completion, and the ending of cycles. *You* will experience many ego deaths. Each one is a step closer to truth. Ego death brings a more pronounced integration of openness, empathy, and compassion. Gently dismantle your ego; each and every story of this massive structure inside *Mind/mind* is a stepping-stone of soul retrieval.

Whatever once held meaning can be loved into nonexistence. But also let the awareness of identity's meaningless nature seed understanding. Create a lighter, more loosely held sense of identity. Glimpse the richness of *Being/BEING* nothing and nobody. But before *You/YOU* can fully grasp and embody these expansive spaces, all ego must be obliterated. *You* will never be without ego. Develop a conscious ego, one that serves *You/YOU* as opposed to *You/you* serving it. As ego dissolves into the background as servant to mastery, true *SELF* will move prominently to the forefront. Then, there will be no doubt of what was illusion and what *IS* real.

The strings and stands of the universe hum of this intricacy. Life creates a symphony of soulful music through which the cosmic story eternally unfolds. While the illusory nature of the world is revealed, your psyche will experience endless transformation. This gradual shift from *self*, to *Self*, to *SELF*, to *ONEness*, to *ONENESS*, *ISness* . . . and *NOTHINGness* and *EVERYTHINGness* is the expansion of Universal *MIND*. From this vantage point, duality is purely collateral dust for chiseling *God/god/GODs* out of form and into formlessness.

At times, energy feels light and simple.
Sometimes, it is dense and complex.
You/you/YOU are the journey. . . of these. . . undulating waves.
Life is the game.
There is no winner.
There is no loser.

They are *One/one/ONE* and the same. . .
as are *You/you/YOU*
and *EYE/eye/I/i.*
Let's play
in the mystery. . .
for all of eternity.

knowing.
Why do i/eye have to put up with their ego?
i/eye can take a look at my ego and ask it to step aside.

Knowing.
I utilize my ego in healthful ways, rather than it using me in unhealthful ways.

KNOWING.
I AM life.

the grace of rebirth.

What is the remembering?

Invite the grace of rebirth.
Consciously initiate this or. . .
let the kiss of decay invoke the aura of the angelic body.
The fragrance of devotion reveals truth.
The flavor of compassion expands energy.
Through love, the visceral form of regret dissolves.
Your essence of intimacy brings forth the alchemy of soul,
bringing *You/you* to common ground.
Receive your precious gifts of human grace.
***KNOW*. . . your presence is enough.**

Every painful experience is birthing the real *YOU* into the world. An inner desire to know *TRUTH* is increasing. Each death is *one* of *being* conditioned, dead and asleep. Each transition is an emulsification process within the cocoon of your life experience, biology, family, friends, culture, and social construct. *You* have always wanted to awaken from the sleep *You/you/YOU* now find yourself in.

Diving into the unknown, and outgrowing your skin, is constricting at times. Sheaths of memory have tightly wrapped and bound your past, present, and future. But this does not mean *You* are stuck, although it may feel that way. At the moment the bands feel the most suffocating, something powerful is actually occurring. Invisible wings are being formed. *You* are in the process of stretching, which means the pressure has to build in order to burst through. The more risks *You/you/YOU* take, the easier transcendence becomes. *You/you* are creating a new *You/YOU,* without even *Knowing/KNOWING*.

It will feel unknown because it is exactly that. And how beautiful that expansive landscape is. But to step upon it means to keep letting go, while holding every single thing that has happened as sacred and holy. Each experience has, in fact, been a beautiful blessing, one that either brought *You/you* here or grew your vibration.

Within the blessing of obstacles and the illusion of identity,
***You/you/YOU* created ego's fights,**
in order to discover the grace of rebirth, as a way of awakening humanity.

Human beings are likened to the plasma that runs through the body. Just as the blood of our human form protects and circulates, *You/I/We/They* are builders and fighters for change. This either results in ongoing expansion or continual decay that cycles into rebirth. For rebirth to begin, decomposition of the old must complete.

Change is a necessity, or everything perishes. It is a function of life, and the breath of experience. Change is a byproduct of itself; an infinite loop of unending creation that is always connected to the greater picture. Yet, it asks *You* to remain present within its movement. Change calls to what is in front of *You/you/YOU*, not what is past or future. However, even they are integral parts. *You* are "change» in and of itself, and an important aspect of collective change.

The Grace of Rebirth	The Remembering	Knowing
The Illusion—Ego's Fight	What has to dissolve?	Aliveness
True Love's Kiss—The Decay	What nature is required?	Creation
Aura of the Angelic Body	What is emerging?	Unification
Fragrance Emitting Devotion	What is the inhale?	Truth
Flavor of Compassion	What is the exhale?	Energy
Melody Through Love	What is harmonizing?	Growth
Visceral Form—Regret	What is being absorbed?	Wisdom
Alchemy of Soul	What can be transmuted?	The Void
Essence as Intimacy	What may be embodied?	Infinite Presence
Forgiving Death—For Giving Birth	What is for giving?	Sovereignty

In moments *You* will be victim or villain. Then, things change and *You* become savior or hero. Some appear as angels, and then, angels in disguise. However, all of these iterations contribute to equalizing and balancing energy. What seems unfair and personal is actually fair in the larger picture of life. Each person and experience takes part in cosmic justice playing out in the right and perfect time. Within those scenarios, *You/I/We/They* are changlings that bridge past, present, and future into the timeless movement of Spirit as form. The sacred stewardship of change requires being visionary, while also embracing each moment as a mystic.

Your points of change become part of life's fabric. The matrix weaves patterns and designs through *You/you/YOU*. Every action, reaction, and interaction engages movement, which creates greater texture, energy, and motion. Within these subtle and grand strokes is the eye of the needle; it is *You/you/YOU* slipping through. When this occurs, your thread weaves into the collective story. Our world is changing and it births us through each change we encounter. Change is the soul's gift to human experience.

The ego will do whatever it can to hold *You* back from your true dreams and desires. It will convince *You/you/YOU* of pathways, goals, directions, or fears. But in holding back, all those connected to your dreams and desires are also put on hold. *You* are the center of a beautiful web of creation that cannot form unless your part is fulfilled. That piece and part is simply your joy and fulfillment. Your stuckness creates stuckness for those related to your experience. Choose carefully between what *You/YOU* want and what others want for *You*. The first choice is how *You* find *Self/SELF*. With the second choice, *You* lose yourself.

There is no need to change anything. . . be with what's here and let it change You.

Chart your own path to wholeness. It will not look like any others or consist of their steps or protocols. There will be those who dream, those who just keep dreaming, and those who do not take time to dream. The ones who realize their dreams align with creative capacity. This cocreation attracts other creatives with whom a new reality is created. In this way, collective rebirth occurs. Tides change. Let the gift of *Self/SELF* inspire a *whole* new world.

If *You* have been hermiting, it is because some aspect of *You* is rebirthing. Your soulful divine *Self/SELF* knows things *You/you* cannot possibly know. It leads *You* to places *you* have never fathomed going. Rebirth requires space. . . and trust. *You* must take a leap of faith and be willing to fly or fall. *You* have so much protection, and guidance is everywhere. As *You* continually dive into the unknown to meet the unknown *Self,* discover essence that distills truth from lies, harvests wealth out of what is barren, and fertilizes communion from inside separation.

You/you/YOU **do not need to do anything.**
The Universe does not hold any expectations.
There is nothing *You/you/YOU* must measure up to.
Life has been blessed by *You/you/YOU*.
The Universe has the pleasure of loving *You/you/YOU*.
The sacred valley lies within. . .
a deep bowl of creativity that awaits. . .
a landscape prepared for new birth. . .
A new life.

knowing.
Why does it feel like i/eye am dying?
i/eye can rise into something higher.

Knowing.
I explore new friends and experiences with an open heart.

KNOWING.
I AM experience.

. . .

TRUE LOVE'S KISS—THE DECAY

What nature is required?

The illusion feels real.
The real feels nebulous.
You are living a dream. . .
within a dream. . . within a dream;
wheels within wheels.
Organic, and through free will. . .
by destiny, and in Divine Will. . .
blessings abound in all encounters.
Individuality dances in a field of duality.
Uniqueness grounds. . . within a ladder of consciousness,
filled with light, color, fragrance, and sound.
All paths converge in a Divine place. . .
Know it by name.
Eternity is your true face.

Once the ground has been cleared, an awakening and inner desire to know *Self* again will rise. In this newfound place, live your life bare naked, vulnerable, authentic, and intending greater alignment. Each and every passing brings awareness of how conditioned, asleep, and unconscious *You/you* have been. This seeds deeper devotion and commitment to *Self/self/SELF*.

The last great frontier is the black hole that resides inside each one of us. The void. It is not simply a place of darkness, but a field of infinite possibility. Here, the most sacred light may be uncovered. This place has unending depths and discovery: yours. Be swallowed up. Discover what is unknown. The inky, multidimensional blackness holds everything. It is the birthplace of creation. This is the womb space. *You* are more infinite than the outer Universe, but only emptiness can illustrate that.

In engaging the path of sage, masked obsessions abound,
creating decay, which has hidden within your earthen ground all along.

At this point, after ego death, the remains must decay. What was deep, jagged, and cutting is still tender enough that your heart may cry out, "*This is too real! I do not want to see or know this!*" But it is yours, and the same is true for others. Our shared pain bridges our belonging to *One/one/ONE* another. The paradox is that all that is decaying feels real. To deny this creates more illusion, but to make it your only reality denies the sacredness of *TRUTH*.

You are always focused upon growth, so the power and importance of decline and decay are often missed. This is an integral part of the transformation process. Decay provides nutrients and compounds for nourishing new life. With the old breaking down and decaying, illusion crumbles away. Truth remains. The valley of death is a hallowed landscape. All death brings new birth.

You must fully dry and wither for something new to be born. In order to flower again, blossom fuller, and shine brighter, allow the organic ending that is desiring to unfold. Let longing and the celebration of this passage be waters that revitalize *You*. Be nourished by the compost of your own death; that your dis-ease become fertilizer for new growth. Don't turn away from the cold, hard ground in which the old *You/you* is now buried. It is this very soil that offers neutrality and renewal.

When *You* hold *TRUTH*, lies have to dissolve. When *You* stand in peace, anger cannot survive. When *You* remain flexible, even the strongest force must decay. Let jealousy, bitterness, resentment, and regret decay. Put your mind in the proper place, and no true harm can be done. Be at peace and hold a vision of love, compassion, and faith.

Keep no skeletons; be haunted by no ghosts.
Let decay and death take everything to a heavenly place.

What *You* discover within may be so sweet, tender, and utterly loving that it seems unreal. But in times of loss and decay, this sacred chalice gets pushed aside out of overwhelmingness. Your holy grail is the grace of forgiveness. Seek to uncover your withheld pain. When your relationship to pain is no longer used to define *You* but instead fuels the fire of your aliveness, the Rebel will emerge. This new emergence will be alive with the fullest expression of love, courage, and commitment. All of a sudden, life shall change from "a play" into play, allowing life and love to be the playground it was intended to be. Ultimately, you will be led into the experience and expression of pure awareness—if ready to hold it all. The expansion that you continually pray for is always born of decay.

Wrap your arms around something you cannot grasp.
Wrap your mind around something that stretches it.
Wrap your heart around something that breaks it.
Wrap your body around something that tests it.
Wrap your will around something that bends it.
Wrap your soul around a world that moves it.
Wrap it all up. . . in Love. . . and dance. . .
simply dance with the movement that *IS*.

knowing.
Why do i/eye feel dead inside?
Who i/eye have been is not who I/eye was created to be.

Knowing.
I engage the process of birth, life, death, and rebirth as a way to keep growing.

KNOWING.
I AM expression.

...

AURA OF THE ANGELIC BODY

What does it look like?

**Until *You/you/YOU* claim the truth
of your precious and sacred nature. . .
You/you/YOU cannot treasure the jewel that *You/you/YOU* are;
nor will *You/you/YOU* treasure the jewels in your midst.
Behold. . . the eight billion sacred gems. . .
that rest within the setting of earth.**

You have been in love with the lower *self*, its drama and illusion. This love has been the addiction, drug, and storyli ne *YOU* have witnessed while *You* wandered in the wilderness. On this day, open to the emptiness that *You* feel. It may be a sense of aloneness or loneliness, but that perspective is illusion. It is openness, a space *You* are not used to. Since *You* need to name it, *You/you* risk falling back on the familiar. But really feel into it; *You* will find this space is subtly different. Rather than pangs of aloneness or the ache of loneliness, a sense of inquiry, wonder, desire, and adventure lie in the nothingness. This is not a wanting, but a waiting. It is awaiting *YOU*. It's not necessary to live life to "the fullest," but it's essential to live your fullness, so to be fulfilled! That will look different for everyone. Some must amass fortunes to feel fulfilled. Others must amass connection. And there are some who amass sacred *KNOWING*, of which there is no greater fulfillment.

**Reflect the energy of ether to expand your aura of the angelic body.
In raising your vibration, the global reflection of wellness also shifts.**

Stop trying to ascend; *You* made the choice to incarnate. Your angelic presence made that choice. Let that angelic essence exude from within, radiating as your auric field through each word, thought, gesture, and energetic vibration. Your aura is a field of radiant light that emanates from an angel who is lit from within. Each person's angelic aura is connected to a light ray that emanates a specific language of frequencies, vibrations, and expressions within the world, when aligned to one's angelic nature. A specific Archangel guides each angel ray community for specific purposes on the earth plane.

Know that *You* are coming out of the pain, and back into your heart. Feel the intuitive nudge when something is off. Love yourself enough to face the *Truth/TRUTH* desiring to rise. Call upon the angel of *Self* and behold how this sacred container of life creates the perfect conditions for empowering one another. There is and will always be love. Sometimes it's front and center; other times, in the background. But it's always here. Sometimes it's distorted; other moments, pure. Yet, it always serves. Embody the highest vibration of love in each moment. That is true angelic service. That sacred activism will change the world.

Angelic Aura	Emanating Mission	Archangel Guidance	Archangle Name & Community Meaning
Blue Light Angel League	Power, Protection, Faith, Courage, Strength	Archangel Michael	Who is like GOD/SOURCE
Purple Angel Flame League	Transformation, Mercy, Forgiveness	Archangel Zadkiel	Righteousness of GOD/SOURCE
Yellow Angel Solar League	Wisdom for Decisions, Beauty	Archangel Jophiel	Beauty of GOD/SOURCE
Pink Angel Peace League	Unconditional Love, Inner Peace	Archangel Chamuel	One who seeks GOD/SOURCE
White Feather Angel League	Harmony, Holiness, Clarity, Purity	Archangel Gabriel	My strength is GOD/SOURCE
Green Angel Healing League	Healing, Prosperity	Archangel Raphael	Healing of GOD/SOURCE
Red Angel Wisdom League	Wise Service, Humility	Archangel Uriel	Fire Light of GOD/SOURCE

You/I/We/They are birds in paradise; take flight and soar into new belonging. . . new beginnings. . . and new states of being. *You/I/We/They* have invisible wings. Just imagine them. Spread them wide. . . and fly. *You* are enough. . . as is your path in life. Soar in celebration of the Divine expression *You/you/YOU* represent. Living life on the edge means having *Trust/TRUST* in your wings. *You/I/we/They* are angels on earth.

Trust the moment;
let it tell *You/you/YOU* when to open.
The most-sacred moments happen
when *You* humbly enter the body.
Bend. Move. Hold. Touch.
Stretch. Expand.
Life is your yoga.

knowing.
Why do I/eye continually judge myself?
It is violent to compare myself to the world around me.

Knowing.
I Am who I Am.

KNOWING.
I Am a unique expression of the Divine.

FRAGRANCE-EMITTING DEVOTION

What does it smell like?

The heart loves.
The mind adores.
The soul cherishes.
Spirit holds.
Being knows.
Devotion does not question.
It is immersed within discipline.

Imagine the gray veil of grogginess that hovers in the air around *you*. As *You* breathe, imagine the indigo flame within glowing and increasing in intensity. When it becomes large and bright, the gray covering will rise and float off. It disintegrates with the light *You* shine upon it. As this occurs, a higher part of yourself is integrated. Do not let another moment pass without fully inhaling the sacredness, fragrance, and flavor of your most sacred *SELF*.

The sweet Love of *Self* happens one step at a time, one foot in front of the other, day by day. Aspire to go the full distance when it comes to loving and being loved. True *LOVE* has no thought. It is cosmic and clear. Love is the embodiment and creativity of Divinity. Life is ultimately teaching *You* to choose yourself, your joy, and your fulfillment. Live in complete devotion to whatever is chosen.

Through growth as spiritual mastery, awaken your devotion
as *You* dissolve the black hole of pride.

Each must walk the path they are given, with presence and perseverance. In the face of all that is distorted and wrong… love, devotion, and commitment create the architecture for a new world. To act in the outer world, without a devotional practice on the inner world, is a futile effort. It will be a waste of life force energy and Divine time. Life cannot support *You* when pushing against it.

At times, *You* will forget this. *You* will question it. In many instances, *You* will turn away. Life will find a way to turn *You* back. It will keep inviting *You* in. Life will pull *You* forward and bring out your gift. It never forgets your greatest wishes. At each stage, when *You* have asked to rise higher… and higher… into the Light, life has known how to get *You* there. It deepens your void and drops *You* into the depths of darkness when necessary. Life exercises and exonerates *You*, to distill the fragrance of devotion.

It could have felt as if life stopped supporting *You* at times; it never did. *You* were merely given space to remember your power. *You* were given opportunities to turn inward. Glimpses of your infinite well were presented so as to cull your own fragrance. Sink into the beauty of that devotion. It shall inspire a grand rapture and romance between *You* and life. Through life's immersion, creation upon creation, make *Love* to every moment.

Be with all of life: the questions, the answers, and the space between. In that is the sorrow and the joy. It holds the misunderstanding, and the stands yet to be taken. Be with it. Do not deny. Do not get caught up in fixing it. Do not run from it... or act upon it. Instead, be holy witness to life in all of its tragedy and comedy. Be present with the *I Am*.

Feel the allness of this partnership and devotion of life to *You*. Feel the spaciousness and the possibility. Feel into the spans of overwhelmingness, suffering, and pain *You* have endured. Be awakened to the wonder, joy, and gratitude for the fullness of experience. At times, *You* felt like nothing; the kind of nothing that is *everything waiting to become*. There have been spans of time where *You* felt like everything; the kind of everything that *waits to uncover emptiness*. Such an emptiness can be defined only by the fullness of what is beyond space, time, and form. Now sink into the depth of prayer and devotion that brings life toward *You*... and *You* toward life. It is rich with sacrament, communion, and blessing. All of life is the sacred text and the embodiment of devotion. Let its multifaceted notes move *You* into ecstatic reverence. How could *You* have ever known that real life was always on the inside. The others fooled *You* into believing what they were bamboozled into believing. They became lost in the world. *You* are finding your way out of the world, and back into your body and *Being*. This *Knowing* is grace.

See everyone and everything with love...
they are merely different versions of *You/you/YOU*.

Life awaits your devotional embrace. It desires to be close and intimate; touching, feeling, caressing, and immersing within *You*. Behold the sacredness of each second, knowing this pure *Love* lies within every moment of your life. Open your eyes; awaken to the sacredness of each and every thing, every one, and even yourself... story... misunderstandings... mistakes... and stances taken. Be in holy matrimony; to have and to hold from this day forward, for better, for worse, for richer, for poorer, in sickness and in health, to love and to cherish, till death do *you* part. Pledge your faith in sacred devotion. Trust in life as Divine counterpart. This sacred covenant is a soulful commitment: *"I will give my best to this life. I will serve life, I will love life, I will be life's hands and feet of aliveness in the world."* Be in holy communion with life. Kneel before it in full submission, filled with gratitude, awe, and innocence. It offers the extraordinary within the ordinary.

You are in exactly the right place, discovering that ordinary and extraordinary are one and the same. It is *You* that creates the difference. *You* are slipping between dimensions. The corridor between those dimensions is like a tunnel and requires a walk of mindful presence to anchor the new dimensional experience. Each time *You* give yourself this devotional experience, you anchor it solidly as your reality. Begin everything with prayer, ecstatic reverence, ceremony, and celebration. Let the fragrance of devotion be carried within the inhale and exhale of each breath.

Devotion is heart having dominion over mind. Engage life completely, so that *You* no longer exist. Become one with life. Devotion asks *You*... to love completely... cherish with great depths... expand each moment... know experience... discover love with on every level, dimension, and experience. Choose complete and utter devotion to life and *Self* as *ONE*.

There is nothing between us,
No separation. . .
because we are *One Love*.
Yet. . .
There is everything between us
because we are Unified Essence.
This means. . .
I don't know what it is to be without *You*. . .
or to be with *You*,
because I am *You/you/YOU*.

knowing.
Why is it so hard to put myself first?
For others to value me, i/eye must value myself.

Knowing.
I have value.

KNOWING.
I AM valuable.

. . .

FLAVOR OF COMPASSION

What does it taste like?

Joy is contagious. . .
spread it like wildfire.
Love is healing. . .
soothe with this balm.
Prayer is powerful. . .
lift it up.

Love and compassion are essential to our nature as human beings. These capacities distinguish us from the animals, except that animals sometimes display more kindness toward one another—and toward people—than we do. The meditative practices of love and compassion purify the mind of resentment, ill will, anger, and callous indifference. They promote communal harmony and break down the barriers that confine us to the ego's prison. By developing love and compassion, the heart expands. Immeasurable good will can be radiated to everyone we meet.

Loving kindness is opposed to ill will and hatred. Compassion is opposed to cruelty and violence. A person of loving kindness doesn't bear ill will or resentment toward others. A compassionate person doesn't wish harm for others. Such a person's heart is stirred on seeing others suffer, and they are moved to act.

Loving kindness is an attitude of openheartedness that allows *You* to see others inseparable from yourself. When *You* cultivate loving kindness, *You* are able to see your fundamental interconnection. All beings are united by a common desire for fulfillment and freedom from difficulty. Loving kindness is friendliness and well-wishing. It is an attitude of benevolence toward self and others. Compassion acknowledges suffering. There is a desire to alleviate suffering of others, and an understanding that presence is the way.

Loving kindness is said to be the basis for compassion, because in order to feel empathy with those who suffer, *You* first must sincerely wish for their well-being, and precisely this is the function of loving kindness. It is the feeling of love for beings that make *You* care about their happiness and suffering. *You* feel their pain as your own and make an effort to relieve them of their pain.

**As *You* endeavor upon truth in action, restore compassion
through the key of innocence.**

Take pleasure in the true happiness of others and its causes, free from attachment and self-interest. Delight in someone else's well-being regardless of your own situation. *You* can cultivate appreciative joy by meditating on the happiness or success of a friend or loved one. Practice this until *You* are able to experience genuine feelings of joy and appreciation. Then gradually build this ability, step by step, and offer this compassionate presence to neutral acquaintances, strangers, enemies, and eventually all beings everywhere. The more solitary *You* are, the more compassionate *You* will be. *You* will be able to hold the world with the tenderness it deserves.

May all beings know their true power. . . May the clearing of consciousness dawn new skies. . . and the vision of sunlight, hot and blazing, be seen now. . . May we imagine the grass, the trees, the flowers. . . May we know children to be in schools or playing. . . May we see couples holding hands in outdoor cafés, lovers kissing in the park, families watching ball games. . . May we truly understand that our presence of fully seeing, believing, and knowing as an ardent prayer that is already done. . . May we see our sisters and brothers dry and safe, unafraid and calm. . . May we not only lend helping hands but anchor thoughts, vision and creation. . .

**Breathe deeply with all that is.
Allow Light to consume all that is not.
In walking the path of Light,
do not take it lightly.
To be Light means
engaging with darkness.
Where else is Light needed?
It is why *You* have the ability to shine.**

knowing.

Why do i/eye have to care?
I/eye can see how my apathy, indifference, and complacency contribute to the issue.

Knowing.
I hold the welfare of others and my world in my awareness.

KNOWING.
I AM the flowering of compassionate presence.

. . .

MELODY THROUGH LOVE—CELEBRATION

What does it sound like?

Can I say I love you?
I am not afraid to say it.
I am not afraid to feel it.
I am not afraid to give it.
I am not afraid to be it.
I am not afraid to let *You* know it.
I am not afraid for the world to see it.

Life can be intense, while also holding spans of monotony. It is a wild and organic endeavor in which *You* discover *Love* as your true identity. This melody courses through every cell of your *Being/being/BEING*. Every experience must harmonize to love. Souls come to experience all that humanness offers—mentally, emotionally, physically, and energetically—but also to transcend these attachments. Whether *You* make choices for short-term human gain or long-term soul expansion, let each one be doused with the essence of Love.

Wisdom through experience shifts *Being* homogenized to *BEINGg enius*;
utilize the melody of love through celebration, as an act of grace.

Most are convinced they have loved or know love. Many may even say they love who they are. Any projections of love onto another must not be mistaken for anything other than the quality of love for *Self/self/SELF*. People can love only to the ability they truly love themselves. Be careful not to slip into patterns of codependence, where *You* require the other's love, attention, and presence to feel loved. Expressions of a needy manner illustrate degrees of Love that are still to be cultivated. But these relationships are vital as a measure for how to better love *Self*. In this way, relationship becomes "praxis."

Stop looking outside for Love. What *You/you* seek exists inside. Let the Lover inside *You* romance the Beloved that *YOU* are. *Self/SELF Love* focuses deeply. Initially, this excludes all others. Once embodied, it overflows onto others... expanding infinitely. *Self* love is the greatest service to offer the world.

Love is in everything... activate it with your presence. Open to... embrace... and receive it. *Love*... is always the answer. Sometimes it can be tough... other times, tender. It must be truthful and telling. With *Love*, all things are possible: healing, growth, justice, empowerment, and connection. Let it flow from *You*, and it will find *You/you/YOU*.

Love... Purely Love... Holy Love... Sacredly Love... Divinely Love...
each and every moment... each and every day... each and every way.

The decision, commitment, and consistency of being your own best friend are essential to the discovery of the Divine. Autonomy, independence, and occasional aloneness are a requirement for creating inner relationship. This is not the time for busying yourself with doing. Even reading, journaling, and meditation are not to be rote activities or ritualistic, but instead to be conducted as experiences of lovemaking. The melody of *Love* must permeate your days. It is here that true *Love* expands beyond boundaries, constructs, and limitations. Any and all experiences of outer *Love* are merely mirrors of the *Love* created within. Intimacy with *Self/self/SELF* playfully flirts with your musings and sensations... impulses and iterations... cravings and desires so that *You* develop a true union within.

Love is neither a step nor a process. True Love... Real Love... Unconditional Love... Lover and BeLoved Love is a path, one that goes into wild unknown depths within your heart, soul, and psyche. This *Love* never hurts. It continually expands, bathes, cherishes, and holds every aspect and dimension of *You/you/YOU*. All have access to this, but embodiment requires devotion, commitment, and courage. This *Love* is not black, white, or shades of gray. The essence of pure *Love* is the infinite appreciation and graduation of color and light. Once *Love* is dissolved into, sacred union can never be severed.

Remain available and open. Become intoxicated by *Love*'s elixir. This drunken ecstasy is eternal, once imbibed. Be in the inquiry... expectation... and exploration of this wondrous state. It creates the ramblings of poets and mystics such as Rumi and Hafiz. Be consumed by *Love*, so that nothing else is seen. The heart is capable of ever-increasing capacities to *Love*. First, achieve human *Love*. Then, move toward unconditional *Love*. Let this explode into Divine *LOVE*.

Love created *You* like itself... let nothing cover that perfection; ever present and overflowing.

There is only one truth... it is *LOVE*. Don't stop until *You* discover its true essence. Anything less than unconditional *LOVE*... is not *LOVE*. This is the celebration that life is asking *You* into.

Can I say I love you?
Will you receive it?
Will you let it in?
Will you embrace it?

You do not need to do anything about it.
You do not even need to respond to it.
Just have it. Receive it. Experience it.
Your presence is enough.

knowing.
Why do i/eye hide from the truth?
It is up to me to discover my truth, and the truth.

Knowing.
I celebrate myself.

KNOWING.
I AM Love.

. . .

VISCERAL FORM

What may be absorbed?

Doubt and negativity nurture weeds.
Get clear on what you are fertilizing.
The past is not for processing;
it was designed for pointing.
What happened to *you*
happened for *You*.
It was not meant to hold *You/you/YOU* back
but was intended to launch *YOU* forward.

In this busy, noisy world, it is vital to recharge and reconnect with the body. Going beyond the addictive need of "doing," phones, technology, work, and "normality" means becoming free of self-imposed conditioning. Delving into this area of the psyche can be "tricky." Do not be surprised about how the ego attempts to derail *You* from fully being present. At times, ego will have *You* act quickly. In other instances, it will stop *You* from taking action. It is in these places of holdback that regret digs in. Laced with the energies of should, would, could and can't, wouldn't, shouldn't is the visceral regret that takes shape. All that could have been, or was not done, further anchors identity and corresponding self-esteem.

Cultivate naturalness as *You* invite unification with the masculine aspect;
deep presence is required to access your visceral form of regret.

Heightened trauma creates an experience known as freeze. Constant anxiety and fear in childhood will create freeze responses that lead to dissociation, greater anxiety, panic, and PTSD as adults. If you felt routinely unsafe and unprotected as a child, the tendency toward a freeze response will occur regularly when triggered. Not being able to fend off danger, or run away, creates immobilization. When so scared that *You* cannot move, systems are compromised. This occurs physically, but also emotionally and mentally when not able to process a situation. Being scared stiff is a result of severe fright and trauma. Panic attacks, obsessive compulsive disorders, and various forms of anxiety also relate to the freeze response.

When dissociating or checking out, *You* leave the body. A lack of intimacy with surroundings, people, and *Self* creates isolation and nonaction. If experiences are never fully acknowledged and given opportunity to "thaw," they remain within the physiology as unconscious disruption. Because they are not consciously accessible and never fully discharged, triggers reengage and compound freeze states. Presence to the pain and sensations supports unnameable trauma in releasing. It also creates the conditions for slow and steady action steps to be implemented.

Eliminating freeze requires the use of multiple therapies. Somatic work, along with psychology, processing, and energy modalities, is often necessary to neutralize unaddressed pain. Community is integral to healing freeze. Those in freeze isolate, feel alone, and suffer in silence. Having one individual that cares will feel extremely supportive. Seek out a sacred witness who can be an unconditional friend and compassionate presence. That individual will hold space for *You* to believe in yourself again. "Freeze" is the face of a small child that was spooked, when everything in the world seems too big. It is okay to come out of the darkness and receive support.

A golden thread that runs through all things.
Low, dense vibrations weave a picture larger than your mind can comprehend.

Continually going back over the "whens" and "whys" of experience only keep *You* living in the past. Overprocessing makes *You* a casualty of unconscious living. Slipping too far into your story can become costly in the present moment, because what is available becomes lost. The stories and experiences that once were now live on as distractions from what is.

Regret focuses on missed opportunities, past decisions, or losses. It becomes a preoccupation with missed opportunities, failures, and mistakes as opposed to living. Regret holds the dominant emotions of shame and sadness. When these emotions are triggered repeatedly, moods will occur. Issues remain unresolved when not taking action toward personal growth. Ironically, this lack of action is the same thing that created regret. In the instances that an action cannot be taken, vulnerability and ownership can be supportive measures.

One small step is enough. After that, try another small step. The way to avoid regret is in continuing to consciously act on what your heart and gut are saying. Get out of your own way and try something new, exciting, and inspired. Change supports the cycle of life. When willing to change directions and move into a new dream, *You* allow another to fulfill theirs by taking the place you held.

Life will continue to bring *You/you/YOU* to the mystery. . .
willingly or unwillingly.
The experience of *YOU* can be experienced only
when *You/you* become authentic, real, truthful, and intimate.
Until then, it's masks and mirrors.
***You/you/YOU* are here to engage in the mystery of life.**
Control is the antithesis.

knowing.
Why won't things change?
i/eye can contemplate my energy, thoughts, and feelings to become aware of
what keeps this experience present in my life.

Knowing.
Who I Am today is not who I was yesterday, nor will it be the me of tomorrow.

KNOWING.
I AM ever changing.

. . .

ALCHEMY OF SOUL

What can be transmuted?

The vessel of inquiry,
a questioning of possibility,
and infinite creative capacity
are the paintbrushes of the soul.
"Experience" experiencing itself
is an eternal ebb and flow
of checks and balances
equilibrating from nothing
to something
and back into the void. . .
as the journey.

The point of life is not to have everything given to *You*, or to simply manifest. The whole journey is for *You* to discover and create aliveness. Give life to yourself. . . as *god/God/ GOD*s on legs, sons and daughters of the Divine Presence.

Free thyself with the gifts of strength, patience, and perseverance;

these blessings allow intimacy to rise.

Taking the road less traveled requires going against the grain. *You* must be mother and child simultaneously. Care for and love yourself as an unconditionally loving, healthy mother would. *You* likely have no idea how to do this, much less know how to receive love of such immense capacity. But the soul desires this experience. It created every obstacle and challenge in a wish for true, pure, unconditional love.

Prior to now, *You* hid your voice, truth, and action on the basis of the inner critic. *You* have condemned yourself for living small, whatever that means. *You* compare yourself to others, who, in truth, have not figured out their own lives. Now, *You* shield yourself from being swallowed by the unknown. Despite this, *You* are required to bear witness to pieces and parts that whisper.

Ripples in the pond of life reveal whom *You* affected and how. *You* cannot hide from your thoughts, words, and deeds. They are as close as your shadow. They cling, not to be cast away. They reveal all of *You,* from your darkest expression to the way *You* radiate light.

These underpinnings rest intimately close but do not touch your essential nature. They are like layers of fabric. Some seem sheer, like gossamer, where *You* see certain sparks of divinity with some clarity and certainty. However, others appear as heavy, dark brocade that blocks all vision and light. These dense veils create uncertainty, beckoning a walk through shadowy unknowns. The darkest of veils will carry *You* through the valley of death, but when finally seen and flung away, they reveal the purest of blinding light.

A meeting will occur where animal, demon, human, and *god/God* come face to face. As each *One/one/ONE* emerges out of your dense fog of *Being/being/BEING*. . . embrace them. . . reverently, compassionately, and lovingly.

All of these filters hover in and around your life. It is how life's scenes are designed. These veils cloak *You* from the truth of your soul and spirit. Encompassed within them are ancestral energies, soul contracts, and self-created karmic lessons. The body can feel weighed down by the virtual storehouse of architectural memory. But beneath this blanket of illusion are specific instructions for making your life a unique expression of soul.

After purification of mind, body, and heart. . . remaining elements unite through the process of conjunction. This provides the simmering necessary for acceptance. *You* are to sit and marinate inside yourself. *You* must soak in the juices of all that has been. It is necessary to savor every aspect of your life experiences and expressions. As *You* discover the truth and understanding of how your mind has worked, the body has held memory, and the heart has felt. . . the faint glow of inner authority will begin to shine. A more authentic expression of *You* is budding.

During this stage of alchemy, unconscious thoughts and feelings bubble up to the surface and into the light of conscious awareness. These nutrients of *Self/self*-awareness support a richer expression of Essence. Continued alone, time, meditation, contemplation, and journaling support the soul's alchemical process. It may feel as if this process is never ending. However, it took *You* a lot longer to get to this point than it is taking to unwind. Be gentle with yourself. Be gentle with your soul.

You/you/YOU are part of a symphony;
an orchestration of creation.
You not only chose to be here,
this moment chose *You/you/YOU* to be.
Your soul song sounds like no other. . .
Harmonize. . .
and life will attune *You/YOU* to its purpose.

knowing.
Is there more to life than this?
i/eye can find value in the valleys.

Knowing.
I live life as a soulful experience and expression.

KNOWING.
I am essential to life; I am Essence BEING.

. . .

ESSENCE AS INTIMACY

What may be embodied?

You/you/YOU are blessed
to have many hearts in your treasure chest. . .
A sacred hideout to explore each night and day,
and a soft cushion of experience in which to play.
Each experience holds many mirrors. . .
familiarities to embrace with soulful rigor.
This fractal of beauty
reveals facets of *You/you/YOU* and *Me/me/ME.*
In some, *You/you/YOU* can see heaven;
in others, witness hell. . .
get to know life's great mystery.

You are 100% organic. . . and so is life. It is not to be controlled, planned, manipulated, or directed. It is to be received. It is wonder full. . . and that means what *You* do not know, *You* will come to know. That which the mind cannot fathom, it will be asked to consider. That which the heart cannot take in, it breaks open to hold. That which the soul has not experienced, it finds in experience. Truth be told. . . *You* are not on a journey. . . *You/you/*

YOU are the journey. . .
Forgiving ego's fight creates the inspiration for giving rebirth to *Self.*

True intimacy comes when willing to discard all that was. It becomes difficult to let go of story and history. Without it, who are *You*? But with it, *You* are headed down a dead-end street. Life has never limited *You*; only *you* have. The true essence of intimacy requires very few words. It would be the full immersion into feeling what brings *You* ecstatic joy. Intimacy invites discovery of what *You* truly desire. Intimacy says. . . dream. Intimacy points toward a wishing well. . . wish. Intimacy would have *You* feel all the feelings that arise.

**Life shall reveal the beauty of aloneness
In that space, discover your wholeness.
Sink into sacredness,
be humbled by greatness.
Learn how to belong. . .
as your soul begins singing its song.
In your aloneness. . .
You/you/YOU shall realize *You are* no one.
In the emptiness,
You/you/YOU discover *You* are everyone.**

knowing.
Why am i/eye at odds with the people in my life?
They are a mirror for how i/eye am odds with myself.

Knowing.
I find common ground with others through vulnerability and softness,
in order to experience greater intimacy with myself.

KNOWING.
I AM in sacred matrimony with my highest SELF.

. . .

FORGIVING DEATH—FOR GIVING BIRTH

What does it smell like?

I forgive life's experience of death.
I forgive this earthen dimension for dying.
I forgive decay.
I forgive destruction.
I forgive change.

I am for giving birth.
I am for giving aliveness.
I am for giving rebirth.
I am for giving creation.
I am for giving flexibility.
I give presence to prayer.
I give way to meditation.
I give in to silence.
I give with naturalness.
I give my human *Self* the grace of rebirth.
I alchemize my energy with the aura of the angel.
I alchemize my inquiry with the fragrance of devotion.
I alchemize my insights with the flavor of compassion.
I alchemize my responses through the melody of love.
I alchemize giving and receiving with the Essence of intimacy.
I am *ONE* with the *DIVINE PRESENCE*;
I transform and transmute all identity through the grace of rebirth. . .
I open to the absorption of all visceral and residual resentment.
May *DIVINE ALCHEMY* dissolve my shadow masculine *self*, bringing innocence
to my pride.
May I adorn the vulture's patience,
so to bridge the illusion of the psychological plane with the reality of the angelic
world.
I step with intention toward a heavenly embodiment.
I am for giving the vulture's gifts of adaptability and innovation,
perception and protection. . . trust and tolerance. . . cleanliness and
resourcefulness.
May these gifts of *KNOWING* be granted by *DIVINE GRACE*.
I am the body of *GOD*.
I AM the breadth of *GOD*.
I AM the eternity of *GOD*.
I AM the internity of *GOD*.
I AM the creation of *GOD*.
I AM the manifestation of *GOD*.

. . .

UP-LEVEL VOICE

COMMUNICATION as your POINT OF ATTRACTION
to shift from

self ——-> *Self* ——-> *SELF*

ego's fight. the grace of rebirth

Be present. Gradually shift into higher octaves of presence, awareness, and perception. Move up the vibrational ladder. Feel your way and ascend to a new reality.

The fifth human grace establishes a new expression from which to speak and be heard. It requires anchoring solidly into expressing clarity and truth. Listen with the inner ear. Hear thy *Self/self/SELF*. The wisdom *You* hold inside is your great service. Share all that has been seen, heard, and acknowledged. Place your experiences upon the altar, with the rest of life's great love stories.

Up-level Voice—by speaking—the truth of who *YOU* are. Move gradually into expression, communication, and sacred creation through focus, vibration, and voice as your point of attraction. As *You* more deeply anchor into your truth—and specifically the *DIVINE TRUTH* within *YOU*—your ability to create a higher expression of *SELF* unfolds. *You* are an ever-expanding, energetic expression of creative capacity. Awaken your *knowing. . . Knowing. . . KNOWING*. Give yourself something new to respond to.

living.
———————————————————
acknowledgment
(slow down and feel.)
———————————————————————————

eye/i am tough. eye/i can beat the odds. eye/i am going to make it. eye/i am a hard worker. eye/i am nervous. eye/i am strong. eye/i am weak. eye/i am a good person. eye/i am not always a good person. eye/i give of my time. eye/i help others, and that makes me feel good about myself. eye/i am a parent. eye/i am a team player. eye/i am nobody. eye/i am married. eye/i am divorced.

being.
———————————————
acceptance
(bring attention to your breath.)
———————————————————————————

eye/i feel. . . stuck. eye/i feel behind. eye/i am better than this. eye/i feel average and ordinary; mediocre. eye/i feel disappointed. eye/i feel I wasn't given a chance. eye/i feel inadequate. eye/i feel small. eye/i feel I have gifts and talents. eye/i feel like people should recognize me. eye/i feel important. eye/i feel imprisoned by circumstances; caged. eye/i feel stressed to uphold an image.

knowing.
———————————————
anticipation
(breathe slowly, deepen into your body.)
———————————————————————————

eye/i may not like obstacles, but life is an obstacle course. eye/i discover how to stretch, leap, and fly because of obstacles on my path. eye/i embrace my blocks and fears and transcend them. Endless doing does not serve me. Life is providing opportunities to balance my divine masculine energy. eye/i am learning the distinction between action and inspired action.

Contrast teaches me to become more deliberate in my actions.

Living.

———————————————

appreciation
(pause and be present to what the moment is asking.)

———————————————————————————

I appreciate my life. I appreciate myself. I appreciate the journey I have walked. I appreciate being on the bridge. I am grateful that I feel more safe today than yesterday. I appreciate feeling more present in each moment. I am grateful I am taking care of my health. I am grateful I am becoming more conscious of my words, thoughts, and actions. I appreciate discerning how I create my reality. I am grateful for what has passed. I am grateful for the genius inside of me.

Being.

———————————————

satisfaction
(connect mind to heart to gut to ground.)

———————————————————————————

I feel satisfied when I start the day right. Beginning the day with gratitude is satisfying. Remembering I am a part of something much larger than myself is satisfying. I feel satisfied when I take time to close my eyes, breathe, and connect with Spirit. I am satisfied when I drift into the ethers. Developing my spiritual self is satisfying and rewarding. The religion of love is satisfying to my soul. Hence I connect to the Universe; I center into soul satisfaction.

Knowing.

———————————————

adoration
(inhale deeply and absorb what is present.)

———————————————————————————

I love how conflict helps me see where I am not loving. I love how conflict turns me back toward my self-care. I love myself. I love being in love. I love being loving. I love being cherished. I adore myself. I love the feeling of love. I love the experience of being lovable. I am the beloved. I love how love inspires. I love how love gives. I am the lover. I love how love heals. I love how love renews. I renew the world when I love myself. I am love in action. I love inspired action. I adore life. I adore animals. I adore babies. I adore smiles, sunshine, and moonbeams. I love the receptivity of love. I love the sacredness of love. Love teaches me so much. I love love.

LIVING.

———————————————

celebration
(rise above and rejoice.)

———————————————————————————

I celebrate wisdom. I celebrate experience. I celebrate my voice. I celebrate sharing my expression. I celebrate learning and growing. I celebrate being an example. I celebrate how obstacles make me stronger. I celebrate my strength. I celebrate my stamina. I celebrate my ability to persevere. I celebrate patience. I celebrate how patient I am becoming. I celebrate that I am cultivating naturalness. I celebrate my natural soul essence.

BEING.

———————————————

exaltation
(ground in sacredness, devotion, and equanimity... unconditionally Love!)

——————————————————————————

*I rest. I imbue. I surround. I immerse. I imbibe. I encompass.
I embrace. I magnify. I materialize.
I contemplate. i dream. I upgrade. I dematerialize. I mirror. I manifest. I vibrate. I spiral.
I master. I move. I dance. I emote. I ascend. I descend. I empathize. I work. I play. I aspire.*

KNOWING.

———————————————

jubilation
(exhale your newly created vibrational reality and... believe!)

——————————————————————————

*I AM comfort. I AM gracious. I AM graceful. I AM adored. I AM wonderful. I AM juicy.
I AM content. I AM empowered. I AM celebration.
I AM common ground. I AM discipline.
I AM OPEN. I AM GENTLENESS. I AM MIRACULOUS.
I AM QUANTUM. I AM RAPTURE.
I AM DEVOTION. I AM EXTRAORDINARY. I AM DYNAMIC.
I AM EASE. I AM JOY.
I AM FUN. I AM GLOWING. I AM HARMONY. I AM ANGELIC.
I AM SOUL. I AM INTIMACY.
I AM THAT... I AM. I AM THAT... IAM. I AM THAT... IAM.*

Always begin exactly where *You/you/YOU* are. Be truthful with how *You/you/YOU* feel. Be authentic in what *You/you/YOU* are thinking. A new human builds from the ashes of your old life. Let your words be catalysts for transformation and transmutation. *You* are the bridge between where *you* are and where *You* want to go. *You* grow into *KNOWING* as *You* ascend the ladder of consciousness. What *You* place into the universal vortex remains in escrow. Belief supports physical presence. *KNOWING* creates change, transformation, and miracles.

NOTES

manifestation.

What has to dissolve?

In a great divide, one became two.
Two became many.
Running to opposite ends of creation,
all was separate, but not apart.
An explosion of energy in motion.
Seeking the wild abandon of realization.
To paint this and sculpt that. . .
to carve then and create now. . .
to melt. . . to smolder. . .
to burn. . . to solder. . .
from formless to form;
no thing and every thing was born.
To reconcile a division that was not real,
the purity of illusion,
in a sense and with nonsense,
was revealed.
This is what *you/i/we/they*
have been creating.
And the realization of this. . .
IS. . .
what *You/I/We/They* have been awaiting.

As ego disappears, often a new one rises. This new ego and identity will convince *You* of desires, passions, and manifestations to be attained. Even though ego identities may surpass one another in terms of vibration, the tactics of delusion are the same whether encountering an extremely dense ego with gross cravings and aversions or a spiritual ego with its desire to heal, lead, or change the world. From these, and all those in between, manifestations will be colored with agendas and intentions.

Manifesting is the collaboration between the seen and unseen. It is the orchestration of energy into matter. The beauty of incarnation is that *You* can be, do, and have anything.

Unconscious wielding of this creative power will produce unconscious random results. Conscious wielding also produces results, but these may be tinged with the shadows of ego. *You* are a genie in a bottle. However, this does not mean sitting back and watching it happen. It is a part *You/you/YOU* must play. This is more important energetically than physically. *You* incorrectly believe that manifestation arises out of doing, rather than *Being/being/ BEING*. Anything you want can be created in your life. Belief is an integral key element.

You are always manifesting. Be cognizant of where *You* manifest from; *Being*... *being*... or *BEING*.

As *You* grew up, the feeling of worth, enoughness, satisfaction, happiness, and fulfillment was equated with external manifestation. Because of this, your trigger switch is always set to act quickly, set intention into motion, and go get what *You* desire. Hustling, building, and manifesting are approached through animalistic hunger. There is rarely the pause that engenders pure creation. For this reason, manifestation temporarily satisfies but briefly lasts. There will never be enough to fill the endless ache for more.

**When manifesting from shadow, *You* get what *you* need.
When manifesting from celebration, *YOU* are the fulfillment of every need and desire.**

Shadow manifestation appears as not enough while having too much. It is wasteful, excess, collecting multiples, and having without fully holding. Manifestation and materialism are like kissing cousins. They might look good together, but something is just not right about the relationship. In the end what looks like a display of abundance will actually stem from a deep inner lack. Excess offers an image of success, only to overcompensate an unconscious sense of smallness. If what exists were to disappear, would the individual still feel valuable, worthy, and confident? Or are the material accoutrements, identity, and persona required to feel valued, successful, and fulfilled? Manifestation is a heavy burden when it is not held lightly and playfully.

One car is not enough; a garage full is required to keep driving, moving, wheeling, and dealing. One home is not adequate; several are needed to stave off boredom, stillness, and true homesickness. Unknowingly, closets of extra things, unused items, and backup materials create added stress, cost, and congestion.

In truth, there is nothing wrong with enjoying life. *You* deserve to have what feels good and brings happiness. But are *You* sitting in the pause and anchoring into feelings of fullness before seeking to fill the emptiness? Love yourself enough to fulfill desires of your heart and soul. Do not become so swept away by what is temporary that *You* miss the real. Your ultimate manifestation is the highest expression of SELF.

**From timeless, boundless, whole space
to a time-bound place...
a deep chasm in which to dive,
a self-created internal divide.
a void manifesting creation, experiments, and unknown reality...**

a black hole of endless separation,
to know. . . and be known
as human. . . as angel. . . and as deity
for the journey as transformation and transfiguration.
What was made manifest
in creation. . .
resulted in many things;
some expansively beautiful and others distorted deviations.

knowing.
Why do i/eye keep manifestating the same things?
i/eye continue reacting and responding in the same ways, so i/eye create the same things.

Knowing.
I Am a conduit for creative capacity.

KNOWING.
I AM a divine manifestation.

NOTES

the grace of self realization.

What is the remembering?

Invite the grace of self-realization.
Consciously initiate this. . .
allow the kiss of rain to invoke the aura of violet flame.
Your fragrance of communion will reveal truth.
Exhaling your flavor of softness expands your energy.
Through inspiration, your visceral ash dissolves;
the essence of vulnerability brings forth the alchemy of soul,
taking *You/you* to neutral ground.
Give life the gift of your human grace.
Deepen into knowing that your presence is always enough.

You live in a wounded world. Wounded people wound others. Forgive every trespass, because they truly do not know what they do. However, hold a vision for each one as capable. . . they are divine and possess the creative divine capacity to overcome their illusions.

The deceptive ego would have you believe everything evil and holy is outside you. Yet, there is nothing outside anyone. It is all a world of our own making. . . your perceptions. . . perspectives and beliefs. The events of the world are beckoning deepened presence and understanding of who *You* are as creator. . . and what *You* have been creating. In becoming more conscious, *You* will begin to realize how unconscious *you* are and have been. Those judged as unconscious are not to blame. . . for no one is to blame. We have all been playing out the dynamic romance of *SELF*-realization.

Within the blessing of darkness and the illusion of evolution,
***You/you/YOU* created manifestations**
in order to discover the grace of *self*-realization, as a way of awakening humanity.

Rather than believe the stories or stay immersed in your story, move into the one that has yet to be told. All prior stories were to have something to rise above. . . now rise. Your power is in your pain; embrace the pain. . . unleash your Power. The one gift most difficult to give, and even harder to receive. . . is complete acceptance.

The dark is light. It is sacred and should be remembered, celebrated, and acknowledged. Not hidden, denied, or forgotten. Your Divinity is all of *You/you/YOU*. Darkness creates the full brilliance of light that eventually shines. Does it mean you must go through the fire? Yes, if *You* feel soldering is required to put things back together. Does it mean *You* must endure the floods? Yes, if *You* have not felt the ocean of emotion that has been lapping upon the shores of your body. Does it mean *You* must endure harsh winds of change? Yes, if *You* are not rooted securely in a foundation of truth and inherent divinity. Does it mean *You* must return to dust? Yes, if *You* have forgotten your earthen self; *You* must till and aerate the ground that is barren, cracked, and dry.

You are moving, although the illusion may have *You* believe the world is spiraling out of control. Each happening breaks *You* down to feel more, see more, hear more, and know more. This great time is opening *You* to greater empathy, sensitivity, intuition, and connection. When *You* allow the fragmented world to fall away. . . a whole new world will nest within your breast, nourished by the milk of every fragmented piece.

The Grace of Self Realization	The Remembering	Knowing
The Illusion—Manifestation	What has to dissolve?	Aliveness
True Love's Kiss—The Rain	What nature is required?	Creation
Aura of the Violet Flame	What is emerging?	Unification
Fragrance Emitting Communion	What is the inhale?	Truth
Flavor of Softness	What is the exhale?	Energy
Melody Through Praise	What is harmonizing?	Growth
Visceral Ash—Resentment	What is being absorbed?	Wisdom
Alchemy of Illusion	What can be transmuted?	The Void
Essence as Presence	What may be embodied?	Infinite Presence
Forgiving Manifestation—For Giving Creation	What is for giving?	Eternity

Every -ingle day, stretch to stay young. Stretch your body, your mind, your beliefs, your love, your service, your passion, your joy. . . Your *Self*! Enlighten every space. Create your own spotlight. Be light. *You* are sacred. *You* need only *KNOW* it. Life is yours to behold. Your Love, yours to experience. Your expression, yours to celebrate.

Stand in the Light. . . YOUR LIGHT! There is no other. It's all *YOU*. Once willing to recognize that, all will be illuminated. Some of life's moments hold such mystery that words are not worthy. Keeping them close is sacred. Find instances of magic that grow the eyes wide with a smile. . . and fill the heart with warm honey. Imagine the surprises of life and the ecstatic rhapsody of being fully alive. Each moment is dependent on how *You* are willing to see it.

Open to the miracle. It's waiting right in front of *You*. . . Look in the mirror. The miracle is in your mind. When *You* let it happen there. . . It happens everywhere. The miracle is *You*. . . But it occurs only when fully realizing it. *You* have worked hard enough. . . Now, let the miraculous side of *YOU* take over. There is only this moment, and it is perfection.

Your pure potential lives beyond the scope of your mind. Fear of that potential lives inside the mind. Do what *You* love to do because *YOU* deserve that. *BE* who *You* are, completely unique and natural, because the world deserves that. Open your heart. Let yourself have what *YOU* most desire by opening your heart to it.

You are each the change in your world. In finding your humanity, *You* serve humanity. Establish a living connection with the *God* that resides inside. Be human in your doing; *God* in your *Being*. The heights to which *You* will soar are equivalent to the depths *You* explore. Dive deep. . . Fly high.

Aloneness reveals who *You/you/YOU* are beyond the skin.
Aloneness is not loneliness;
it is an opportunity for knowing what is within.
My aloneness taught me
about my togetherness.
I was never alone.
Instead, I discovered all oneness.
In my aloneness,
who I was dissolved
into who I AM.
In that allness,
I never feel lonely again.

knowing.
Why am i/eye here?

Knowing.
I give meaning to life.

KNOWING.
I AM Divine.

. . .

TRUE LOVE'S KISS—THE RAIN

What nature is required?

Fall in love again and again. . .
endlessly do.
To the point where *You* wonder

if there are enough words. . .
adequate words. . .
the right words. . .
even though *You* know there are no words.
Let it feel flirtatious and playful. . .
wondrous and beautiful.
Be filled with joy and happiness. . .
with glee.

Sadness has a profound and positive purpose. Those sacred tears wash *You/you/YOU* of all that is false—in belief, experience, and life. That cleansing releases discomfort and pain, lies and limitations, beliefs and boundaries, fear and indifference. All tears are the holy anointing of the Divine. These moments open the heart. When sinking into a pool of sadness, a tender, warm embrace can be felt. A sacred presence is always near. This holy communion not only brings *You/you/YOU* closer to the Divine, but also closer to the embodiment of the Divine.

There will come a change in the rain. It will no longer be the storm or the flood. It will not be charged with thunderous booms or lightning strikes. As *Self*-realization comes, soft rain will sprinkle. It will glisten with happiness. The misty moments will feel warm and appreciative. *You* will experience immense gratitude that *You* made it through.

In engaging the path of the mystic, spiritual obsessions abound;
creating rain, which hid within your earthen ground.

Standing in the rain is the most wonderful place. It allows *You* to feel nurtured; to be cleansed and to grow. When in that place, magic happens. The tears are no longer dripping with grief; instead they flow with gratitude. *You* are able to make new choices and see events in new ways so that *You* can do a different thing.

Flowering always comes after the rain. Beyond the most painful, traumatic, and tragic moments is a space that holds and nourishes with seemingly endless sacred waters. Tears are a communion between soul and body. . . Spirit and separation. Your new voice will feel steady and strong. . . loving, tender, and compassionate. What initially bore through your ground as pain now becomes fertilizer for a new expression.

Sometimes it is necessary to look at life and see what needs to change. . . what needs to remain the same. . . and what needs to be left behind. Place your prayers in the water. . . in the rain. . . in the shower. . . and in your tears. If water is coming, bless it. Ask it to gently do its job; to help *You* trust what is happening as part of the Divine plan. Commune with nature so that *You* understand her ways.

The final stage of spiritual power is through opening the heart. Remain in celebration of life. *You* are learning how to *be in the world but not of it*. *You* realize that there is no separation, because everywhere there is *Self*. *You* see commonality rather than difference. *You* feel with love, instead of indifference. There is no death, only ever-expanding life. No need exists because everything exists within *You*. There are no victims; all are seen as capable. *You* rain upon everyone in a renewing, soft, loving way. *You* see them. *You* know them. *You* acknowledge them. *You* are them. This is the beauty of the rain.

Life is not the paradox. . .
***You/you/YOU* are.**
It is not about the words or silence. . .
Open to grace. . .
the tender touch. . .
the innocent kiss. . .
the cosmic giggle. . .
that returns to memory.
Weave your divine golden thread
with filaments of humanity.

knowing.
Why do i/eye feel so much sadness?
i/eye am being cleansed.

Knowing.
I sing in the rain.

KNOWING.
I AM abundant.

. . .

AURA OF THE VIOLET FLAME

What does it look like?

Be lit. . .
Let the fire blaze.
A violet cauldron. . .
An indigo elixir. . .
A purple spray. . .
A lavender mist. . .
A white feather. . .
A golden tip. . .
A sacred point
of light.

In this moment, *You* are not being asked to walk through the fire. Life is inviting *You* to *BE* the fire that cleanses long-imprinted patterns and tendencies in the world. It's asking *You* to be the fire of presence, warmth, and expression. It is asking *You* to be the flame of Light that sets off a blaze of change.

Through Violet Flame Alchemy comes the wisdom of descension. It supports the embodiment of high-vibrational Source Energy within your physical body. This energy of Divinity is alchemized through your humanness. The violet flame, or light, is the color of freedom and has the quality of mercy. It is the energy of transmutation. Violet light in the aura denotes that the soul is free to commune with *God*.

Reflect the energy of fire to expand your aura of the violet flame.
In raising your vibration, the global reflection of security also shifts.

Your alignment to higher degrees of embodiment allows for a powerful impact upon the planet. As *You* stand in the purity of your light, your mere presence is enough to create transformation and transmutation. In fact, there is no need to will anything, or intend. Your frequency and vibration are enough to create change in the environment around *You*. Your work in absorbing and owning all that was misaligned has served to make *You* a powerful anchor within the world. A soul who truly owns the wholeness of their darkness and light becomes a walking vortex in the world. It is not by what is said or by what is done. The vortex of *BEING* simply *IS*.

To maintain this powerful field, it is important that *You* remain in a state of creative play. Partake in activities that bring forth joy. All of your creation will be infused with the crystalline energies of the violet flame, thus having the same impact on whoever experiences them.

Your confidence is vital. You must *KNOW* who *YOU* are. This is from a place of complete humility. It is a quiet reflection. Confidence and creativity are cornerstones that empower true creation.

Be the earthen substance.
Be the flint.
Be the match.
Be the friction.
Be the spark. . .
and the flame.
Roar into a fire. . .
and call out the Divine name.
Burn away the dross.
Reclaim innocence again.
knowing.
Why am i/eye afraid?
i/eye am always being given opportunities to find my power.

Knowing.
I feel confident.

KNOWING.
I AM powerful.

...

FRAGRANCE-EMITTING COMMUNION

What does it smell like?

YOU are dreaming a dream
that *You/you/YOU* are awakening.
As *YOU* awaken,
You/YOU long for others
to wake up with *You*.
Here... there... everywhere...
the dreamer, the dream, the nightmares,
and the awakened
are one and the same.

Aloneness is not loneliness, it is comfort with knowingness... of *self*... *Self*... and *SELF*. True communion is found inside aloneness. The most important relationship *You* will ever have is inside your eternity. Sacred aloneness reveals what *You* are made of. It allows *You/you/YOU* to move beyond the illusory constructs of thought, word, and deed. Aloneness reveals who *YOU* are beyond your skin. *You* will meet *ISness* when stepping into aloneness.

Tap into the immense feeling of aloneness that surfaces as *You/you/YOU* are stripped of the security in false selves. Let the barren open space fill every ounce of your being. Feel the ache of loneliness. Experience the deep chasm of separation that has lived inside *You/you/YOU* for eternity. Let this be alchemized with the profundity of aloneness. The gift of feeling completely alone is that *You/you/YOU* get to rediscover *You/you/YOU* have never been alone. *You/you/YOU* have always been connected.

Once purification is underway, integration begins. *You/YOU* will have new awareness, aha moments, and breakthroughs that must be fully integrated into the body and life. *You/YOU* will ground into a new level of daily practice. *You/YOU* now know how easy it is to fall asleep and go unconscious. Each day, the process of distillation will begin again. Here, *You/YOU* are purifying further by consciously choosing how *You/YOU* will live. Your choices will be moment-by-moment, day-by-day conscious assertions.

Through practice *You/YOU* cling less to identity and embrace more of the unknown. *You/YOU* aim to awaken each day with fresh eyes of innocence. In addition, *You/YOU* close each day releasing all that occurred. This is the practice of dying each night and awakening each day. Doing so engages a practice of continuous inner transformation and self-realization.

As *You* play within the world of form, begin creating differently than before. Move gently into reality creation. Let thoughts rest in pure reality, not fantasy or filter. Anchor into the field that lies beyond logic, ego, or story. Practice embodying consciousness rooted in higher truth, worth, love, and presence. Then, create your *reality/illusion/dream* with that flavor of gentleness. Hold each moment as if a fragile heirloom for future generations. Then, carefully place your imaginings into the vehicle of time.

Shift experience by placing presence upon what *You/you/YOU* cannot yet see. Behold life with a lucid-dreaming quality. Be with everything in your current experience, but hold the imaginal realm closest to your naked *BEING*. Do not base new creation on what your physical eyes see. Feel into all things without sight; use insight. Touch the world like an early explorer. Seek to discover a new and better world. Hold that vision as real.

Through growth as soul mastery, awaken to your communion,
as *You* dissolve the black hole of gluttony.

Find compassion rather than judgment and see the simplistic beauty of being human… in addition to the vast power of your Divinity. The world is calling for Love. It's not about the words, it's the subtle and sacred awareness of what lies beyond the words. The many voices that you hear, inside or outside, stem from the same source. Enlightenment is the embrace of the simple, ordinary life.

Your "name" is spoken forth by Creation… heard by the Creator… until remembered as the same. It is *You* speaking, until hearing the sacred *One* who speaks. *You* are Light, Sound, and Color. Light shines through *You*, as softly as an ember to that of a brilliant raging fire. Sound comes forth from within *You*; in silence and whispers, to ranges of laughter, song, screams, and cries. Color expresses as all manner of experience. *You* embody as human attributes of fear, perseverance, resilience, and self-realization. *You* are the Divine Feminine attributes of birth, receptivity, and power. *You* are the Divine Masculine attributes of initiation, action, and strength. *You* eternally exist as the Hue-Man, or God-Man, being of Sacredness, Connection, and Presence.

You are experience… *You* are relationship… *You* are every conversation of the Universe. *You* are unwinding your way into the great expanse of the Void from which all things originated. This revealing requires your outer engagement in relationship, bringing into union and with communion what has been projected far and wide. Your separation was part of this sacred communion. Contrast is necessary for texture, dimension, and dissonance. It creates completion for wholeness, so that full remembrance of knowing may be inhaled. Such an inhale is long awaited after a full and deep exhale. None of this is logical. It was never intended to be. The mere thought might make *You* feel crazy. It will drive the ego insane.

You are man. *You* are woman. *You* are fear. *You* are love. Ultimately, *You* must come to terms *Being* the peace of death and the frenzy of aliveness. As *You/you/YOU* disintegrate, *You* become more *SELF*. Integration brings understanding. Disintegration brings the unknown. To take pause honors remembering. Be bored. It is your moments of emptiness that hold the greatest value. *You* are Light, the most Divine kind. Own it.

You are a lotus; cultivate deep in the mud.
Your beauty emerges as a gift for the sun.

Fall in love with emptiness… endlessly do. Discard the drama of the world. It is filled with endless distractions. The world is a drug. Too many are addicted without even realizing. It feels flirtatious and playful to explore and express in the outer world. It also feels relevant… and yet, it is not. Your relationship with the outside must be laced with the fragrance of communion so that the eye remains single. When both eyes are open, *You* become closed. When the eyes are closed, *You* open.

The Lotus represents the rebirth of the sun. It blooms by day and closes by night. Gods and goddesses sit on lotus thrones, as it represents *Self*-awareness. The lotus represents the mind opening up in the journey to eternal spiritual enlightenment. Just as the lotus goes through so much before it blossoms, so does human consciousness before it can reach enlightenment. Without the difficult lessons of being human, the beauty of consciousness unfolding would not be realized.

May every woman dance in her radiant femininity... May every man revel in strength while embracing his sensitivity... May your humanity be the open doorway to meet and greet every other... May the God within recognize the God within all others... May they smile in recognition of each other...

You, the dreamer,
are dual in your awakening;
which is proof that *You/YOU* are still sleeping.
The *ONE* who imagines
is eternal Oneness...
where there is no day or night.
There is no separation...
or plight.
It is all holy communion...
You are the sacrament.
It is all in imagination.

knowing.
Why is toxicity around me?
i/eye am seeing what needs to be released.

Knowing.
I attune my words, thoughts, and actions toward positive living.

KNOWING.
I AM that I AM.

. . .

FLAVOR OF SOFTNESS

What does it taste like?

May hearts open more each day...
and minds expand in broad ways...
May souls remember their essential nature...
and ego sacrifice its constriction and structure.
May all beings recognize

**the softness of true BEING. . .
and release the hardness,
struggle, and toil
they have been living.**

Each step taken helps delicately reveal subtle flavors that your heart, body, and soul require. Breathe. Focus your love with such deliberation that *YOU* see through the *i/eye/I*'s inside *You*. Experience each revelation rippling upon the murky pond of your existence. Breathe. Let the soul's rhythmic beat lead *You/you/YOU* into the harmonic chamber of *SELF*'s high heart. Allow the wonder of this divine dance. Let it stir within your belly. Innocently and curiously, open to life. . . one millisecond at a time. As each step becomes slower and slower, watch life speedily move *you* and *You* toward *YOU*.

You/you are continually dying, while constantly being reborn. In this way, *You* are the eternal newborn—reincarnated second by second. Imagine your eyes are closed, unable to see but fully aware. Innocence is a fresh foundation for aliveness. Breathe. Stretch your body. Unfurl. Uncurl. Yawn. Expand and then return to fetal comfort. Feel into the safety of life's womb space. Breathe. Let each sensation be a new experience of the unknown. Be willing to *unknow* all that *you* have known. Touch the earth often. Lie upon the ground. Smell the skin of the great mother. Let her scent remind *You* of your gentle nature. Rediscover how to innocently be human.

Let the body have infinite experiences of sensory and sensual exploration with *Self* through earth, water, air, and fire. Create *Self/self*-love practices and rituals that allow energy to move. Walk. Bathe. Exercise. Breathe. The body was born to writhe, rise, curl, and stretch. Muscles ache to explore. Filaments yearn to slide past one another. . . stretching, contracting, exhausting, and strengthening. Oh. . . the ache! Let the gentle ache of growth and expansion seed regularly within your physiology.

Taste each day. Swallow every second, and touch the timelessness of oncoming moments. Smell your experiences. Inhale what surrounds *You*. Be enamored with the stinky, funky, and rotten. Lean into the ecstasy of the aromatic, perfumery, and confectionary. Listen with deafened ears, in order to hear the sacred sound of silence. . . the heavenly music of your spheres. . . and the joyful noise resounding within. Let discordant noise pull forth what is resonant from within *You/you/YOU*. Let the mind be blind, so that *You* perceive from childlike eyes and a divine, loving heart. Be *consciously unconscious* so that *You* meet every hidden aspect of yourself. With gentleness. . . with love. . . and with devotion. Be so gentle that life's harshest moments are held softly and gracefully. Soften. . . soften. . . soften.

As *You* endeavor upon truth in silence, restore softness through the key of fulfillment.

The world conditions people to hold, take, collect, hoard, and use, as if we are containers. Closed containers grow old and stagnant. They fester and get cloudy. An open container fills and refills, continually washed clean of things it has held. We act as containers, yet we are not. *I/you/we/they* are conduits. In this way, energy simply flows through. *You* do not get stuck by it, nor does it become stagnant within you.

The world purports ideas that harden *You*. The concept of strength is perceived in a distorted manner. The world appears to value being *tough*. However, that idea has hardened your barriers, walls, guards, and calcifications. Every heart is a walled garden. Seek a heart not hardened like dry land, but soft soil tilled over again and again. Let us be like soil, moistened with the tears of love, the remembrance of Spirit, the love of a friend, or the warm breath of a lover. This is the soil that was worthy of receiving life.

Life does not always make sense; it is not supposed to. When things become uncomfortable, life is still working in your favor. All manner of experience will occur to support softening. Life was never designed to be as hard as humans make it. *You* have forgotten how to rest. . . how to relax. . . how to organically flow. Live in the rhythms that organically occur. Consider living in a manner that sounds too good to be true. . . and *You* may discover it is the truth and all good. Relax into yourself. . . your body. . . your life.

Come. Take my hand. Feel its softness. Know its touch. It seeks only to embrace. It lies open to feel held. It is here to give unto *You*. Yet, it is also open to receiving. It can close, but only to grasp the essence of the moment. Softness is kind, generous, and humble. It offers before it asks, and it rarely demands. What beauty exists in someone whose heart has become soft, open to life, and receptive.

May mankind behold all sisters and brothers. . .
in a manner that allows love for one another.
May all that experience unrest
experience complete bliss. . .
May the misguided realize their illusions
and trappings of ignorance.
May every life know beauty,
and each person, their uniqueness. . .
May all know they are holy
and celebrate completeness.

knowing.
Why do i/eye feel so tired?
I/eye am aware of how i/eye feel.

Knowing.
I soften into life.

KNOWING.
I AM the sweet elixir of divine play.

MELODY THROUGH PRAISE—EXALTATION
What does it sound like?

Don't forget where *You* came from;
where all came from.
Sing...
Clap...
Dance...
Shout...
Create...
Prostrate...
Pray...
Rise to the *heights*
***for which You* were made.**

Sometimes being struck with illness brings blessings. The moment a job is lost, a relationship ends, or life falls apart can be the answer to a long-held prayer. They may be pivoting *You* to a greater good. These moments offer time and space to decide who *You* want to be, what *You* want, and how to create that. As this happens, something else shall die... and it will be something that needs to go. The cycle of life is fluid and organic when we allow its rhythm.

Wisdom through unity shifts *Being* visionary to *BEING* mystic;
utilize the melody of inspiration through exaltation, as an act of grace.

This is time to let your old patterns, behaviors, and beliefs go. Despite what you see happening, hold a strong and firm vision of a world *You* know is possible. This is the battle to overcome... the one inside your mind. Lift your consciousness to higher ground as *You* partake in the final steps of letting go. Be deaf to what others think. Be inwardly focused and listen. Develop a discipline that takes your mind from the chaos. Sanity arises from a consistent daily spiritual practice. Otherwise, insanity takes over. Let each step of your life be your meditation. Breathe in your surroundings. Know your Oneness. Let both the mystical and the mundane meet in your mind... because they exist within one another in this earthly experience.

In these experiences, do not to pray for anything. To do so affirms the lack, the loss, and the experience. Do not ask for situations to change or something to heal. Do not add energy to that which *You* do not want. Focus in this manner only prolongs what is in place. The current experience is based on past seedlings. Do not fertilize old sprouting. What *You* create now in the fertile landscape of heart, mind, and soul creates your tomorrows.

Find your rhythm. Be the focus. Take it all in. Let it all go. Have gratitude whatever arises. Then, even the hard, challenging, and crazy becomes fuel for your awakening. Open to receiving; be the allowing. Awaken to all that life offers with intimate receptivity.

Hold a space of gratitude for all that *You* celebrate about life. Remain in the conscious presence of unconditional love for what has happened. Praise the seen and unseen for what is present. Raise a celebration within the sacred temple of your heart. Fill it with beauty and harmony, trumpeting sound and praise. Breathe. Listen. Relax. Have gratitude. Love. This is the practice of praise. The only real way. This engages, integrates, and unifies. It creates ripples exponentially. This is power, grace, and truth of your Divine inheritance of creative capacity.

Collective change occurs through partnership with Source. *You*, as life, are always moving, even when standing still. Attract what *You/you/YOU* want by becoming that internally through your praise and worship. Claim your true power and partnership with Spirit, with gratitude as your binding agent. It does not matter how big or small the imaginings; *YOU* need only rest it upon the altar of GOD's love. This melody of praise can produce all manner of miracle and manifestation in an instant.

What is in your mind today is of no consequence. What is in your heart is what matters. Stay within your heart and move forward in your life. Expect one miracle after another. Praise and gratitude bring about new beginnings and blessings that shall open your heart in ways *You* cannot imagine. Embrace every moment, cherish every experience, and drink of each expression. *You* are the sacrament of Source. Feel the Love. Be the Love. Give the Love.

Sing your praises and lift your spirit high. Tell life about itself, "*Thank you for being the sacred mother that nurtures me. Thank you for being the heavenly father that provides for me. Thank you for being the tree of life that feeds me. Thank you for being the ear that hears me. Thank you for being the experiences that move me.*"

Become attuned to the melody of praise. With sincerity and understanding, call upon Source. Humbly stand before the door of devotion and establish celebration and joy as an indwelling atmosphere. With the energy of belonging, seal each word in sacred alliance with Infinite Presence. Have trust. Have faith. Let gratitude become *You*.

It is your nature to vibrate high.
It is natural for *YOU* to be totally alive.
All *You/you/YOU* really sacrifice are the lies.
Say goodbye.
Open channels of inner delight.
Vibe up your holy temple; fill it with Divine Light.
Surrender. . . not to your story,
but to your Most High.

knowing.
How do i/eye commit to myself?
i/eye can create a daily practice.

Knowing.
I give praise for my life.

KNOWING.
I AM exalted.

. . .

VISCERAL ASH

What may be absorbed?

Your journey from "Me" to "We"
parallels your path of "fear" to "Love."
The original sin is separation.
The miracle is Love as connection.
May every heart be filled with Love. . .
and every mind be cleared of ills.
May each and every life be set free.
May all human beings remember
their innate harmony.

You projected *God/Source/Essence/Universe*, and various *powers/gods*, outside *You*. Your *ALL-THAT—IS*ness became *ONE*ness; the *ONE* became *One* and shrank down to *one*. Separation continued separating and individuating. This reality's been maintained through the belief that *Higher Self/Spirit* is beyond the body, that *GOD* is outside *You/you/YOU*. It is up to *You* to return *God/god/GOD* back to your cells, your heart space, and your *Mind/mind/MIND*.

As *You/you/YOU* deepen divine integration, pure consciousness shall descend into your *Being/being/BEING*, reclaiming dominion within your kingdom as *Knowing/KNOWING*. The false world *You/you* created will dissolve. Humanity is your doorway for *dis-integration*. When *you/i/we/they* receive this holy "indeavor," a sovereign state shall once again reside with majesty.

Enlightened living is attainable. It is not some distant mystical encounter or galactic escapade. It is here, amid every present moment. It lies within the common happenings of life, and inside your cells. It is beyond the material glow of positive or negative addictions. . . intellectual absorption. . . affirmations. . . goals, techniques, or rituals. Plunging into your darkness activates alchemical grace. Going to the darkest of regions of *Self/self/SELF* is where *You* find the brightest spark of illumination. The *Light* of your Essence rests beyond the reaches of time and space, inside your void of nothingness. . . emptiness. . . and hollowness. Paradoxically, grace appears in the midst of this immense hopelessness, helplessness, surrender, and sacrifice.

What *You* experience, only *You* can know. No other will feel or understand, until they experience something similar. Even then, neither of *You* knows the intricacies and intimacies of each other's life. No matter how *You* attempt to share it, your perception is as unique as *You* are. It was built out of your defenses. Thus, your life is the unfolding ripples of your constriction and conflict, celebrations and moments of bliss. But one commonality exists as visceral ash. It is the hopelessness and helplessness of being human. It is the meaninglessness of life. It will tear *You* down time and time again, sinking You into tarp its of depression. But your beautiful human Spirit is so strong that it will not stay down.

**Cultivate presence as *You* invite unification with the devil aspect;
deep presence is required to access your visceral ash of resentment.**

Visceral ash becomes the fertilizing agent for living a misaligned life. Do not condemn, criticize, or minimize yourself. It is not worth it. *You* have been *Self*-conscious. Your doubt, disbelief, and lack of confidence are the ashes of other fires *You* have walked through. This insecurity does nothing other than repeat experiences. Criticism limits your expansion. It keeps *You* from any sense of power, or empowered creation. Self-condemnation removes the ability to align with Divine Being. Internal noise creates distortion. Do not allow ghosts of the past to rise from the ash.

To own your power may seem terrifying. *You* have spent so much time not believing in yourself that it feels impossible to find the confidence to do so. Shift what the mind says. Deep down, *You* "think" *You* are not good enough. Although you're scared of remaining who *You* are, there is more terror in being powerful. For this to occur, *You* must let go of the soot *you* carry. This ash no longer serves. Lay down your burdens of resentment.

Resentments are like splinters. If not removed, they fester into infection. This complex emotion will linger inside, gnawing at *You*. Resentments build into grudges and the inability to forgive. Resentment avoids conflicts externally, while raging battles internally. It bases life on should and expectation, often holding others to unrealistic standards. Resentment is self-obsession at its finest.

You choose pain. . . out of an unconscious desire to feel a close connection to others. But this is codependent attachment. True connection to others has no pain. None. Because it is from a place of wholeness, detachment, honoring, and love for the journey of *Self*. Pain is the drug of illusion. It is how too many shoot up and stay strung out in delusion. Pain is an addiction. Having it in your life has served in some way. Bless it, but now choose again. Choose to be nobody. With no identity, there can be no pain.

Love will always bring up anything unlike itself. Allow the distortions of *love* to serve you, without resistance to how they appear. Acknowledging your self-absorption is a leap into self-realization. Releasing resentment fo *Self* and others frees *You* in a way nothing else can.

**What *You/you/YOU* perceive
can be real, distorted, or false.
What *You/you/YOU* hear
is a version of truth. . .
someone's truth,
not everyone's truth,
much less the real truth.
What *You/you/YOU* embody
becomes your experience,
is lived as your truth,
and expresses as knowing.
Leave no residue.**

knowing.
How did i/eye reach this level of burnout.
i/eye receive exhaustion as a profound message from my soul.

Knowing.
I rest and rest some more.

KNOWING.
I AM divine relaxation.

. . .

ALCHEMY OF ILLUSION

What can be transmuted?

Life is the canvas.
You are art.
Be enlightened by your still-small voice,
hearing its soft whispers, feeling its gentle nudges,
experiencing its romantic gestures,
and knowing its everlasting presence.
You/you/YOU are not form. . .
You/you/YOU are formless.
I AM. . . You are. . . We are. . .
this temple of. . . *ISness.*
In this space
at this time. . .
let us not only walk together
but also witness every step.

Humanity can be experienced only when willing to fully own your anger, frustration, disappointment, or other dense emotions held toward another or yourself. Rather than reverting to politically correct behaviors of dutifully forgiving, forgetting, walking away, or just moving forward. . . be present to where *You* are.

With attention upon aspects of life *You* wanted to turn from in the past, *You* gain balance that reaps rewards far greater than *You* could have dreamed. The challenge of being with life exists only when there is a challenge of being with the *self*. The challenge of being with *self* is parallel to your denial of being Divine. The need for distraction, restlessness, endless consumption, and projections and the inability to spend long periods alone or truly present to others are how *You* run from your true power.

Accept thyself with the gifts of stillness, breath, and doing more nothing; these blessings allow vulnerability to rise.

In the murky waters and dark hallowed places, there are streaks of light that shine through. These cast perspective upon ignorance and ego in a whole new way. *You* will likely to be shocked by the violence of your reality. *You* will see the apathy, indifference, and stubbornness *you* inflict upon the world in subtle and unconscious ways. Behind these faces, intimately touch the feelings that hardened such masks into being. *You* will discover how separate *you* have always felt; how isolated and lonely. *You* have held yourself as different, unacceptable, and unloveable. What *You* unconsciously think and feel makes the light seem too bright... distant... and unattainable. However, the spark is reignited here. *You* will feel the urge to do better and be better. But before that can happen, *You* must rest in your final ravine of separation. There are many weeds and vines tied to feeling alone, abandoned, victimized, and forlorn. Do not leave this space of abandonment too quickly, lest *You* create that experience again in manifest reality.

You are entering the alchemical surge of coagulation. *You* are cracking open and breaking through. *You* have been able to stop the leakage of the past into the present. *You* have paused the dripping faucet of negative energies, thoughts, and words. *You* are becoming free of mind and matter. Your conscious awareness is connecting to greater consciousness in a more powerful way. Your soul is discovering its relationship with Spirit. The kindling of hope is once again being placed into the fires of your longing. The physical universe is not separate from spiritual reality. It is a reflection of it. All of this lives inside *You/you/YOU*.

There is more than one of "*You*" here. This becomes evident with *Self/self/SELF* discovery. *You* are the *One* to discover... that *You/you/YOU* are the *ONE*. *You/you/YOU* are not just a rainbow in the dark, but also the gold, and the storm. A divine courtship lies in wait within this field of light, shadow, color, and sound. Your humble surrender leads to an everlasting gaze into the *i/eye/I/I AM*, which encompasses the horror of *being* monstrously demonic, the maddening hunger of *Being/being* animal, the excruciating heartbreak of *Being/BEING* human, and the exhilarating awe of *BEING* Divine. *You* are the common denominator in all of these. *You/you/YOU* are the world. The universe lives inside *You/you/YOU*. Not only have *You/you/YOU* had it backward, *You* had it inside out.

Within your circumstances—through the shadows of *self,* and choices of *Self*—is a wormhole for realizing *SELF. Knowing/KNOWING* rests inside your experiences. Willingly immerse mind, body, heart, and spirit with what is presented. Become lost, and deeply so. Within the thick forest that life surrounds *You/you* with, the real *YOU* shall be found. Each step reweaves strands of your DNA. Visceral vines illustrate where *You* bind your *Self/self/SELF* and how your eternal nature has been restricted. Open to emptiness within this ladder of consciousness. Rest within your silent gasps. Relax into your resounding sighs. Recline further. Each time the work feels barren and boring, there is more to uncover. Divine expansion lies in wait, within the places *You/you/YOU* do not want to see, hear, and acknowledge. Step into the void. Shed your skins of time... all of them. Miracles occur when illusion and ignorance dissolve. It is all illusion. The only thing that is not... is *YOU*... the Divine *YOU*.

Meet me in the center;
that place of softness,
vulnerable and deep.
Cracked open by life,
burned by its heat.
The pain of the world,
held within the palms of your hands. . .
Each one baptized by breath
as each purifying their eyes.
Meet me there. . .
in the places where others hurt.
Let us free them of burdens
by doing the inner work.

knowing.
Why??? When??? How???
i/eye do not have to know.

Knowing.
I step into the unknown with arms wide open.

KNOWING.
I AM the Unknown.

. . .

ESSENCE AS PRESENCE

What may be embodied?

As *You/you/YOU* journey
within the grand realm of earth. . .
a mandala of life is created.
The sands of time
crystallize a holy experience
across many moments.
It is the memory (all)
of what has been experienced
emotionally, spiritually, mentally, and physically.
Life is a sacred hideout
a magic lamp. . .
of wishes and dreams. . .

that is to be polished and shined. . .
so to release your Essence.
***You* are a genie in a bottle.**
Your wish is your command.

Radiance reveals by fully feeling everything. It is in the vulnerability of an open heart. Feel every emotion to the fullest, so that *You* are alive within the nutrients of each moment. Sometimes, that means exploring the varying hues of pain and sadness. That also means feeling the fullness of joy, laughter, happiness, and ecstasy too! These spectrums are energies and wave forms of tone, color, and frequency. These feelings are weather; sunshine and rainstorms. . . each serving, replenishing, and restoring the soul's ecosystem.

Forgiving manifestation creates the inspiration for giving self-realization to *Self*.

When meditating, do not run from the thoughts that come. Do not push away the sensations that arise. Know it all. Feel it all. Be with it all. Let these things arise, so that they may pass. Do not let illusions of yourself be more important than the truth. Nothing should alter your path to belonging. Once the false has poured through *You*, emptiness will settle inside. It will feel spacious. For a time, nothing may occur. Seek for nothing to occur. Simply be with the *Self*.

Find a rhythm where *You* are unaware if the breath is moving in or out; become the breath. Breathe to the place where *You* cannot distinguish if *You* are breathing or being breathed. Let it feel infinite, so that *You* are the flow. Breathe in a manner that *You* experience the outside breathing. . . inhaling. . . absorbing. Become no-body. . . become no-thing. . . become no-one. . .

The "unknown" *You/you/YOU* is a vast frontier waiting to be explored, holding treasures and riches in escrow, until ready to fully receive yourself. In every step, through every experience and expression, is the full power of your Eternal Radiance. The ownership of that is your most vulnerable place. To hold that magnitude of power means letting go of all that *You* have been.

Oneness encompasses being so intoxicated that *You* cannot find form any longer. It disappears yet is completely present. Set your sight at the highest point you can imagine. It is beyond who *You* are; it is not your body, but your Being. It is larger than life.

You are a vessel. . . of pleasure and play. . . imagination and creation. It's what you have done all along. It's automatic! Nothing. . . no one. . . no experience can keep your Light from shining. It just does. The true playground of infinite possibilities is purely. . . child's play. Breathe out the bubbles of creation and watch them burst into reality!

You/you/YOU **birth for one thing, and one thing only.**
To Love and Be Loved.
You/you/YOU **awaken via one path, and one path only.**
To Forgive and Be Forgiven.
You/you/YOU **ascend with one knowing, and one knowing only.**
Presence is Enough.
In this way of Living. . .

By this truth of Being. . .
In this life of Knowing. . .
We are One.
We are the Ones.
We are The *ONE*.
knowing.
Why don't they see my perspective?
i/eye can become neutral.

Knowing.
I value all perspectives.

KNOWING.
I AM Presence.

. . .

FORGIVING MANIFESTATION— FOR GIVING CREATION

I forgive life's experience of misaligned manifestation.
I forgive this earthen dimension for distortion.
I forgive lies and manipulations.
I forgive secrets and conspiracies.
I forgive control and deceit.
I am for giving alignment.
I am for giving conscious, inspired action.
I am for giving truth.
I am for giving creation.
I am for giving a sacred space.
I give presence to words.
I give way to inspiration.
I give in to creativity.
I give from my heart and soul.
I give my human *Self* the grace of *Self/self/SELF*-realization.
I alchemize my *being/Being/BEING* with the aura of the violet flame.
I alchemize my breath with the fragrance of communion.
I alchemize my actions with the flavor of softness.
I alchemize my touch through the melody of inspiration.
I alchemize my speech with the Essence of vulnerability.
I am *ONE* with the *DIVINE PRESENCE*;
I transform and transmute spiritual obsession through the grace of *Self/self/*

SELF-realization. . .
I open to the absorption of all visceral ash and residual gluttony.
May *DIVINE ALCHEMY* purify my darkness and illuminate the false *Self/self*.
May I adorn the hawk's wings,
for bridging the illusion of evolution with the truth of involution.
I step with faith, belief, and *Knowing/KNOWING* toward a heavenly
embodiment.
I am for giving the hawk's gifts of courage and strength,
seeing and dreaming, focus and awareness.
May the gifts of *KNOWING* be granted by *DIVINE GRACE*.
I AM the ether of *GOD*.
I AM the fire of *GOD*.
I AM the water of *GOD*.
I AM the earth of *GOD*.
I AM the air of *GOD*.
I AM the spirit of *GOD*.

. . .

UP-LEVEL VISION

INNER VISION shifts your POINT OF ATTRACTION
to shift from

self ——-> *Self* ——-> *SELF*

Be present. Gradually shift into higher octaves of presence, awareness, and perception.
Move up the vibrational ladder. Feel your way and ascend to a new reality.

The sixth human expression of grace establishes a new lens from which to see and be
seen. It requires anchoring within the silence and stillness of ever-present meditation. See
with the inner sight. See all of *Self/self/SELF*. Through receptivity, new worlds are created.

Up-level Vision—by seeing—the divine reality of who *YOU* are. Transform into
unity, community, and sacred oneness through focus, vibration, and voice as your point
of attraction. As *You* more deeply anchor into visionary insight—and specifically DIVINE
SIGHT within *YOU*—your ability to create a higher expression of belonging unfolds.
You are an ever-expanding, energetic expression of the cosmos. Awaken your
knowing. . . Knowing. . . KNOWING. Give the world something new to respond to.

living.
————————————————

acknowledgment
(slow down and feel.)
————————————————————————————

*eye/i am evolved. eye/i will make myself better. No matter how hard things get, eye/i will
keep going. eye/i am growing. eye/i am learning. eye/i hold a higher vibration than they
do. eye/i don't have shadows. eye/i have done my work. eye/i healed my issues. eye/i am*

past that. eye/i don't associate with negative people. eye/i don't watch television. eye/i am not that kind of person.

being.

—————————————————

acceptance
(bring attention to your breath.)

—————————————————————————

eye/i feel. . . dark sometimes. eye/i feel resentful and upset; eye/i fume. eye/i feel hot. eye/i feel eye/i can't get enough. eye/i feel insatiable; eye/i want everything. Others should hurt the way eye/i hurt. eye/i feel disrespected and ignored. eye/i feel gossiped about, so eye/i gossip. eye/i feel like being mean. eye/i feel bad. eye/i feel like a devil; eye/I am always fighting my demons.

knowing.

—————————————————

anticipation
(breathe slowly, deepen into your body.)

—————————————————————————

eye/i am uncomfortable in the unknown, but it also holds dreams. eye/i feel afraid of darkness, but something valuable resides there. Within the darkness are parts eye/i can reclaim to become whole. Instead of pointing a finger at the world, eye/i can bring light to those places within myself. As eye/i curl up in the darkness, eye/i can shed my skin. eye/i can look upon the darkness as a guide to higher awareness. eye/i can embrace devil energy with angel wings.

Living.

—————————————————

appreciation
(pause and be present to what the moment is asking.)

—————————————————————————

I appreciate the rain. I appreciate how the rain sounds and feels inside me. I appreciate when cleansing showers flow through. I am grateful that I increasingly embrace my feelings. I am grateful for all of my emotions, I appreciate my mystical side. I am grateful for the magic and mystical encounters. I appreciate the growing compassion I show myself and others. I am grateful I am willing to face my shadows. I am grateful for healing and wholeness.

Being.

—————————————————

satisfaction
(connect mind to heart to gut to ground.)

—————————————————————————

I feel satisfied in accessing the ember of my soul. I feel satisfaction in knowing the beauty of my soul journey. I feel satisfied with how I am simplifying my life. I find simplicity satisfying. Finding fulfillment within life, relationships, and purpose is satisfying. I feel warm when I am satisfied. I am satisfied that my inner flame is growing stronger. I am deeply satisfied with who I am becoming. Being devoted to the journey of my soul is spiritually satisfying.

Knowing.

———————————————

adoration
(inhale deeply and absorb what is present.)

———————————————————————

I love how conflict helps me see where I am not loving. I love how conflict turns me back toward my self-care. I love myself. I love being in love. I love being loving. I love being cherished. I adore myself. I love the feeling of love. I love the experience of being lovable. I am the beloved. I love how love inspires. I love how love gives. I am the lover. I love how love heals. I love how love renews. I renew the world when I love myself. I am love in action. I love inspired action. I adore life. I adore animals. I adore babies. I adore smiles, sunshine, and moonbeams. I love the receptivity of love. I love the sacredness of love. Love teaches me so much.

LIVING.

———————————————

celebration
(rise above and rejoice.)

———————————————————————

I celebrate the magical. I celebrate "aha" moments. I celebrate synchronicity. I celebrate mysticism. I celebrate the breath; each inhale, exhale, and pause. I celebrate stillness. I celebrate doing more nothing. I celebrate Being. I celebrate the darkness for the richness that it holds. I celebrate the darkness for the light that it reveals. I celebrate light. I celebrate presence. I celebrate that my presence is enough. I celebrate that wholeness comes from darkness and light.

BEING.

———————————————

exaltation
(ground in sacredness, devotion, and equanimity. . . unconditionally Love!)

———————————————————————

*I spark. I glow. I flicker. I warm. I flame. I burn. I fire up.
I blaze. I radiate. I illuminate. I light.
I incarnate. I recognize. I redirect. I redesign. I re-create.
I reincarnate. I remember. I connect.
I increase. I enlist. I enlighten. I hold. I yearn. I long. I belong.
I witness. I love. I liberate.*

KNOWING.

———————————————

jubilation
(exhale your newly created vibrational reality and. . . believe!)
————————————————————————————

I AM bold. I AM confident. I AM calm. I AM powerful.
I AM peaceful. I AM relaxed.
I AM silence. I AM stillness. I AM serene. I AM hope. I AM wealth.
I AM prosperity. I AM truth.
I AM TRANQUILITY. I AM UNLIMITED.
I AM ENLIGHTENED. I AM EXALTATION.
I AM BRILLIANT. I AM RADIANT. I AM DELICIOUS.
I AM MAGNIFICENT. I AM LOVE.
I AM TRANSCENDENCE. I AM AUTHENTIC.
I AM INTELLIGENCE. I AM ALIVENESS.
I AM THAT. . . I AM. I AM THAT. . . IAM. I AM THAT. . . IAM.

Always begin exactly where *You/you/YOU* are. Be truthful with how *You/you/YOU* feel. Be authentic in what *You/you/YOU* are thinking. A new human builds from the ashes of your old life. Let your words be catalysts for transformation and transmutation. *You* are the bridge between where *you* are and where *You* want to go. *You* grow into *KNOWING* as *You* ascend the ladder of consciousness. What *You* place into the universal vortex remains in escrow. Belief supports physical presence. *KNOWING* creates change, transformation, and miracles.

oppression.

What has to dissolve?

Your presence is enough.
The time *You* give *Self/self/SELF* is love.
There is nothing that *You* have to do.
There is nowhere *You* have to go.
There is no one *You* have to be.
There is no purpose that must be fulfilled.
These are the lies that oppress *You*.
One lie requires another lie,
that requires another and another. . .
Each belief becomes a cage that holds *You* hostage.
Be mindful of what *You/you/YOU* believe.
All things are temporal.
This ephemeral world is a mirage.
Your life is built upon illusions. . .
your illusions and delusions.
Only love is real.
Let it shine through.

What appears "small" has the "GREAT" within it. Each human experience is calling for its higher expression of humanity, and divinity. Rather than sinking into disempowerment, fear, or oppression. . . pause and reflect upon why *You/you/YOU* called forth a human experience. It is intimidating to be David against Goliath. Incarnation in and of itself is wrapped in limitation and oppression. Human beings inherently hold the desire to overcome. Oppression was built into your storyli ne as "the hero's journey." Certain situations and moments bring triggers to the forefront. Triggers allow *You* to see what is up for absorption, recognition, and balancing.

Human experience not only introduces oppression but eventually also offers the realization of *being* your only true oppressor. *Self/self/SELF* oppression begins with negative thinking, criticism, doubt, and fear. Oppressive experiences arise out of the "law of cause and effect" and "the law of correspondence." Oppression comes from what you think, do, and believe. These elements are directly related to *Self/self/SELF*-absorption, making your small *self* bigger than everything else. This is how *You/you/YOU* imprison and oppress yourself.

With pressure seemingly coming from the outside, focus remains external. That only keeps *You/you* reactive and distracted. Let the outside point to thoughts, feelings, and sensations that internally hold *You/YOU* back and bog *You/YOU* down. In truth, your thoughts, perceptions, and perspectives are the true oppressors.

No one can come into your energy unless *You* allow them.

With oppression, there are two paths. One path encounters shadows and darkness but holds an opportunity to discover the brightest of light, should *You* stay the course. Light is found in your devotion to the darkness and what it asks of *You/you*. With immersion, the trappings of complexity, attachment, passion, resistance, ego's fight, manifestation, and oppression are shed. It is a path of spiritual mastery and maturity that awakens *Self/self/SELF*-awareness, compassion, and loving kindness.

The other path is one of vertical alignment. The highest *HOLY SELF* emerges from your commitment to *LIVING* and *BEING* the sacred embodiment of unconditional love aligned with Essence. This very disciplined and devotional path is often a solitary experience. It means integrating and embodying presence and heightened consciousness in a very distracted and unconscious world.

Ultimately, both paths lead to the same place. However, the first path offers the realization of multiple levels of *self, Self,* and *SELF,* spiritually, mentally, emotionally, energetically, and physically. This recognition leads to profound realizations of creative capacity. The second path also attains actualization but does not contain the full depth, breadth, texture, contrast, and dimension. The vertical road is void of the exit ramps, stops, and detours that are met upon the scenic route. However, both are beautiful paths. *You* came for the full experience of life. *You* can have it *All/all/ALL*.

Oppression brings forward an unjust or cruel exercise of authority. It imposes burdens, making others feel weighed upon or pushed down. Power that causes harm is oppression. Here, actions and agendas are about conquests. Taking control and having "power over" encompasses the ability to dominate others and to control resources, and enforcement based on agenda. Restrictions placed upon an individual, group, or peoples often bring about low self-esteem, exploitation, and dehumanization. Conformity is subtle oppression. Homogenization creates oppression. As time has passed, systems and structures are geared to homogenize. Some of these structures involve religion, education, and government.

All people are equally powerful, unless *You/you* choose to see them otherwise.

We live in a world that rewards forcefulness. Overdoing, multitasking, and spending time toiling disturbs the *Wind* element. Additionally, the *Wind* element builds in negative polarity when indulging in raw or processed food, excess, alcohol, or drug use. Force is an addiction to always controlling, improving, analyzing, worrying, or planning life. Thinking about life replaces actually living it. The number of hours spent "doing" opposes health and well-being and far outweighs time spent being human.

Oppression is a form of mental pressure. Outside forces victimize, control, or project onto people, groups, systems, structures, governments, etc.. . . But systems, paradigms, and constructs that limit, control, and hold *You/you/YOU* hostage are only mirrors of how *You* limit your expression, control your experience, and hold back life. These systems and forces cast shadows to court *You* into awareness and empowerment. The external flirts with *You/you/YOU*. Whether or not *You* choose to be empowering or disempowering is your choice. Focus your mind on what is creative and new. Don't waste time and energy looking back.

Today, rise above your identity. . . race, creed, color, religion, economic status, political party, and other identifiers. Rise above them. See yourself as part of the human family. . . a global community of friends and lovers. . . the soul collective. . . a divine kaleidoscope. See yourself as *ONE*, knowing no stranger; expansive and free. See your world in a higher expression with all wanting good blessings. . . more love. . . more joy. . . more pleasure. . . more happiness. . . more fulfillment and purpose. For change to root. . . it must build from the ground up. Be the root. . . a strong, healthy, vital root cause of higher love, kindness, consciousness, and compassion. *You/you/YOU* would not meet situations if *You* did not have the wherewithal to handle them. Big *BEING*s face big things. . . and create huge change. Be the antidote. Be the cure. Be the healing. Let the Divine medicine of loving kindness, hope, and faith express as *YOU*.

You **are not on a journey.**
You **are the journey.**
The message became the messenger
and turned into a mess.
Time to circle back. . .
and redress.
What goes around
comes around. . .
You are the creator,
the created,
and the creation.
There is only *ONE* **in the room. . .**
You **and** *God*. . .
Let the Divine express.
Life seeks your holy *YES!*

knowing.
How do i/eye overcome this?
i/eye persevere.

Knowing.
I Am strong, capable, and persistent.

KNOWING.
I AM the vessel of Spirt, through which all things are possible.

...

THE GRACE OF FREEDOM
What is remembering?

Invite the grace of freedom.
Consciously initiate this.
Let the kiss of wind invoke your aura of holiness.
The fragrance of majesty reveals truth.
The flavor of wholeness expands your energy.
Through inspiration, the visceral flight of remorse dissolves;
the essence of humility brings forth the alchemy of Spirit,
taking *You/you* to fly ground.
Give this gift of human grace.
***KNOW*. . . your presence is enough.**

To truly be free, *You* must risk losing everything: who *you* have been, how others see *you*, what *you* identify with, what *you* believe, and, most importantly, what *you* know. This sounds scary and painful. That is why *you/i/we/they* don't do it; at least, *you/i/we/they* think we don't. Heartbreak is unconsciously created for that purpose. There is power in your pain. Nothing is ever wasted. Some part of *You/you/YOU* knows what is necessary to remember *Truth/TRUTH*; this *one* is the instigator of heartbreak.

In your willingness to break down who *You/you* are, true desires reveal themselves. They may be entirely opposite of everything *You* once wanted. Do not be surprised when the material world no longer matters as much. What touches the heart and fills the soul might be of greater meaning. The illusion was that material things and a superficial existence could fill you.

Within the blessing of death and the illusion of war,
***You/you/YOU* created oppression,**
in order to discover the grace of freedom, as a way of awakening humanity.

When heartbreak occurs, embrace it for the gifts that it brings. Gold rests in the darkest places. Sink into the moments that introduce *You* to your depths. There is nothing more beautiful than your ooey-gooey, soft, molten center. Let it ooze. . . everywhere. Get messy; let your humanity grace everything. Your soul seed is destined to grow into what it *IS* designed to be. Get your mind out of the way and trust. Let your body be the vessel and your voice be the conductor. Let Spirit rise within *You* and express the harmony, union, and communion of sacredness.

This is not choice between the red pill or the blue one. This is an invitation for a life enamored with life, love enchanted by love, loss beguiled by loss, death dying to die, and liberation mesmerized by its own freedom. There is nothing outside *YOU*, or any rabbit hole to venture down. *YOU* are the pill and are to be swallowed whole. Let Spirit be your intoxication, and your full expression of Essence be the high. Life is but a dream.

The only true control lies in the choice to let go of the idea of control. That is your first step toward real freedom. Although creative meanderings of ego shall still occur, it can serve something greater than itself. True freedom is not escape from anyone or anything. It is the embrace and command of oneself, unbound from past and future need, unfettered from emotional baggage and egoic manipulation.

The Grace of Self Freedom	The Remembering	Knowing
The Illusion—Oppression	What has to dissolve?	Aliveness
True Love's Kiss—The Wind	What nature is required?	Creation
Aura of the Holiness	What is emerging?	Unification
Fragrance Emitting Majesty	What is the inhale?	Truth
Flavor of Wholeness	What is the exhale?	Energy
Melody Through Inspiration	What is harmonizing?	Growth
Visceral Flight—Remorse	What is being absorbed?	Wisdom
Alchemy of Spirit	What can be transmuted?	The Void
Essence as Humility	What may be embodied?	Infinite Presence
Forgiving Oppression—For Giving Possibility	What is for giving?	Infinity

Freedom is your soul's birthright, placed within *You* from birth. Freedom is also a human right. Although this may not be your physical experience, it is always available mentally, emotionally, and spiritually. Choice and perspective are yours to wield however *You* choose. Things are never happening to *You*; they can only happen through *You*. Essence always *IS*, even when buried beneath veils of false thoughts, beliefs, and perceptions. *You* are free to make anything your truth. The freedom to feel pain or joy is equally yours. Oppression, imprisonment, struggle, and suffering are among many choices present.

You/you forgot *You/YOU* are free, and became serious about the stories *Being/being* told. Each and every circumstance arises out of your birthright of freedom. What will *You* choose to see, experience, and *Know/know/KNOWING* in the freedom of *Being/being/BEING*? No war, hate, or ill will can be held after realizing that *You/you,* and only *You/you,* hurt yourself. No other has the power to do so. Attitudes, beliefs, and thoughts create freedom or enslavement. Your consciousness creates the world *You* experience.

In time and through timelessness, every soul awakens to *Creator SELF.* This is initiated by sparking, burning, and melting away all that is unlike *LOVE.* It is accessible through *any/every* path of life. Awareness eventually comes to all of us, regardless of whether on a path of isolation, aloneness, a householder's existence, or a celebrity expression of global reach. Each will encounter their own moments of oppression, for the purposes of remembering that they are, and always have been, free.

Divine awareness comes when releasing time, form, and identity. By seeing what remained unseen, a wormhole opens for *Being/being/BEING* to be catapulted into recognition. When what was forgotten is remembered and what was separate is reunited, acceptance comes. This remembrance brings forth new life choices toward personal and soul sovereignty. Inner conflict ends. *Self/self/SELF*-doubt and deficit cease. *Self/self*-hate is no longer tolerated. *Self*-abuse is not allowed. *Self/SELF*-oppression ends. A new era begins, one in which focus centers upon healthful choices for conscious living. The anticipation of your new form will outweigh the lethargy of your past.

Be nothing. Embrace everything.

Pursue personal and collective goals through the joy of developing your creative faculties. When focused upon fun, play, love, and laughter. . . the way for flow, abundance, and joy is opened. Nothing. . . no one. . . and no experience can keep your Light from shining. It just does. To live life freely, regardless of your human condition, is to experience divine liberation.

Immerse in the human experience as a child getting lost in their play with wonder, enthusiasm, and curiosity. Let that depth of *BEING* cause laughter in saints, sadhus, and gurus. It is from this sweet place that life's secrets trickle into many that are considered crazy, weird, lost, and homeless. Depths of wisdom are quietly carried as they walk invisibly among *You*. The least among You are often more liberated than those who flaunt their freedom. The one who has much to lose cannot be free until they have lost everything, especially themselves.

Celebrate everything.
What *YOU* choose already chose *You*.
Now release what *You/you* were,
and *You* will remember the truth *YOU* have always been.
This is your adventure of a lifetime.
An infinite journey. . .
that spirals.
What is whole comes full circle.
***YOU* are free.**
***YOU* have always been.**
***YOU* are the Essence of Freedom.**

knowing.
i/eye feel as if my hands are tied.
If my hands are behind me, my heart can be out front.

Knowing.
I Am free.

KNOWING.
I AM freedom.

. . .

TRUE LOVE'S KISS—THE WIND

What nature is required?

You/you/YOU **are the Universe in all its splendor. . .**
the Angels. . . the Ascended Masters. . . Spirit.
Let the winds of change raise *You/you/YOU***.**
Extend your arms. . .
Bridge what is human to that which is Holy.
Your life is a sacred text.
Your body is holy ground
You/you/YOU **are sacred.**
You/you/YOU **are pure perfection;**
even your imperfections.

There are times in life where resistance keeps *You/you/YOU* from fully participating in life, love, and your pursuit of real happiness. But moments of hardening make softening enriching. By resisting, pushing against, or staying away from any *person/place/thing*, *You/you/YOU* do not allow the awareness, healing, gift, or Love available from that experience. There is no real separation. There is no true ill. There are merely distortions in how *You/you/YOU* perceive. There can only be good. Moving beyond the illusions of life requires embodying living gratitude. Release your grievances as an active expression of giving thanks. When *You* clear the lens of perception. . . love, gratitude, and abundance can remain.

As *You* get older, *You* have an opportunity to become wiser. . . to hold gratitude not only for the loving, beautiful, successful moments, but especially for the challenging, heart-wrenching, and low ones. Time presents endless opportunities to open and flower. . . to learn to receive by giving. . . and to understand that loving *Self/self/SELF* is the secret door to being loved. Ultimately, *You* incarnated to experience life as a state of joy and unconditional love. *You* came to experience the full expression of your humanity as the gateway to *God/GOD*hood. Your true mission is compassion, kindness, and presence. Your perfect vision sees good in all things, and the Divine in everyone. That expanse of awareness is Grace.

In engaging the path of love catalyst, mental obsessions abound,
creating winds, which hid within your earthen ground all along.

The Element of Air relates to your state of *Being/being/BEING*. Air's spiritual quality is this pure basis of *Being/being/BEING* so immersed within something, active or inactive, that *You/you/YOU* become *ONE* with it. Through an aligned *Wind* element, *You* have great, unforced capacity for work. Healthy Wind is connected to focus and an intuitive quality of seeing the abstract or deep connections of things. Inspiration conveys the Wind element, naturally creating effortless stamina and enthusiasm for life.

The rhythms and cycles of nature are always at work. Healthy Wind is the alignment of movements and cycles within the body in regular rhythm and timeliness. There are neither excess movements nor trembling sensations. Sleep is easy and undisturbed throughout the night. Life's difficulties are handled without anxiety or excess stress. In returning to balance and naturalness, winds of change recalibrate *You*. Give everything over to Divine Power. Release your hold and allow what IS larger than *You/you/YOU* to take over. But this means that *You* must flow with the wind and not cling to the past.

> **Being the change is an inside job.**
> **In every situation. . . each experience. . . and condition. . .**
> ***You/you/YOU* are being served.**

Inherently, all people are innocent, even those who commit what is named awful, villainous, and devious. Every reaction and action stems from programming. What was learned came from those who were also programmed. They, too, were innocent. Every action, word, thought, and deed is based in innocence; especially the most-unconscious ones. In your innocence, *You/you/YOU* became the very play that *YOU* enacted. *You/you* got carried away. *You* forgot the innate power of "command meant." It was never designed to be a question; this is an affirmation of confidence and creative capacity. . . *Who I AM*. Ultimately your combined experiences expand your realization of *BEING DIVINE*.

There is a gift within the great story—your story, my story. . . his story, her story. . . and the mystery—and everything it is wrapped and bound by. It is a beautiful *present*. Sacred stories are known by stepping through the doorway of the holy *ONE*. Divine Natural Intelligence weaves through all of it. Our strings and strands weave and wind with one another, becoming knotted and bound in order to become untangled and free. Herein is the dance and nurturing space for remembering eternal aliveness and Divine alignment. DNA. . . Divine Natural Ability. You're born with it, imprinted uniquely. Your supreme ladder of consciousness rests here; dive into your strings and strands. With each stretch of growth, *You* will experience contraction.

> ***Who am I?*. . . If *You* ask this question, therein lies the illusion.**
> **It was never meant to be a question; it is a command.**
> **It got turned around in time.**

Contractions become more frequent with increasing awareness. Releasing each and every identity, personality, and form reveals more of who *You/you/YOU* are, and serves the vision of the soul. The deepening immersion of *Self* into *soul*. . . and into *Essence*. . . is your drama. . . your karma. . . and your holy dharma. Breathe deeper and deeper as each identity falls away. Breathe into any pain that is present. Within mind, heart, energy, and body lies an untapped unknown. This cannot be accessed by the known. Go where there is no path, and possibilities will come into view.

What is meant will stay with *You*. What is not shall go as quickly as it came. There will be those who cannot handle your love. They missed it; *You* didn't. They may not feel anything. People love to the best of their ability. Don't cling to what doesn't want *You*. It does not deserve *You*. Let the winds of change bring change. What *You* want wants *You*.

Be authentic in your expression. Share the best of *YOU* every time. Flow like the wind; do not hold what desires to leave. Stand in the gap, the place between if and when. Life will stir things up so that everything moves. Remain in the place between breaths. This is the bridge between conscious and unconscious, the divide in which to merge as *ONE*.

You eventually understand being fully human is okay. Feeling the full spectrum of emotions is humanity. Experiencing the grand expanse of your polarity and using all the colors in your crayon box is the glorious experience of humanity. Holding back from experiences, expressions, relationships, or places blocks receptivity, keeping fulfillment and peace elusive. *You* are a star*seed,* designed to grow, flower, and prosper. You came to Earth for an adventure. Celebrate the full expanse of the life *You* have been given, and the profound strength, tenacity and will with which *You/you/YOU* have lived it.

Compassion is dressed with freedom and adorned with wholeness.

You are gracefully broken along the way. This learning, growing, and discovery will one day be seen for all of its tragic beauty. Each human, regardless of their circumstances, is forever held in that Divine grace. In innocence, continually ask only one question: "*What's possible?*" Then, let the Universe, with its infinite wisdom, show that to *You*. When *You* ask a question, a vacuum is created. The Universe must fill that with an answer. Life offers that continual grace.

Being conscious, awake, and aware requires seeing all things through the eyes of this *LOVE*. Hold steady the *KNOWING* of every person as a great *Master/Creator/God. You/I We/They* are *Divine Essence.* Embody the humility of th*IS Divine Presence.* Through this ever-present practice, all are returned to an awakened realm of pure sacredness. You are elemental in nature. Awaken the gentle fire. Stand solid as the earth. Flow as water. Dance as the flame. Flow softly as the air. Be flexible like wind. When allowing winds of change. . . enlightenment is instantaneous.

To immerse within the euphoria of *BEING*. . .
Be in Joy, of Joy. . .
with Joy, and a
s Joy.
To activate *PRESENCE* within *LIVING*. . .
Be in Light, of Light. . .
with Light, and as Light.
To embody the ecstasy of *KNOWING*. . .
Be in Love, of Love. . .
with Love, and as Love.
***KNOW* Thyself. . .**
as the Way, the Truth, and the Life
of the Infinite.

knowing.
Why won't anything change?
i/eye am the change i/eye wish to see.
Knowing.

I invoke the winds of change.

KNOWING.
I AM the elements of nature.

. . .

AURA OF HOLINESS

What does it look like?

The soul longs to be held in a sacred way.
The soul came to share the Universal heart,
and to be the voice of Universal Love.
The soul longs to be wrapped in essence. . .
as it wraps the world in an aura of holy favor.
The world soul is in discovery
of its beauty and intelligence.
The world soul did not come to create history through separation;
it is the dream of reuniting and remembering.

You are the bridge between the visible and invisible; the connective tissue between life's longing and belonging. *You* are the staircase that connects mortality to eternity. This *Self/ self/SELF*-realized integration is attained by facing life completely, open and committed to whatever it brings. It is the courageous journey of the open-hearted, free-spirited, untethered human. It is the visionary's dream. . . the mystic's embodiment. . . the spiritual rebel's expression. . . the humanitarian's experience. . . and the love catalyst's inspiration. Each of these facets energizes your holy rays of auric expression.

Dying is not a human condition. It is a natural cycle of creation. To repeatedly die, and keep living, is a birthright of *God/GOD*hood. It is eternity in the making; the language of life and a continual courtship of divine expansion. Presence is the only pure and mutually beneficial exchange between *Being/being/BEING* human and *Knowing/knowing/ KNOWING God/god/GOD*. Within the purity of this, *You* meet an essential truth; there is no death, only life. . . and life after life. . . and life after afterlife. This is the essence of freedom. Through *afterlife, You* can realize your endless nature.

Reflect the energy of creation to expand your aura of the holiness.
In raising your vibration, the global reflection of information
and technology also shifts.

The romance of a lifetime lives inside *You/you/YOU*. Seek to love. Pray to remember. Kneel to rise. Submit to *Oneness*. When truly awakening, there will be nothing left to say. The presence to others. . . the honor of listening. . . the beauty of seeing. . . and the blessing of acknowledging. . . will far outweigh the need to be seen, heard, and acknowledged. Your doorways of consciousness are many. They have everything to do with your senses, emotions, and thoughts. Let each one reveal a different space in which you create, experience, and express. You are not only human; you are multidimensionally divine. When *You* embody the frequency of higher *SELF,* as opposed to that of lower *self, YOU* awaken to many sensory layers of life. Until then, let the aura of holiness be emitted through your alignment with life. That is the sacred practice of yoga.

Quiet the *Mind/mind,* so that *Spirit* speaks. Then, *Mind* can follow as faithful servant, setting about the logistics necessary. However, these actions will not be frenzied or hurried. Life will begin feeling like a dance. Life will flow. Synchronicities will increase. Things will fall into place. Essence does not push or force. It has no agendas or goals. Essence is organic.

The heart is vast. The soul even more so. And these are but a speck of who *YOU* are. Dissolve your identity into the expanse of all that *IS.* There is nothing outside that remotely compares to what is within. Worth is inherent. When seeing your full *Self/self/SELF, You* will see every single moment as holy. Do not only dream a new dream; see, be, and embody it. Let your life epitomize your dream.

Every experience must be fully absorbed to squeeze the juice out of life.
Don't judge your life; drink from it.

Within *You* exists depravity and divinity. Life's dual landscape is the doorway for yoking humanity with sacredness. Through this union, the last vestiges of separation can be dismantled. The vulnerable face of your humanity cracks open the unconscious and unfeeling facade that veils your true experience. Immersion into full feeling dissolves these masks of delusion. In gaining recognition of all that *You/you* have been, the awareness and illumination of *GOD* reveal wisdom and truth that illuminate the darkness of your world. With full participation and ownership of your life, the *god/God/GOD* of your understanding comes into view. Once the lower expression of *god* is realized, the countenance of *God/GOD* radiates brightly from within.

In meeting *god, God*, and *GOD*, a revelation will emerge. *You* created all of it; *You, you*, and *YOU* created every moment, experience, and circumstance of your life. Every situation, relationship, and outcome was initiated by *You/you/YOU,* through your energy, intention, and attention. You have been conscious, but mostly unconscious; likely 99 percent of the time. Your illusions derailed your personal power, purpose, and peace. Place these illusions upon the altar of your heart to be forgiven, dissolved, absorbed, and released. Your endless deaths and disintegration are transformation, transfiguration, and alchemy.

By deeply inhaling life as it *Is/is/IS*, the Divine is more powerfully embodied. By expansively exhaling, the Divine exudes from within *You.* The *I AM* experience is a devotional *One/one/ONE*, integrating every level; from false *self* to awakened *SELF.* As *You* absorb all of *Self/self/SELF*, your aura of holiness expands. Let go of effort, trying, learning, and doing. Embrace pure *Being/being/BEING.* Within the blessings of life is the desire to know *Self* again, and again, and again. This is the spiraling of the Infinite. A divine designer creates this world, and this sacredness lives inside *You/you/YOU.*

Love thy god.

Love thy God.
Love thy GOD.

Ultimately, life boils down to *LOVE*: fierce loving advocacy, self-love, compassionate love, kind *Love*, and unconditional *LOVE*. *Love* thy *god*; the raging, harsh, judging, punishing, and terrorizing *god* within *You/you*. *Love* thy *God*; the fickle, game-playing, strict, temperamental, and disciplining *God* with *You*. *Love* thy *GOD;* the tender, compassionate, forgiving, adoring, and gracious *GOD* within and beyond *You/you/YOU*. Have compassion, presence, and love for what each of these divine aspects created within your life. Through these faces, *You* became aware of your creative capacity, which included depth, dimension, polarity, and paradox.

In fully owning your creative power, embracing the full spectrum of your power from demonic to daemon and divine, *You* garner the ability for generating pure *Self/self/SELF*-love and healthy selfless *Love*. This renewed expression of *YOU* can create without agenda, force, manipulation, or need. Your expression reigns with compassion as *YOU* see yourself in every person. *YOU* behold others' actions as innocent, allowing them to be who they choose to be. *YOU* identify as oneness, rather than separation, duality, or defense. *YOU* see how the Divine Plan collectively balances all things. *YOU KNOW* that life, with all of its contrast, is simply energy balancing and equilibrating itself. Nothing is personal, and yet it all is. Every aspect of life is revered as a beautiful dance of texture, dimensional experience, and energetic expression.

The Divine *SELF* is a pure expression of love. Your alignment establishes sacred ground from which the power of humanity may anoint, bless, and grace others. This begins with *Self/self*. Mastery at this level is majesty. Namaste is invoked by the *self* (the animal within you) and *Self* (the shadows that veil you). These two aspects in sublimated prayer are the bones and earth of the most Holy *SELF*. Embodied sovereignty exudes the yoga of compassion, kindness, love, and vision. Blessings now correlate to your new view of *Self/self/SELF*. Through unconditional love and nonjudgment, *You* are graced by the illumined Essence of your eternity. By giving this holy anointing to *Self/self/SELF*, *You* greet all others as Divine; in *LOVE*, of *LOVE*, with *LOVE,* and as *LOVE*.'

You. . . are **Star Stuff.**
You. . . are **Light.** *You*. . . are **Heavenly.**
You. . . are **Divine.**
So *IS* the one next to *You*, across from *You*, in front of *You*, and behind *You*.

In moments of clarity, *You* shall emerge with a growing awareness that your holy Essence is bigger than *You/you/YOU*, your story, or your life. Until then, follow your script as part of the universal storyli ne. Within the infinite is the infinitesimal. Within the tiniest particle is the blueprint of an entire Universe. Do not underestimate your *self*. . . *Self*. . . or *SELF*. . . and how they echo. *You* are a part of an intricate flowering, a petal amid many in an endless field. *You/I/We/They* are unfolding together.

Bring clarity to what has been divided. . . harmony to what has been in chaos. . . and communication to deafened protest. Amid what is crying out from within chaos and confusion, holy presence is witnessing. Focus upon your power of holy presence— realizing the Sacred *IS* within every cell of your *Being/being/BEING*. Guide the scared *You/you* into becoming the sacred *YOU*.

Be led as a moth to a flame. Let the glow of holy aura burn away your flimsy wings of false humility. Let blinding light replace your body of *knowing* with the fire of *KNOWING*. Let the incineration of illusion become the illumination of sacred presence. Let the death of false embodiment be the reincarnation of Holy grounding. Becoming enlightened requires *You/you/YOU* be stripped of the layers that led to a life of repeating cycles of pain. Sacrifice your lower form and open to the experience, expression, and embodiment of your highest Holy Essence.

You are nearing the end, but not quite there. Gather all of the awareness, wisdom, and self-realization available. Then, the symphony can finish. Whether you choose to stay or go, completion has everything to do with your personal growth, spiritual mastery, and awakened humanity. Gather your insights and hold them close. They are holy. Anticipate your blessings, grace, and abundance. Know these to be true and receive your due! Anchor into the richness *YOU* are inside. . . for the mirror of this, the Universe cannot hide.

Whisper words of passionate celebration. . .
Ecstatically dance in emanation. . .
Celebrate your illumination. . .
and look deeply into your *eyes/i/I*'s of Oneness.
Slip into *Me/me/ME* as *Eye/i/I* slip into *You/you/YOU*.
Let's make love within the illusion. . .
and have a holy reckoning
between the sheets
of time.

knowing.
Do i/eye matter?
i/eye am not my circumstance.

Knowing.
I matter.

KNOWING.
I AM Holy.

FRAGRANCE-EMITTING MAJESTY

What does it smell like?

Your body is a grand cathedral. . .
Your life, a ring that binds. . .
Your commitment, the holy vows. . .
Your love, the sacred container. . .
Your devotion, the seal. . .
Your discipline, the eternal love knot.
It is your Divine Right to be happy.
It is your Divine Right to be in love.
It is your Divine Right to be free.
It is also within your Divine Right to believe otherwise.
And it is your Divine right to choose not to.
The enlightened *BEING* is no different than *You*;
they simply make different choices.

We—*You*, the other, and I—are part of a magnificent process of accounting that brings all things into balance. This has everything to do with your life, as well as before and after your lifetime. As an individual being, *You/you/YOU* are a point of light that impacts the collective. Each thought, every emotion, all actions are part of the collective unfolding. Life could not, or would not, exist without *You*. How could there be history if *You* were not here to perceive it?

You are the rose. . . in all of its beauty;
a tight bud. . . a display of petals. . . a fallen flower. . . and every thorn.

The rose fragrance can be mysterious, evocative, romantic, and even surprising. No two people experience this scent in the same way; a difference that's due to the genetic makeup and growing conditions of the roses themselves. *You* are like the rose; as a unique expression of life and, especially, when engaging your piece of the divine puzzle. Much like roses, the scent of a human is determined by many factors: the soil it grows in, the amount of rain (emotion) and sun (courage) it experiences, and the manner (love) with which it is tended.

The rose fragrance represents sacredness. Its gentle, layered, and beautiful appearance offers a glimpse of a masterful, active presence. As this fragrant flower blooms, its buds gradually open to reveal blossoms with many beautiful layers. This is how spiritual wisdom unfolds. This is also symbolic of the human journey. Have faith in your yesterday's, today's, and tomorrow's. Have faith in yourself, life, and the universe. Have faith in the gentle and precious moments. . . and the strung out erratic ones. Have faith because *You* are always held; that one truth is eternal.

Through growth as mastery of the unknown, awaken to your sacredness as *You* dissolve the black hole of wrath.

Each individual is to live life on their terms... to transcend the *Mind/mind/MIND*... to expand their consciousness. Every person has conditioning, fear, and oppression. This is why it is important to go inside instead of outside... to follow your gut instead of the crowd... to discern truth in a world of illusion... to seek your knowing instead of following the path that others say is the way to go or not go. Your YES must arise out of deep soul searching. Some YESses are identity and conditioning. Some YESses are fears stemming from shadows. Some YESses arise out of unconsciously tapping into the collective. Some YESses are impulses, reactions, and restlessness. To discern what is in the higher interest, *You* must stop and feel into your majesty. The soul YES is always deeply grounded, not attached, and never concerned with the opinion of others. In some cases, it may not be an easy walk, but that YES will always serve your best life and the greater good.

There is nothing *You* must do to get life right... No specific purpose or path, calling or direction, doing or no doing, pleasing or playing of the game. *You* came for the right to experience life fully, through the full experience of Source living, being, and knowing through *You*. Simply let Essence flow... it will always bring *You* to each moment in right time, right awareness, and right *Being*. Simply let go and receive where *You* are.

The unknown is always in the embrace of unbecoming.

The greatest service *You* can give others and the world comes in your approach to your most difficult, divisive, and challenged relationships and experiences. Instead of running out to change the world... begin where *You* are. Changing the relationships and experiences closest to *You* is what changes your world and the nature of the world. Situations and experiences arise to support the rise of majesty. The first step is always love... self-love, unconditional love, selfless love, deliberately loving.

There can be only good. Anything other than that is an opportunity for greater good. *You* are the magic lamp... the genie... and the one who holds it. The only difference is *You* have infinite wishes. Wish beautifully and let the genie in your bottle grant you heart's desire. That's the power of consciousness.

Beyond all perceived boundaries, peer through any set of eyes, from any timeline. *ISness* is at the center of all things. As *ONE* soul with eight billion sets of eyes, there is no stranger. There is no enemy. There is no family, friend, or foe. There is no past or future. There is no experience beyond *You*, because *One/ONE* of *YOU IS* experiencing that. *ONEness IS* the megastar. *ONEness IS* the unknown, indigenous, aboriginal, and alien. *ONEness IS* the president of a country, and the most poverty-stricken citizen. *ONEness IS* simultaneously the drug addict and the drug... the saint and the sinner... the winner and the loser... the atheist and the monk... the mother, father, and child. Regardless of whom *You* look at, see what *GOD IS*. See the *Self/self/SELF* as *ISness*. There is no savior. There is no Satan. There is no past. There is no future. Wherever *You/you/YOU* are *God/god/GOD IS*. Wherever *You/I/We/They* are... *God/ god/GOD IS*.

There is *LOVE* inside that is greater than anything *You* have ever known or experienced. Let it flow effervescently and shower upon everyone. The *LOVE You/YOU* share is the ultimate expression of Essence. It will dissolve everything that is no longer yours, while also inviting the *LOVE You* deserve. . . from *Self*, from others, and from life. Love and be loved. *You* are *LOVE*; you are *LOVE*able. We all are.

The intoxicating elixir that quenches your thirst is this recognition. *YOU* are not awakening to something outside; *You* are awakening to the fact there is nothing to awaken from. Life just *Is*. . . what it *IS. YOU* are. . . *ALL that IS*. This dawning of sacredness is self-realization, flowing fragrantly from every pore of *Being/being/BEING*. Drink of each moment slowly, as *You* savor the fragrance of majesty that *You/you/YOU* are. *Self/self/ SELF*-realization is your life's mission. *You* are a galactic supernova returning to cosmic awareness. Welcome to the mystery, your majesty.

LIGHT *IS*. . . **a sea of stars**
SOUND *IS*. . . **a symphony of undertones.**
COLOR *IS*. . . **a spectrum of consciousness.**
In each timepiece
rests the peace of timelessness.
Release. Embrace.
Let go. Allow.
Be everything. Be nothing.
*IS*ness *IS*. . . **Demon. Monster. Animal. Human. God.**
You **are the paradox of th***IS*.

knowing.
How do i/eye get through this dark night of the soul?
I/eye light my candle.

Knowing.
I Am a divine child of the universe.

KNOWING.
I AM Divine Creator.

. . .

FLAVOR OF WHOLENESS

What does it taste like?

Expect nothing.
Seek nothing.

Want for nothing.
You are a vessel for energy to flow through.
Be open. . . be clear. . . be pure.
This world is for your experience.
Life is beautiful.
There is nothing to take with you. . .
nothing to hold on to. . .
nothing you need.
Your presence to anything
provides a whole and holy experience.

To be human can hurt deeply. Being Divine offers pure bliss. The embrace of both is not duality; it is wholeness. Fully face your humanity. . . in its frailties, rage, pain, hate, and hopelessness. Stand vulnerably in the *TRUTH* that nothing needs to be healed. It need only be experienced, felt, and embraced every time the feelings, sensations, or experience rises. Keep ascending the ladder of consciousness, spiritual majesty, and *SELF*-actualization. Until knowing all of it, *You* cannot be whole or free. The power and presence of your divine majesty must be fully embodied, not intellectualized or imagined. By *BEING* unconditionally loving, compassionate, and equanimous, *You/ you/YOU* are already held in this flavor of wholeness; simply remember. This yoking of form and Spirit is where your holy *LIGHT* resides.

Life is intended to be a wholehearted experience; not only for manifestation, but also for experiencing transformation and transfiguration. Your experiences are intended to be both sensory and beyond the senses. Through the shadows of the physical expression, *You/you/YOU* begin an organic course of unfolding. This flowering moves *You* across the spiraling ladder of consciousness. Venturing into the land of opposites offers the full sequencing of your creative capacity. Wholeness encompasses knowing your shadow forms, unconscious expressions, conscious expressions, higher forms, and *IS*ness beyond form.

Your life purpose is for embodying unity instead of duality. To think otherwise is a futile play of hide-and-seek. To do otherwise keeps *You* asleep. Within *You* lies the power, potential, and presence of the entire Universe. Do not squander your wholeness on self-doubt, separateness, or silly noise. Do not put others on a pedestal or follow them blindly. Raise yourself up; be led from within. *You* are discovering inner authority, autonomy, and interconnectedness. *You* are opening to the presence of *Self/SELF* without the prerequisite of *doing*. A great understanding is dawning. *You* are not required to be, do, or have anything or anyone to feel complete, whole, and worthy.

Revel in the body of work that *IS* your life story. *You/you/YOU* are an individual *god/God/GOD* spark, derived from the womb of creation. *You/you/YOU* are the Garden of Eden. . . the tree of knowledge. . . the serpent of transformation. . . the divine masculine. . . the divine feminine. *You* are the apple. . . the bite of the apple. . . and the *ONE* who took the bite. *You*, beautiful *One/one/ONE,* have taken many bites of the apple, and for this the scales keep shifting until balanced. Forgiving oppression creates the inspiration for giving freedom to *Self.*

When there are no wings with which to fly; nest.
They have been tucked away only for *You* to remember how to fly.

The topography of your heart holds hidden secrets. Within it, longing fuels a desire for sacred union. Devotion and trust lead to the soul's diamond cave of belonging. *You* inhabit a moving temple. *You* are the embodiment of an enormous spirit. . . nonjudging, everlasting, and forgiving. Although *You* have played within human storyli nes of perspective and perseverance, the realization of sacred *One/ONE*ness is continually dawning. True surrender comes when *YOU* become everything and *You/you* dissolve into nothing.

You/you/YOU will one day recognize *self* as the ultimate soulmate. The part of *you* entrenched in boundaries, limits, structure, and form has unconditionally loved and served *You*. Through *self's* sacrifice, *You* have come to *Know/KNOW* the ascent toward beauty, boundlessness, formlessness, and timelessness. Now, through the sacrifice of *Self*, *YOU* will *KNOW* infinite expansion, cosmic awareness, and the sacred unknown. What was once imbalanced attains divine justice, creating balance and abundance. The embodiment of *self IS* for Mastery. The embodiment of Self *IS* for the Mystery. The embodiment of *SELF IS* for majesty. These unite to create a trinity of inner community and communion.

Accept "the thought" that *You/you/YOU* are human, but *KNOW* the *TRUTH* of *BEING DIVINE*. Walk upon the planet as an inspired human whose footsteps illumine the sacred path of *Divine Expression*. *You* are a Master. . . a *god/God* walking. . . a Great and Mighty *ONE*. . . without question. *You* are not of this world; neither is anyone else. *You* are not on a journey; *You/you/YOU* are the journey. *You/you/YOU* are *Experience/experience/EXPERIENCE* experiencing itself. As *You* stand in awe of the Universe, know that it is a mere reflection of the Universe within *YOU*. Explore your *YOU*niverse and be awed by brilliance.

As *You* endeavor upon truth in humanity, restore humility
through the key of wholeness.

Duality, darkness, and density are aspects of w(h)ol(i)ness. Within nondualism, reality is seen as a creative play enacted by the Divine Absolute where no thing is wrong. From this overarching perspective, all of life aligns to a Divine Plan where everything serves the greater good; every single thing. Even the ego—whose purpose is to fulfill itself—has always served what *IS* greater than itself. The flavor of wholeness encompasses responsibility for all that *IS* above. . . and all that *IS* below. In this unified sacred vision of *EYE/eye/i/I*, all that *IS* separate transforms and transmutes misaligned perception into the pure recognition of *ONE*ness.

Source is the entirety of form and formlessness. It is *KNOWING*. . . the Allness. . . the Everything and the Nothing. Transcendence is possible only through a humbled *Mind/mind* and pure heart. To know wholeness. . . embrace the whole of darkness, light; everything between and beyond. When *You* can truly be with all of *You/you/YOU*. . . an experience of wholeness will ground. *You* must be your own best friend. . . soulmate. . . partner. . . companion. . . and caregiver.

Humility is the full acknowledgment and grounding of Source as *YOU* rather than apart from *You/you/YOU*. This is not boastful, arrogant, or forceful. It is the manifestation of majesty, holiness, and sacredness. It is the awakened realization that every great Master and Prophet has spoken. Humility is the divine realization of the great within the small. True humility carries this *Divine Confidence* and *Divine Creativity*. It is fully embodied *KNOWING* as *Creator* held as sacred stewardship. Th*IS* power must be decreed with deliberate and conscious intention, presence, and prayer. *ONEness IS* intoxicating. Do not become drunk with power; be intoxicated through *PRESENCE*.

You are born of Oneness,
emerging from empty space, in order to know the
wholeness of physical experience.

There is no need to go in search of anything. *You* are remembering your *Self/self/SELF* from inside out and outside in. Everything comes by way of acknowledgment. This is why *You/you/YOU* are a paradox. *You* exist within life, and life exists within *You/you/YOU*. It is not something to go in search of. Simply get still. To change your outsides, shift your insides. You are magyckal. Surrender to that.

Boundlessness is available within quiet pauses, where seen and unseen states of presence avail *You* of mystical possibility. Regardless of the positive or negative nature of your experience, gratitude alchemizes the energy and always raises *You* to a higher spiral. Ascend the ladder of consciousness by grounding into the energies of gratitude, appreciation, and satisfaction. Do not think them; feel them. Emanation of feeling increases your light and aura. Be wholly present to what holds the greatest satisfaction for *YOU*. Then, confidently be *ONE* with that. Praise that *ONEness*. Verbal praise in jubilation increases your magnetic ability. Activate your magyckal, mystical, majestic *SELF. God/GOD*hood is ultimate *MIND*ful, sensory experience of soulful worship.

You are the designer of your life. . .
the creator and psychic vision keeper.
Approach everyone and everything
with love, beauty, and celebration.
Giving and receiving
are the same.
Energy must flow.
This was true in the beginning. . .
This truth has existed all along. . .
This infinite movement of wholeness
will be what remains in the end.
In mastering your *self*,
***YOU* create the world *You* deserve.**

knowing.
Will i/eye always feel broken?
i/eye will until i/eye won't. i/eye do until i/eye don't.

Knowing.
I Am whole and complete.

KNOWING.
I AM divine majesty.

. . .

MELODY THROUGH INSPIRATION—JUBILATION
What does it sound like?

You are not a drop in the ocean;
You/you/YOU are the ocean.
To see the great *SELF*, *You* must align with that.
Each word is your command.
Each thought is your prayer.
Each sound. . . each tone. . . and each expression
is the wand of God.
Each knowing. . .
is the divine breath of inspiration.
You are a *LIVING* moving temple
for *BEING* and *KNOWING*.

Your work is meant to be play. Your seriousness was intended to be light. Your agendas are to be released. *You/you/YOU* have the right to choose struggle, toil, and lessons. . . or the choice to flow with the divine harmony of grace, play, and ease. Both will lead to the same destination. The former is a longer, more turbulent road. This path of wisdom arises with experience, learning, and growth. The latter also has adventure but reaches certain destinations more quickly. It is built upon creativity, imagination, and communion. This one rests in *Knowing*, intuition, and trust. The melody of inspiration flows within both. Seek to know that harmony. Be in relationship with it. Open your mind to it. Behold the brilliance that is. . . *YOU;* be inspired by th*IS*.

Before beginning any task, become very clear on your ultimate vision and experience of fulfillment. Align to what *IS* required for alignment with that embodiment. Unite with what inspires the vision. Find your muse. Also, find a true believer; another who *KNOW*s your vision as already done. *"Where two or more are gathered. . . there I shall be also."* The Divine is in everyone. Right union brings forth Divine manifestations. Do not share with too many people or the energy is dissipated. Only choose an individual who lives with integrity and commitment.

Wisdom through presence shifts *Being* revolutionary to *BEING* a spiritual rebel; utilize the melody of song through jubilation, as an act of grace.

Model the melody of inspiration; *You* are not to teach. Teaching gratifies one's own need for importance. Inspire by recognizing the beauty and capability of others. Teaching holds a shadow of hierarchy. Modeling exemplifies equality. The beauty is that there are no replicas in life, only melodies of Divine inspiration. The revelations of inspired creation ripple out, inspiring others. Creation is the flowering of Source, just as a bud opens to a flower. As each person steps into their power of inspiration, another is sparked to do so. If not sparked, a healing journey will ensue as a model of inspiration. Either way, individual melodies form harmonies. Be in service to your heart. All other service flows from there.

You/you/YOU are an offspring of the Divine Heart, free to fly. Spread your wings. Leap. Create a new world experience of aliveness that becomes the praise of Creation. Where a void of nothingness once existed, the womb of creative possibility now resides. It is neither empty nor full; it *IS* what *You/you/YOU* make of it. It becomes what *You/you/YOU* are inspired by.

Your choices will move *You/you/YOU* to what is finite, or that which is infinite. The mind seeks the tangible; the infinite knows everything beyond that understanding. It is inspired by the silence of the heart and presence of the soul.

Holding back your voice not only diminishes your unique, melodic expression of cosmic creation but also creates dissonance through "the missing." With true genius, the ego steps aside. It does not manage, manipulate, control, or force voice and expression. It moves to cosmic rhythm. When living from the neck down, the body and heart move to the melody of inspiration. In fine-tuning yourself, your natural tendency will be toward higher expression. This catalyzes openings of inspiration. The method and medium of creation do not matter. The willingness to experience and express is of importance. Be your own inspiration. Create a life story that has you look back and say, "WOW." Celebrate your beauty, courage, strength, and impact. The world needed and needs your genius. . . your love. . . your expression and your light.

Each voice carries a vital and necessary tone. Sound vibrations, frequencies, and tonalities supply resonant or dissonant reflections of energy. When unclear about words spoken, tone reveals with clarity. Tone is vital in bringing forth the frequency required for harmony. The tone of one's voice tells their truth. When tuning in with deep sensitivity, *You* can discern what is love, indifference, lie, or *Truth/TRUTH*. Every person expresses a unique soul signature. Each individual is not only a soul song but also a sacred melody of inspiration within our collective, compounding memory of harmonic intelligence.

The Divine looks through your eyes; *You* are the altar of Spirit.

The *Unknown* holds new connections. . . new revelations. . . new experiences. . . and new relationships to people, places, things. . . even money. Let yourself dissolve into nothingness. That is how the Universe was born. And my dear. . . *YOU* are a galactic supernova. . . here to create vast new worlds. Be nothing. Embrace everything. Be new with each experience and moment. In the nothingness is everything! Inspiration is the dance of masculine and feminine energies. The melody of inspiration begets more inspiration and infinite creation.

Each person has a specific path of genius that is unlike any other. This genius is the

Divine Thread. Everything common about your life is conditioning. *YOU* are Spirit that cannot be broken. Yet, it is also what makes you uniquely *You*. No one else can fulfill that piece of the Divine Plan. Reflect the world as *YOU* desire it to be. Divine *KNOWING* is embedded within your cells. Live the life *You/you/YOU* are inside. Your aliveness, dreams, and truth live there. Be wild and free.

Soulful aliveness arises out of ever-deepening *Self/self/SELF*-acceptance and devotional surrender. *You/you/YOU* are always in a state of transition. *YOU* have no beginning and no end. *You/you/YOU* are life. However, *You/you/YOU* are also energy, engaging the process of *Living/living/LIVING, Being/being/BEING,* and *Knowing/knowing/KNOWING* this.

Soulful commitment to the life *you* unconsciously created is your purpose.
Shifting from unconscious living to conscious presence is your dharma.

When receiving guidance, don't ask *how*, just say *yes*. Your way will be made. Life has the ability to orchestrate plans beyond mental understanding. Life always leans into serving the greatest good. *You* are life's muse and inspiration. *You/you/YOU* are a dream in the awakening... *You/you/YOU* are a Divine Child with whom life is well pleased. Come out of the shadows. You are loved. You have always been. Be embraced by the fullness and purity of unconditional love.

You/you/YOU are a *Divine Idea* created in the heart and mind of a *Divine Source*. *You/you/YOU* are a *Divine Revelation*. Let life be a romance. Let Love fall for *You/you/YOU*. In that sacred love and longing is your belonging. Here *You* have lain, sleeping in the meadow. The fresh smell of New Earth is beginning to awaken *You* from an open-eyed slumber. *You* toss and turn, leaving the earth matted from the weight of burdens *You* chose to hold... *Your* spirit flies above *you*... beckoning *You* to Let Go. Laughingly your Spirit whispers... *You have been GOD Being/being/BEING all along.*

Your sacred walk will create the path.
Your design was genius all along.
Share your gifts... and Giggle.
Expand your energy... and Dance.
Amp up your energy... and Pray.
Bask in your Light... and Praise.
Align your life... and Inspire.

knowing.
Will the pain ever end?
There is a powerful being hidden beneath my pain.

Knowing.
I Am inspired and I inspire.

KNOWING.

I AM the illumination of Spirit.

. . .

VISCERAL FLIGHT

What may be absorbed?

You/you/YOU are not awakening to something outside;
You/you/YOU are awakening to the truth
there is nothing to awaken from.
In whatever way *You* desire, play.
Choose the dark of night,
or the Light of day.
You/you/YOU are safe.
Enjoy this journey as life,
with its many landscapes.
Run through fields of thought;
surf emotion's waves.
Dive into the deep blue;
ride upon the sun's rays.
Embrace all that Earth has to offer. . .
In light. . . love. . . and laughter. . .
your destiny was always written to prosper.
Sleep child, as long as *you* like.
Eternity shall be here when *You* rise.
There is no error in *Being/being/BEING*;
only error in judgment.

Feelings of restlessness are telltale signs of visceral flight. It begins with an inability to focus. You might find yourself pacing. You will become distracted. With the slightest sign of discomfort or danger, you will leave your body. Sometimes for no reason at all, you will feel the need to leave. This is what keeps addictions going. It is the vibration that keeps attracting that same villain in your life. The undercurrent of restlessness will have you looking for reasons to do something different, be somewhere else, or have a new life.

**Cultivate generosity as *You* invite unification with the Divine aspect;
deep presence is required to access your visceral flight of remorse.**

Toward the end of a cycle, *You/you* will feel caged in. The sense of feeling trapped intensifies anxiety. Your restlessness will increase. *You/you* will pace, ponder, and position different options. Confusion will cloud the *mind*. Panic may settle in. *You* will become fidgety. Every reason to leave where *You* are will rise again. But do not. You are in flight mode; specifically, visceral flight. Visceral flight is deeply embedded memory of the physiological, emotional, and psychological pathways that led to *You/you* leaving your body. Your body is here; *You* are not.

Instead of becoming distracted, feel the feeling of being caught, trapped, stuck, and imprisoned. Change your unconscious flight patterns through grounding. Time with experience dissolves these phantom chains that seemingly bind You. The flight response is fear trapped within the body from early life. Stay with the feeling. Breathe through it. Move your body. Be present. Often times, toward the end of healing, a moment will arise that reminds *You* of the trauma experienced. In this instance, *You* will be hypersensitive to the reactions of the body. It is as if *You* are able to witness what trauma has done to *You*. *You* will feel the the ramblings of remorse and escape deeply embedded within the cells of the body. *You* will also feel a deep sense of compassion for being human. . . being a child of trauma. . . and being innocent.

What rests within the body must be given space to ascend into the Light of awareness. It's important from time to time to evaluate your life. *You* have outgrown certain situations and people. To make way for the new, *You* must cleanse your life, your space, and your energy of all that has come before. Peace is always in the present moment. Within that is the new. . . new life, new relationships, new love, new experiences, new expression, and renewed aliveness.

Visceral flight does not rise to further bind *You*.
It appears so that *You* free yourself.

Recognize how *You/you* disappear and fly off, in moments that are most challenging. Your spirit hovers at a distance, witnessing. The desire to escape is strong in humans. Much of this comes from feelings of remorse. This is not just regret regarding consequences; it is the regret of what *You* did, why *You* did it, and to whom. This is the regret of motive, agenda, and unconsciousness. It encompasses your deeply held guilt for the wrongs committed. Remorse comes from knowingly, purposefully causing pain, hurt, detriment, and anguish to another. Whatever was done changed relationships, lives, and outcomes in a deeply profound and negative manner. Remorse can arise only out of true empathy. It flowers from deep inner work, introspection, and forgiveness. When remorse rises in consciousness, there is no way to run away, escape, or leave. *You* will stand authentically in all that was good, bad, and ugly. You will own your darkness and negativity. *You* remove places of division, separation, and illusion by being with them.

Being with these times is servant leadership at a different level. Every step, shift, transformation, and transmutation is to assist ancestral healing. A wave has been building for centuries, and it resulted as you. . . your release. . . your discipline. . . your healing. . . your expansion. . . your contraction. . . your unknowing. . . and your dissolving. The generational elements, wounds, curses, conditions, secrets, lies, traumas, and traditions must all be dissolved and absorbed to know truth. *You* are healing yourself and all those who came before *you*.

When moving from one octave of experience to another, *You* become the bridge between what was and what will be. It is important to keep your heart grounded in the soil of Source. It is equally necessary to keep your mind lifted into the heavenly realm of infinite possibility. As the bridge, *You* must be built into *BEING* by *KNOWING* the new experience *YOU* desire as *LIVING*. *You* are the bridge of animal writhing into human understanding. . . human understanding into humanity. . . and humanity *Being/BEING* to divine *Knowing/KNOWING*.

Peace is a present state of mind. Judgment, angst, conflict, gossip, and chaos may seem to be about the present but always stem from the past. Your current discomfort comes from past wounding, stemming from a completely different issue. Wherever *You* are, whatever *You* are doing. . . if not breathing peace into a world of aliveness, life is *being* breathed into a past that is already dead. Silence is integral. Rise in the wee hours and sit in the quiet. This sacred and special time is when the world is still. Communicate with the body. Let it know it is supported. Hug and hold yourself. Let the sacred see through your eyes, speak from your lips, and touch through your hands.

Each moment of life will expand *You*. That is life's love and intention for *You*. This will come through the gentle ease and flow of experiences that feel good, or life will provide contrast that cultivates the alignment required for mastery and magnificence to exude from *YOU*. Time is irrelevant, as a work of art takes as long as it takes. And *You/you/YOU* my dear, are a masterpiece. Now. . . master peace, patience, and personal power.

Believe not in your beliefs.
You are more than thought.
Believe not in your wounding.
You are more than your experiences.
Believe not in your illusions.
You are more than human.
Believe not in your failures.
You are more than your choices.
Believe not in your mistakes.
You are more than your identity.
Believe not in your fear.
You are more than your freeze, fight, or flight.

knowing.
Why does my body tremble and feel cold?
My body is signaling me to love myself, to listen to myself,
and to expand beyond my perceptions of Self/self.

Knowing.
I Am a master of peace.

KNOWING.
I AM the wings of Spirit.

...

ALCHEMY OF SPIRIT

What can be transmuted?

Is this one of many bubbles of possibility?
Is life predetermined? Is it fate? Is it destiny?
Do your choices determine the path?
Ego stakes its claim,
saying *You* have control.
The soul remains silent,
as universal secrets to gently unfold.
Essence is simple;
it requires no thing
because it *IS* the answer.

Essence exists inside *You*, living simultaneously within everyone. This is *your/my/our* eternal connection. If not present to the interwoven *Essence* between us, *You/I/We/They* cannot take responsibility for *your/my/our/their* part in collective creation. What *You* encounter does not arise for the purposes of victimhood, martyrdom, survival, empowerment, or thriving. It is not for engaging an agenda, attainment, or ambition. Nor is it for drama or entertainment. Everything occurs in order to enhance the awareness of *what is alive* within *You/you/YOU*.

See thyself with the gifts of aliveness, peace, and joy;
these blessings allow humility to rise.

You are like a fish in water, yet feeling disconnected from the water, even though *You* feel wet. Disconnection from the water, fishbowl, or outside environment is not the issue. Problems result from identifying as a fish. Identity is the issue. *You* convinced yourself that *You* are a fish. Others, also believing they are fish, treat *You* like a fish.

Misidentification, perception, and perspective create the illusion that *You* live, be, and know. Until *SELF*-realization emerges, *You* remain a victim of your *Mind/mind*. Instead, consider that all aspects of the story are *You*—the fish, water, fishbowl, world beyond the bowl, and the world beyond that. When identity drops, expansiveness *IS* present. Remove your skin so that no boundary remains between *You* and the air; *YOU* become the air. Living in the fishbowl of Earth, *You* do not see what lies between the visible and invisible. By removing boundaries created through naming, your ability to see the allness of *You* is available. Expanding beyond boundaries and names expands your awareness of *IS*ness.

The real does not seek to be seen, or heard. It just *IS*.
Only the false strives to *be, attain, and accumulate* more... and more... and more.

Each soul is a cell in the Universal Mind of Creator Consciousness. The parameters of infinite storyli nes are preset by each soul. All possibilities are laid out. Your soul chooses every step. Alternate paths and choices were also created so that all possibilities and resulting pathways are available. Whatever *You/you/YOU* are not experiencing within this timeline and point of view, *You/you/YOU* experience in another. *YOU* are infinite. When expanding your level of consciousness and vibrational frequency, *You* leap into a different bubble of experience, and its trajectory. No right or wrong experience exists, because life *IS* experience experiencing itself in all ways, spaces, and times. The human condition began long before the *ONE* known as *You* came into a body. *You*, and every fragmentation of *You/you/YOU/I/We/They*, play life's game of hide and seek.

ILLUSIONS TO. . . FORGIVE/DISSOLVE/ABSORB/RELEASE

HUMAN GRACE	FORGIVE	DISSOLVE/ABSORB	RELEASE
Simplicity	Complexity	Rage	Negative Attitude
Detachment	Attachment	Frustration	Complacency
Dispassion	Passion	Bitterness	Dissatisfaction
Forgiveness	Resistance	Jealousy	Projection
Rebirth	Ego's Fight	Regret	Sikken Attitude
Self-Realization	Manifestation	Resentment	Perspectives
Freedom	Oppression	Remorse	Perceptions

The soul made your freewill choices while designing the life *You* were born to live. *You* do not have free will as a person. If *You* are meant to increase in frequency and leap into another experience, it occurs because the soul made that freewill choice before *You* incarnated. If *You* shift out of a career and economic status, it occurs because the soul's freewill choice mapped that for your life. All of your destinations are predetermined, with blessings and points of grace placed along the way. Destiny and fate are out of your control. Your divine design and soul blueprint *IS* what it *IS*. Do not despair at this. Revel in it. The truth *IS, You* cannot make an incorrect move, because the move *You* make was the one intended.

Whether or not *You* believe in fate, destiny, cocreation, or karma. . . they exist simultaneously. Within your soul's choices, the life options, timeline, experiences, and body were laid down. Even synchronicity is the orchestration of a divine plan directed by soul. Your soul planted every sign, symbol, and synchronicity on your behalf, to prompt the choice *You* will make. The experience is what your soul learns from; how *You/you/ YOU* feel, emote, express, react, and respond.

VERTICAL ALIGNMENT—EMIT/EMBODY/ EMBRACE/EXPRESS/EXUDE

HUMAN GRACE	EMIT	EMBODY	EMBRACE	EXPRESS	EXUDE
Simplicity	Beauty	Gentleness	Anticipation	Higher Ground	Clarity
Detachment	Union	Tenderness	Appreciation	Sacred Ground	Tranquility
Dispassion	Wisdom	Kindness	Satisfaction	Solid Ground	Purity
Forgiveness	Reunion	Groundedness	Adoration	Fertile Ground	Generosity
Rebirth	Devotion	Compassion	Celebration	Common Ground	Intimacy
Self-Realization	Communion	Softness	Exaltation	Neutral Ground	Presence
Freedom	Majesty	Wholeness	Jubilation	Holy Ground	Humility

Is life created, predetermined, ordained, or already done?
Yes, yes, yes, and yes.

Your destiny, or call it fate, has been prerecorded. The ego, frustrated by this idea, will fight for its power of choice. It cannot fathom having no control. Ego wants credit for its successes and failures. It needs to believe in its ability to transcend circumstances. Your identity will argue that it made specific choices, but look closely; *You* will see. What *You* choose is what destiny designed. A thought that arises is preordained. Making a choice, and willingly doing the opposite, is exactly what was intended. *You* have all the power in the world, and yet none at all. *You* believe there is choice, but are following a plan set in motion long before this life began. *You/you/YOU* think there is control over your circumstances, but there is nothing to control. There is nothing *You* can do that is not already planned for *You/you/YOU*.

This is life's brain-teasing paradox. The ego will keep wrestling to prove its worth, power, and position. But the soul beams at the brilliance of its creation. The Divine *ONE* laughs while *You/you/YOU* plan, heartily guffawing at the cosmic paradox of freedom. This is the enigma of life.

Is life free will, Divine will, fate, or destiny?
Yes, yes, yes, and yes.

There is real peace within the hopelessness and helplessness this brings up for *You*. Be with how it feels in your body to have no control. How do *You* judge your life? What do *You* keep running from? What if *You* accept your life as *IS*? What if *You* accepted all that *IS*? Doing so would allow *You* to relax into *Self/self/SELF* more deeply.

Life is a dream that *You* have already lived. *You* are asleep and do not know it. This life has already played out. It is a memory. Your point of "review" might be at the beginning or middle or within the ending of this story. It could be the last experience of an endless array of lifetimes, or among the first of many. The primary purpose is for experience. Life is the past, present, and future in the most timeless of ways. Something new always appears to be unfolding yet also appears as if it already happened: Memory—Deja vu—Premonition—Past Lives—Dreaming—Channeling—Creation. Contemplate these phenomena. They have nothing to do with time. They connect to timeless *BEING*.

Each day, *You* are awakened. . .
into the ashram;
not deep in the woods, or upon a mountaintop.
This spiritual retreat,
your sacred sanctuary,
is all of life;
in every exercise,
through each engagement,
and the deepening practice these provide.
***You/you/YOU* will feel twisted and contorted**
until *You* yoke with life;
its illusions, blessings, and graces.
***You* are the circle of life.**
Dive into your deaths.
Take time to ponder.
Be present to where *You/you/YOU* roam.

knowing.
Where am i/eye in this?
i/eye am the contrast, polarity, and duality.

Knowing.
I Am the bridge.

KNOWING.
I AM Oneness;
the unifying principle of God, Source, Divine Universe of all things.

ESSENCE AS HUMILITY

What may be embodied?

A *YOU* beyond form witnesses
from a heavenly realm.
Bring that to earthen awareness.
Your task is not to ascend to Heaven,
but for Spirit to descend into form.
A vast universe exists within.
Hidden within *You/you/YOU* are the raw materials for alchemical change.
All manner of Gods, Goddesses, Angels, Guardians, and Guides reside there.
Have a heavenly experience on Earth.
It is your Divine Right.
Upon *YOU* rests a Holy Crown.
Life is your Kingdom.
Stand in majesty,
Your Highness.

Experience is the sacred divining rod. Life's ongoing saga heralds every son and daughter as King and Queen of their creation. Your nobility was granted at the point of divine conception. Your expression is uniquely special and filled with majesty. *You* are the extraordinary in the ordinary. There is no other like *You*... *you*... or *YOU*.

Your experience is not just a human story; it is a divine one. This is not simply the hero's journey; it is an infinite, legendary epic of intergalactic, cosmic proportion. Majesty is your birthright and the pleasure and play of the holy *ONE*. *You* are an experience of prayer and an embodied meditation of the *ONE*. The Divine *ONE* meditates upon *YOU*. Th*IS* presence resides within *YOU* fully and completely. Meet that divine presence through communion.

You are alchemy. Life is the alchemist. Be malleable... nonresistant... transformative... and ever changing. See what life makes out of *You/you/YOU*. Be willing to be nobody, so that you are *lead/led* into *gold/GOLD*. Discover the majesty of living, beyond identity. Don't just step into the void... leap into *IS*ness, wide open and untethered.

Within a vortex of earthen space, singularity centers within a black hole, condensing into a small space where gravity takes over. Pulling inward... inward... and further inward... into a single point of infinite creative capacity, focus and vision begins to expand. Amid strings and strands... superstrings and plancks... a *God* particle of *IS*ness sparks a harmonious light that shines new life. This *IS*... zero point; a unit of light... a photon... a massless property of waves and particles.

The vibration conducts electricity, light, and sound waves, brimming with potentiality and possibility... and ripe with malleability for shape-shifting. Vestibules of frequency resound, as a sacred cathedral of crystalline light forms. Holy resonance filters at light speed, through a liquid measure of pure creative capacity.

EMBODIMENT OF HUMANITY & DIVINITY	NATURE	AURA	FRAGRANCE	FLAVOR	MELODY	KARMIC RESIDUE	ALCHEMY	ESSENCE
Grace of Simplicity	Storm	Master	Beauty	Gentleness	Move-ment	Visceral Memory	Mind	Clarity of God
Grace of Detachment	Flood	Light	Union	Tenderness	Balance	Visceral Weight	Body	Tranquility of God
Grace of Dispassion	Snow	Crystalline	Wisdom	Kindness	Peace	Visceral Fight	Heart	Purity of God
Grace ofr Fogiveness	Drought	Rainbow	Reunion	Grounded-ness	Service	Visceral Smoke	Earth	Generosity (of God)
Grace of Rebirth	Decay	Angelic	Devotion	Compas-sion	Love	Visceral Form	Soul	Intimacy of God
Grace of SELF Realization	Rain	Violet Flame	Communion	Softness	Inspiration	Visceral Ash	Illusion	Presence (of God)
Grace of Freedom	Wind	Holiness	Majesty	Wholeness	Song	Visceral Flight	Spirit	Humility (of God)

In the emptiness of space *IS*. . . *IS*ness. In the vastness of no thing, a quake and a spark create a quark. . . moving and undulating. . . breathing and exercising. . . expanding and contracting. In the timelessness of no time, no matter, and no thing *IS*. . . the *IS*ness. . . of electrons. . . protons. . . neutrons. . . atoms. . . and molecules. This rests in the mighty kingdom and queendom of majesty, where sons and daughters of light are born. . . to remember. . . they are of no-bility. Each must rise to the crown, meeting all they are subject to. Vibration moves. . . to the action and activity of noble decree. The word is the command. Divine Grace is given. However, human grace is the key to your kingdom.

Let life lead; it will take *You/you/YOU* places never imagined. It will grow and expand *You/you/YOU* through blessed experiences that seem like challenge, upset, or unfairness. However, these experiences polish, shine, and refine *You*. As scales balance, stand within the glory of your mastery and majesty. The beauty and strength of your human spirit have the power to shine through any experience. This *IS* the sacred dance of *Spirit* in form.

When *You* embody the *KNOWING* of. . . "*My Presence Is Enough*". . . awakening will be instantaneous. Until then, play within the shadows of your illusions, and unconsciously within the sands of time. Resist nothing about your experience. Embrace everything. It is all simply. . . experience, experiencing itself.

Create as *God/GOD* through *Being/BEING* and *Knowing/KNOWING* the clarity of your desires with full feeling. That divine gift, skill, and talent is the vibrational ladder of creative capacity. First, prime yourself with what *Is/is/IS*. Accept where *You/you/YOU* are; fully receive all that it has to offer. There's *GOLD* in them there hills and valleys! Accepting and acknowledging where *You/you/YOU* are offers realization of what *You* do not want. It also gives you a peek into what *You* do want. Use where *You/you* are to an advantage.

SENSATION-ALL INTEGRATION

	self/being absorption	Self/Being Grace	Embodied Sensation
Step 1 of Aligning to a Higher Octave	Complexity	Simplicity	Anticipation
Step 2 of Aligning to a Higher Octave	Attachment	Detachment	Appreciation
Step 3 of Aligning to a Higher Octave	Passion	Dispassion	Satisfaction
Step 4 of Aligning to a Higher Octave	Resistance	Forgiveness	Adoration
Step 5 of Aligning to a Higher Octave	Ego's Fight	Rebirth	Celebration
Step 6 of Aligning to a Higher Octave	Manifestation	Self-realization	Exaltation
Step 7 of Aligning to a Higher Octave	Oppression	Freedom	Jubilation
Creative Capacity IS	Void Spaciousness	Sacred witness	Awakened Aliveness

**There is no need to change anything.
Be with what is here, and let it change *You*.**

Engaging the seven steps of vibrational increase supports moving into a different octave of experience. It is necessary and important to anchor into confidence and creativity. Linger within each step devotionally to harness the energies. Use visualization, imagination, and dreaming to see and believe your new reality. Reality creation is an inner experience, first and foremost. These steps of creation require deep focus and feeling immersion. With each step, relax into the ease and grace of *KNOWING*.

1. ANTICIPATION—*inner* excitement and expectation of things, inside and out
2. APPRECIATION—*inner* joy and love for things, inside and out
3. SATISFACTION—*inner* fulfillment for what exists in this moment, inside and out
4. ADORATION—*inner* overflow of love, respect, and connection that nears worship
5. CELEBRATION—*inner* heightened pleasure of things, inside and out
6. EXALTATION—*inner* happiness and praise worship about *Self/Life*
7. JUBILATION—*inner* joy and victory for life, inside and out

Merge with your great OverSoul. Higher guidance always led when it was most needed. Your soul is a fertile garden prepared to experience increasing depths of feeling. Love so deeply that *You* cannot separate the love for another from the love *You* have for yourself.

Sit... Close the eyes... Let your lips and face smile... Let your heart smile. Now focus on each chakra, smiling and expanding as you move up the rainbow within: root—red, sacral—orange, solar plexus—yellow, heart—green, throat—blue, third eye—indigo, crown—purple... expanding all around *You* and becoming brilliant Light. You are a rainbow... and the pot of gold at the end of it... Remember.

The power of creation is simple. It rests within the arms of joy. Majestic Creation is the most sacred of sensations as it is reflective of your Spirit bubbling over with Essence. Aliveness is replete with elements that arise from inspired, active integration. This is not the egoic attachment of process or the shadow reflection of constant acquisition or egoic manifestation. Spirited creation is a constant buoying of ever-lifting energies embracing life from a heart-centered space of *KNOWING* and realization.

Curiosity is the child of wonder. Expansion, duality, and multiplicity are grandchildren and great-grandchildren in the generational legacy of thought, form, and energy. In the end... this infinite expansion of *IS*ness will spiral back into the void for another exploration of space... curiosity... and *knowing/Knowing/KNOWING*. Once again... "*In the beginning*"... will be "*the word.*" And, the experience of timelessness will once again birth in "time."

There is only One... Truth be thy name.
Thy creations come... Thy will be done...
On earthen ground as *IS* in the heavenly realm of consciousness.
In the believing, shall be the experiencing
of your trespasses, illusion, grace, and flowerings.
In temptation will be treason.
For giving creates receiving.
The return to presence is secret passage.
Close all other doors; meet thy heavenly maker and all that th*IS* graces.
***You* are the echo of a timeless nature and a spaceless being of boundless capacity.**
***You* are the body of *Christos* and the blood of such ancestry.**
You are the Divine Child and the lineage of *Light*.
***You* are *Creation's Child*... Crown thy*SELF* your Majesty with Divine Right.**

knowing.
Who am i/eye really?
i/eye am god.

Knowing.
Be still and know that I Am God.

KNOWING.
I AM GOD.

...

FORGIVING OPPRESSION—
FOR GIVING POSSIBILITY

I forgive the experience of force and victimization.
I forgive this earthen dimension for dominance and manipulation.
I forgive obsession, oppression, and suppression.
I forgive conditioning, gaslighting, and brainwashing.
I forgive fears, patterns, behaviors, and blocks.
I am for giving empowerment.
I am for giving freedom.
I am for giving peace.
I am for giving love.
I am for giving truth.
I give presence to purity.
I give way to innocence.
I give in to wonder.
I give off laughter.
I give my human *Self* the grace of freedom and possibility.
I alchemize my experience with the aura of holiness.
I alchemize my expression with the fragrance of sacredness.
I alchemize my unconscious nature with the flavor of wholeness.
I alchemize my conscious nature through the melody of song.
I alchemize my life with the Essence of humility.
I am *ONE* with the *DIVINE PRESENCE*;
I transform and transmute obsession, oppression, and suppression
with the grace of freedom...
I absorb of all visceral flight and residual remorse.
May *DIVINE ALCHEMY* harmonize my thoughts and cool the wrathful *self.*
May I adorn the hummingbird's heart,
so to bridge this illusion of opposites with the reality of *ONE*ness.
I hum with *KNOWING*, finding holy ground within a heavenly embodiment.
I am for giving the hummingbird's gifts of joy and lightness,
sweetness and positivity, presence and playfulness, swiftness and resilience.
May the gifts of *KNOWING* be granted by my human grace and open me to Divine
Grace.
I am the holiness of *GOD.*
I AM the sacredness of *GOD.*
I AM the wholeness of *GOD.*
I AM the harmony of *GOD.*
I AM the humility of *GOD.*
I AM the eye of *GOD.*

UP-LEVEL INNER AUTHORITY

CONFIDENCE shifts your POINT OF ATTRACTION

to shift from

self ——-> *Self* ——-> *SELF*

Be present. Gradually shift into higher octaves of presence, awareness, and perception.
Move up the vibrational ladder. Feel your way and ascend to a new reality.
The seventh human expression of grace establishes a new posturing from which to stand in light. It requires *Knowing* who *You* are. It means relaxing into *KNOWING*. Claim your Divine Inheritance. Pray yourself up. Raise your vibrations. Hold vigil for the sacred. The clarity and consistency of your practice is devotional service. In this way, *You* become a disciple of life. You become the sacrament, and the anointing of grace.

Up-level Inner Authority—with confidence—by standing fully in your creative capacity. Move gradually into power, presence, and sacred peace through focus, vibration, and voice as your point of attraction. As *You* more deeply anchor into *Knowing*—and specifically into *DIVINE KNOWING*, all things become holy. *You* are an ever-expanding, energetic expression of wholeness. Awaken your *knowing. . . Knowing. . . KNOWING*. Give the universe something new to respond to.

living.

————————————————

acknowledgment
(slow down and feel.)

————————————————————

eye/I can't make my mind stop. eye/i keep having negative thoughts. eye/i don't want these memories. These stories keep looping in my mind. eye/i cannot get away from my past. eye/i don't want to become my mom. eye/i am not my dad. eye/i am right; they are wrong. This is good; that is bad. It's me against the world. eye/i am not going down without a fight. eye/i am at war.

being.

————————————————

acceptance
(bring attention to your breath.)

————————————————————

eye/i feel. . . afraid. eye/I blame others. eye/i feel like leaving; eye/i don't want to be here. eye/i feel shame. eye/i feel moments where eye/i want revenge. eye/I don't want to admit that eye/i hate. eye/i feel. . . remorse for how eye/i treated some people. eye/i feel rage toward some people and things. eye/i feel eye/i am fighting for my life. eye/i am exhausted.

knowing.

————————————————

anticipation
(breathe slowly, deepen into your body.)

————————————————————

eye/i am dying to all that is illusion. eye/i rebirth when eye/i let old parts die. eye/i open to the new when the old passes. All that decays is compost for a healthier beginning. eye/i can see the light at the end of the tunnel. eye/i realize that each death experience is birthing a more authentic and divine expression. Each day eye/i spiral higher in awareness. eye/i raise my vibration every time eye/I let the dense dissolve. eye/i love my self to death and love my SELF into aliveness.

Living.

————————————————

appreciation
(pause and be present to what the moment is asking.)

————————————————————————

I appreciate forward movement. I am grateful for change. I appreciate the winds of change. I am grateful for how I have changed. I am grateful for the new things coming into my life. I appreciate being a spiritual rebel. I am grateful for my unique genius. I appreciate diving into the things that fulfill me. I am grateful to spend time with people I love and who love me. I appreciate creating in areas that feel like play. I my grateful that my endeavors bring joy.

Being.

————————————————

satisfaction
(connect mind to heart to gut to ground.)

————————————————————————

Resting in the void is satisfying. I feel the satisfaction of possibility within the void. I feel the energy of creation within the void. I feel satisfied with how I navigate life. I am satisfied plunging into the unknown. I find satisfaction in shedding masks and false selves. I experience satisfaction when expanding beyond my comfort zones. I am satisfied with releasing all story, identity, and structure. I feel satisfied with what I am creating now. I find satisfaction in creativity.

Knowing.

————————————————

adoration
(inhale deeply and absorb what is present.)

————————————————————————

I love my cycles and rhythms. I adore discovering my humanity. I love flowering. I adore each and every feeling and expression. I love letting go of the old for something new. I love birth and rebirth. I love awakening truth when a falsehood dies. I love the depth and texture of each emotion. I love that I can feel so deeply. I love myself for embracing all that I AM. I adore harmony. I love harmonizing experiences. I adore how the sound of God comes through me.

LIVING.

――――――――――――――

celebration
(rise above and rejoice.)

―――――――――――――――――――――――――

BEING.

――――――――――――――

exaltation
(ground in sacredness, devotion, and equanimity. . . unconditionally Love!)

――――――――――――――――――――――――

I wonder. I wander. I design. I create. I birth. I sponge. I grow. I expand. I know. I circle. I integrate. I experience. I express. I contract. I shrink. I disintegrate. I dissolve. I absorb. I decay. I die. I empty. I still. I void. I rebirth. I rise. I relax. I renew. I regenerate. I vision.

KNOWING.

――――――――――――――

jubilation
(exhale your newly created vibrational reality and. . . believe!)

―――――――――――――――――――――――

I AM JUBILATION. I AM ECSTASY. I AM CERTAINTY.
I AM KNOWING. I AM BEING.
I AM EXQUISITE. I AM PRECIOUS. I AM GOD/GODDESS.
I AM VICTORIOUS. I AM SPIRIT.
I AM INFINITE. I AM BEAUTY. I AM ILLUMINATION.
I AM GRACE. I AM ALIVENESS.
I AM BLISS. I AM AMAZING. I AM DELIGHTFUL.
I AM IRIDESCENCE. I AM GOLDEN.
I AM DIVINE. I AM MAGICAL. I AM MAJESTY. I AM SACRED.
I AM HOLY. I AM ESSENCE.
I AM THAT. . . I AM. I AM THAT. . . I AM. I AM THAT. . . I AM.

When creating your own ladders of creation. . . always begin exactly where *You/you/YOU* are. Be truthful with how *You/you/YOU* feel. Be authentic in what *You/you/YOU* are thinking. A new human builds from the ashes of your old life. Let your words be the transformation and transmutation that lead to ascension. *You* are the bridge between where *you* are and where *You* want to go. Absorb the whole of *You/you/YOU* each step of the way. *You* are growing into *KNOWING* as *You* move up the ladder of consciousness, and into rainbow light. What *You* initially place into the universal vortex remains in escrow. Your belief supports physical awareness. *KNOWING* creates change, transformation, and miracles.

. . .

THE LADDER OF KNOWING.

How have you been served?

**What lay amid *You/you/YOU*,
however messy, beautiful, or painful,
is a living practice of personal growth
that awakens *Self* to belonging.
Endings need closure.
Beginnings require opening.
Embrace your eternity.**

You have been shown a multidimensional ladder of consciousness. Through immersing your life into these three books: *Living, Being*, and *Knowing, You* are privy to three levels of *Self* existing simultaneously, in time, and with timelessness. *You* can travel vertically, horizontally, and dimensionally in any experience and expression.

   You are solely responsible for creating your reality. The life *You/you/YOU* were given was destined to be the life *You* were given. *You/you/YOU* eternally are and have always been *Purely Divine. Divine Truth, Divine Power*, and *Divine Presence* are always with *You*. Acceptance, celebration and honoring are the path for aliveness to flower.

layer of absorption #1. . . dis-integrate complexity

The Grace of Simplicity	The Awareness	The Remembering	Knowing
The Illusion	Complexity	What has to dissolve?	Aliveness
True Love's Kiss	The Storm	What nature is required?	Creation
Aura of the Master	Expression	What is emerging?	Unification
Fragrance Emitting Beauty	Woodsy	What is the inhale?	Truth
Flavor of Gentleness	Walking	What is the exhale?	Energy
Melody Through Movement	Anticipation	What is harmonizing?	Growth
Visceral Memory	Rage	What is being absorbed?	Wisdom
Alchemy of Mind	Negative Attitude	What can be transmuted?	The Void
Essence as Clarity	Higher Mind	What may be embodied?	Infinite Presence
Forgiving Complexity	For Giving Simplicity	What is for giving?	Space

The Grace of Detachment	The Awareness	The Remembering	Knowing
The Illusion	Attachment	What has to dissolve?	Aliveness
True Love's Kiss	The Flood	What nature is required?	Creation
Aura of the Light Body	Experience	What is emerging?	Unification
Fragrance Emitting Union	Gourmand	What is the inhale?	Truth
Flavor of Tenderness	Painting	What is the exhale?	Energy
Melody Through Balance	Appreciation	What is harmonizing?	Growth
Visceral Weight	Frustration	What is being absorbed?	Wisdom
Alchemy of Body	Neutral Attitude	What can be transmuted?	The Void
Essence as Tranquility	Sacred Ground	What may be embodied?	Infinite Presence
Forgiving Attachment	For Giving Detachment	What is for giving?	Neutrality

The Grace of Dispassion	The Awareness	The Remembering	Knowing
The Illusion	Passion	What has to dissolve?	Aliveness
True Love's Kiss	The Snow	What nature is required?	Creation
Aura of the Crystalline Body	Strength	What is emerging?	Unification
Fragrance Emitting Wisdom	Spicy	What is the inhale?	Truth
Flavor of Kindness	Bathing	What is the exhale?	Energy
Melody Through Peace	Satisfaction	What is harmonizing?	Growth
Visceral Fight	Bitterness	What is being absorbed?	Wisdom
Alchemy of Heart	Complacent Attitude	What can be transmuted?	The Void
Essence as Purity	Solid Ground	What may be embodied?	Infinite Presence
Forgiving Passion	For Giving Dispassion	What is for giving?	Equanimity

The Grace of Forgiveness	The Awareness	The Remembering	Knowing
The Illusion	Resistance	What has to dissolve?	Aliveness
True Love's Kiss	The Drought	What nature is required?	Creation
Aura of the Rainbow Body	Creativity	What is emerging?	Unification
Fragrance Emitting Reunion	Pungent	What is the inhale?	Truth
Flavor of Groundedness	Dancing	What is the exhale?	Energy
Melody Through Service	Adoration	What is harmonizing?	Growth
Visceral Smoke	Jealousy	What is being absorbed?	Wisdom
Alchemy of Earth	Projection Attitude	What can be transmuted?	The Void
Essence as Generosity	Fertile Ground	What may be embodied?	Infinite Presence
Forgiving Resistance	For Giving Acceptance	What is for giving?	Peace

The Grace of Rebirth	The Awareness	The Remembering	Knowing
The Illusion	Ego's Fight	What has to dissolve?	Aliveness
True Love's Kiss	The Decay	What nature is required?	Creation
Aura of the Angelic Body	Truth	What is emerging?	Unification
Fragrance Emitting Devotion	Fruity	What is the inhale?	Truth
Flavor of Compassion	Singing	What is the exhale?	Energy
Melody Through Love	Celebration	What is harmonizing?	Growth
Visceral Form	Regret	What is being absorbed?	Wisdom
Alchemy of Soul	Sikken Attitude	What can be transmuted?	The Void
Essence as Intimacy	Common Ground	What may be embodied?	Infinite Presence
Forgiving Death	For Giving Birth	What is for giving?	Sovereignty

layer of absorption #6 ... dis-integrate manifestation

The Grace of Self Realization	The Awareness	The Remembering	Knowing
The Illusion	Manifestation	What has to dissolve?	Aliveness
True Love's Kiss	The Rain	What nature is required?	Creation
Aura of the Violent Flame	Confidence	What is emerging?	Unification
Fragrance Emitting Communion	Aquatic	What is the inhale?	Truth
Flavor of Softness	Play	What is the exhale?	Energy
Melody Through Praise	Exaltation	What is harmonizing?	Growth
Visceral Ash	Resentment	What is being absorbed?	Wisdom
Alchemy of Illusion	Perspective	What can be transmuted?	The Void
Essence as Presence	Neutral Ground	What may be embodied?	Infinite Presence
Forgiving Manifestation	For Giving Creation	What is for giving?	Eternity

layer of absorption #7 ... dis-integrate oppression

The Grace of Freedom	The Awareness	The Remembering	Knowing
The Illusion	Oppression	What has to dissolve?	Aliveness
True Love's Kiss	The Wind	What nature is required?	Creation
Aura of the Holiness	Illumination	What is emerging?	Unification
Fragrance Emitting Majesty	Floral	What is the inhale?	Truth
Flavor of Wholeness	Imagining	What is the exhale?	Energy
Melody Through Inspiration	Jubilation	What is harmonizing?	Growth
Visceral Flight	Remorse	What is being absorbed?	Wisdom
Alchemy of Spirit	Perception	What can be transmuted?	The Void
Essence as Humility	Holy Ground	What may be embodied?	Infinite Presence
Forgiving Oppression	For Giving Possibility	What is for giving?	Infinity

NOTES

From timeless, boundless, whole space
to a time-bound place. . .
a deep chasm in which to dive,
a self-created internal divide.
A void, manifest creation, experiments, and unknown reality. . .
lead to a black hole of endless separation.
You. . . you. . . YOU
have come to *know. . . Know. . . KNOW*
and be known
as human. . . angel. . . and deity. . .
for the journey as transformation, transfiguration, and alchemy.
This is your soul's dharma,
so joyfully engage with your human karma and samskaras.
Make the most of your life;
do not run or tarry, or fear or worry.
There is more than enough time;
You have all eternity.
In unwinding the illusions *You* created,
do so with reverence.
Becoming human. . . *Knowing God. . .* and
Being a Divine Presence.

knowing.
How do i/eye receive grace?
i/eye fully receive what is in front of me; this is human grace.

Knowing.
I Am the energy of jubilation.

KNOWING.
I AM Holy Ground.

NOTES

multidimensional sheaths.

What are your layers of Being?

In the beginning was *the word. . .*
before that, *silence;*
the word created everything.
Between vision and veils
a world hath prevailed.
Expressions of the Divine,
experiencing space, form, and time;
manifesting into a spiraling of sheaths,
and a multitude of dimensions.
When all is said and done
the echo of *KNOWING* is all that remains.

A spiraling layer of sheaths cocoon within your consciousness. They encompass a stairway of vibrational frequencies—from least conscious to an all-encompassing unified presence of consciousness. These dimensional levels do not require analysis, processing, or even understanding. They simply await your awareness and embrace. Not hierarchical, or stepping-stones, these layers exist in dormancy and aliveness at all times.

SHEATH ONE

1	LIVING	BEING	KNOWING
	BLESSING OF LIFE	**ILLUSION OF TIME**	**GRACE OF SIMPLICITY**
Engages	Path of Seeker	Emotional Obsessions	The Storm
Reflects	Energy of Spirit	Global Reflection of Energy	Aura of Master
Awakens	Growth as Contemplative Mastery	Hole of Slothfulness	Fragrance-Emitting Beauty
Restores	Truth in Questioning	Key Whole of Devotion	Flavor of Gentleness
Reveals	Wisdom through Inquiry	Teacher to Example	Melody through Movement
Invites	Unification with the Wound	Cultivating Listening	Visceral Memory
Allows	Gifts of Signs, Symbols, and Synchronicity	Hear Thyself	Essence as Clarity

SHEATH TWO

2	LIVING	BEING	KNOWING
	BLESSING OF CHALLENGE	ILLUSION OF DUALITY	GRACE OF DETACHMENT
Engages	Path of Rebel	Secret Obsessions	The Flood
Reflects	Energy of Water	Global Reflection of Climate Change	Aura of Light Body
Awakens	Growth as Emotional Mastery	Hole of Lust	Fragrance-Emitting Union
Restores	Truth in Grounding	Key Whole of Tenderness	Flavor of Tenderness
Reveals	Wisdom through Expression	Egoist to Humanitarian	Melody through Balance
Invites	Unification with the Child Aspect	Cultivating Appreciation	Visceral Weight
Allows	Gifts of Creativity, Imagination, and Talent	Receive Thyself	Essence as Tranquility

SHEATH THREE

3	LIVING	BEING	KNOWING
	BLESSING OF CONFLICT	**ILLUSION OF MONEY**	**GRACE OF DISPASSION**
Engages	Path of Visionary	Material Obsessions	The Snow
Reflects	Energy of Air	Global Reflection of Fashion	Aura of Crystalline Body
Awakens	Growth as Mind Mastery	Hole of Greed	Fragrance-Emitting Wisdom
Restores	Truth in Essence	Key Whole of Trust	Flavor of Kindness
Reveals	Wisdom through Witnessing	Businessman to Philanthropist	Melody through Peace
Invites	Unification with the Creative Aspect	Cultivating Connection	Visceral Fight
Allows	Gifts of Light, Love and Compassion	Heal Thyself	Essence as Purity

SHEATH FOUR

4	LIVING	BEING	KNOWING
	BLESSING OF CHAOS	**ILLUSION OF HIERARCHY**	**GRACE OF FORGIVENESS**
Engages	Path of Humanitarian	Personal Obsessions	The Drought
Reflects	Energy of Earth	Global Reflection of Human Rights	Aura of Rainbow Body
Awakens	Growth as Physical Mastery	Hole of Envy	Fragrance-Emitting Reunion
Restores	Truth in Stillness	Key Whole of Balance	Flavor of Groundedness
Reveals	Wisdom through Listening	Politician to Servant Leader	Melody through Service
Invites	Unification with the Feminine Aspect	Cultivating Conversation	Visceral Smoke
Allows	Gifts of Communication, Empathy, and Intuition	Know Thyself	Essence as Generosity

SHEATH FIVE

5	LIVING	BEING	KNOWING
	BLESSING OF OBSTACLES	**ILLUSION OF IDENTITY**	**GRACE OF REBIRTH**
Engages	Path of Sage	Masked Obsessions	The Decay
Reflects	Energy of Ether	Global Reflection of Wellness	Aura of the Angelic Body
Awakens	Growth as Spiritual Mastery	Hole of Pride	Fragrance-Emitting Devotion
Restores	Truth in Action	Key Whole of Innocence	Flavor of Light
Reveals	Wisdom through Experience	Homogenized to Genius	Melody through Love
Invites	Unification with the Masculine Aspect	Cultivating Naturalness	Visceral Form
Allows	Gifts of Strength, Patience, and Perserverence	Free Thyself	Essence as Intimacy

SHEATH SIX

6	LIVING	BEING	KNOWING
	BLESSING OF DARKNESS	**ILLUSION OF EVOLUTION**	**GRACE OF SELF REALIZATION**
Engages	Path of Mystic	Spiritual Obsessions	The Rain
Reflects	Energy of Fire	Global Reflection of Security	Aura of the Violent Flame
Awakens	Growth as Soul Mastery	Hole of Gluttony	Fragrance-Emitting Commitment
Restores	Truth in Silence	Key Whole of Fulfillment	Flavor of Softness
Reveals	Wisdom through Unity	Visionary to Mystic	Melody through Inspiration
Invites	Unification with the Devil Aspect	Cultivating Presence	Visceral Ash
Allows	Gifts of Stillness, Breath, and Doing More Nothing	Accept Thyself	Essence as Vulnerability

SHEATH SEVEN

7	LIVING	BEING	KNOWING
	BLESSING OF DEATH	**ILLUSION OF WAR**	**GRACE OF FREEDOM**
Engages	Path of Love Catalyst	Mental Obsessions	The Wind
Reflects	Energy of Creation	Global Reflection of Information and Technology	Aura of Holiness
Awakens	Growth as Mastering the Unknown	Hole of Wrath	Fragrance-Emitting Sacredness
Restores	Truth in Humanity	Key Whole of Purity	Flavor of Wholeness
Reveals	Wisdom through Presence	Revolutionary to Spiritual Rebel	Melody through Song
Invites	Unification with the Divine Aspect	Cultivating Generosity	Visceral Flight
Allows	Gifts of Aliveness, Peace, and Joy	See Thyself	Essence as Humility

NOTES

NOTES

glossary of dimensions.

What dimension do You/you/YOU create from?

In the delight of your spirit,
witness as *You* wander.
Open to the vastness of *Mind/mind/MIND*
and your ability to ponder.
Imagine and decree...
manifest creations and miscreations...
as *You* uncover and discover your *Self/self/SELF* in each.
Bring forth endless iterations...
searching far and wide... for something already within reach.
When what was not spoken is spoken aloud...
it is no longer absent, separate, or denied.
Healing occurs.
Wholeness reveals.
Dimensions are clear.

Many aspects of language make up your multidimensionality: tone, texture, staccato, speed, volume, intent, and reference. Tone connects with sound, while texture relates to taste, and staccato to touch. Speed is linked to smell. Volume refers to hearing. Intent is vestibular, connecting to the inner ear. Reference point is proprioception, meaning a sense of positioning, or the sixth sense. The use of the senses is important in comprehending, communing, and intuiting what dimension of *Being/being/BEING* is energetically expressing, and which aspect of *Self/self/SELF* is speaking. Life is a prism that fractals into endless possibilities of light, sound, and color.

Language	Sensory Perception
Tone	Sound
Texture	Taste
Staccato	Touch
Speed	Smell
Volume	Hearing
Intent	Vestibular
Reference	Proprioception

The following terms delineate dimensions of personhood, from shadow to Divine. These books are written in this manner to emphasize multiple dimensions within your singular expression. The language of dimensions supports recognizing who, how, and where an individual is operating from vibrationally and perceptually. By bringing presence to dimensions of personhood, cellular memory is triggered and unlocks what has been hidden or denied. In this way, awareness is catalyzed. Greater oneness is available, individually and collectively.

**Much of what *you/i/we/they* are yet to discover
exists in subtle ways.**

A second intent for writing these books in this manner is to support seeing the dimensions in which language, action, thought, and focus relate to the shadow *self*, identity *Self,* and higher *SELF.* You can review any word to deepen how *You/you/YOU* approach life. For example:

self/being	Self/Being	SELF/BEING
intimacy	Initimacy	INTIMACY
creation	Creation	CREATION
experience	Experience	EXPERIENCE
expression	Expression	EXPRESSION

Lowercase *intima/*refers to surface experiences within the world. Here *intimacy* refers primarily to *sex* at the level of *self,* often filled with lust or hunger at a base, animal, or task level. *Intimacy,* with an uppercase "I" and remaining lowercase letters, pertains to vulnerability; meaning transparency, realness, and opening up to others with a deepened closeness of language, relationship, or sexual connection. However, this level of *Intimacy* can exist without sex being involved. Communion and safety exist. It also engenders greater presence and commitment. *INTIMACY* pertains to sacred union within oneself. This can also be in relationship to the Divine, which is coined as the Lover and Beloved experience and expression.

Lowercase *creation* refers to the act of making something. For example, art, building, or crafting items. *Creation,* with an uppercase "C" and remaining lowercase letters, refers to manifestation in conscious and unconscious ways. *CREATION* is the conscious intent of aligned masculine and feminine energies within an individual. It is the partnership with Inner Spirit (*IS* or *IS*ness) in creating reality. *CREATION* can also encompass all of life and the Universe.

All words have multidimensional meanings and expressions. Each one carries a vibratory range that carries tone, texture, staccato, speed, volume, intent, and reference point.

What is said is deemed important,
particularly when recognizing *who* **is speaking.**
Through these distinctions,
an experience reveals the speaker.
Expressions portray the listener.
Your presence is enough.
Embrace. . .
Allow. . .
Inhale. . . Exhale. . .
and repeat.

knowing.
Will duality always plague my life?
i/eye lean into the contrast.

Knowing.
I Am paradox.

KNOWING.
I AM Infinite.

NOTES

glossary of terms.

What are the terms of your expression?

You are innocent;
your walk must be as well. . .
in the inhale. . .
in the stretch. . .
in the exhale. . .
in the expression. . . and the expansion.

being—This expression of personhood is the unconscious, lower vibration and hidden shadow nature.

Being—This expression of personhood is the identity that surfs existence between lower and higher nature, unconscious to somewhat conscious.

BEING—This expression of personhood is of a higher nature that aspires to deeper presence and conscious living. This is the closest to divine presence that one can become in human form from the perspective of the mind.

Being/being—This expression of personhood is the merged experience and expression of the unconscious, shadow nature, and identity that surfs between lower and higher nature, unconscious to somewhat conscious.

Being/BEING—This expression of personhood is the merging of identity that surfs between somewhat conscious and the higher nature that aspires to deeper presence and conscious living.

Being/being/BEING—This expression of personhood is the unified expression that soul came to experience, express, and witness.

DAEMON—A supernatural power that is the unification of all aspects of light, sound, color, and space

demon—The aspect of personhood that is the shadow. This may be unconscious and hidden and is always active to some degree.

Demon—The expression of personhood, hidden or active, that is shadow nature, which is the raw animal nature

demon/Demon—The expression of personhood, hidden or active, that is darkness. It is the expression of the monster inside. It is the raw animal plus a more intense shadow expression.

DEMON—The expression of darkness that is the same intensity but opposite polarity to LIGHT. This is the devil within.

demons/Demons/DEMONS—The unified expression of darkness; the devil, monster, and raw animal nature

god—The unconscious expression of personhood as an active creator of reality

God—The somewhat conscious expression of personhood as an active, more intentional creator of reality

GOD—The creator of all reality: good, bad, or indifferent

God/god—This is creatorship and manifestation capacity of the unconscious lower expressions of Self/self.

God/GOD—This is creatorship and manifestation capacity that lean toward higher expressions of Self/SELF.

God/god/GOD—The unified presence of cocreatorship regarding reality, life, experience, and expression

god/God/GOD—The incremental unified presence of cocreatorship

Home—The physical space of inhabitance; the body or a structure

HOME—The place of belonging; a structure, space, and sacredness

Home/HOME—The unified integration of the body as a sacred vessel of belonging, while also at one with existence and higher expression of creator

i/you/we/they—The collective shadow or unconscious

I/You/We/They—The collective semiconscious

love—The expression and field of experience that is dual, shadowed, and codependent within relationship

Love—The expression and field of experience that is dual. It moves between shadowed and codependent to light and independent within relationship.

LOVE—The expression and field of experience of oneness. This is a field of unconditional presence that integrates life in an interdependent way.

Love/LOVE—A dance within the field of experience that moves between shadow and light. It leans toward more-healthful expressions that are independent with a leaning toward unconditional and interdependent.

love/Love/LOVE—The unified field of expression that holds relationship at all levels among codependent, independent, and interdependent

knowing—The stance of ego, identity, or shadow based on conditioning, knowledge, or arrogance

Knowing—The stance of identity or ego based on knowledge, intelligence, and intellect

KNOWING—A pure integration, understanding, and expression of intuition and intelligence

knowing/Knowing/KNOWING—The union of intellect, intelligence, knowledge, and arrogance

light—An expression of positivity and illumination that might also be a mask

Light—An expression of positivity, leadership, and illumination that serves in the world but also possesses a hidden aspect of shadow in thought, attachment, and/or agenda.

LIGHT—Purity of thought, expression, and service, with no attachment and no agenda

light/Light—An expression of positivity and illumination that might also be a masked shadow of artificial lighting, while also illustrating positivity, leadership, and illumination that serves in the world

Light/LIGHT—An expression of positivity, leadership, and illumination that serves in the world, but with some attachment and/or agenda while also leaning toward higher expressions that have no attachment, agenda, or need for recognition

LIGHT—Purity of thought, expression, and service, with no attachment and no agenda

light/Light/LIGHT—A unified expression that moves in waves between dim to bright

mind—The realm of unconscious thoughts, patterns, behaviors, shadow, and woundings

Mind—Intellectual, knowledge-based space of questions, process, analytics, and thinking. This operates in both conscious and unconscious ways.

MIND—Higher intelligence. The cocreative power of the Universe.

Mind/mind—The expanse between unconscious thoughts, patterns, behaviors, shadow, and woundings and intellectual, knowledge-based space of questions, process, analytics, and thinking. This operates in both conscious and unconscious ways.

Mind/MIND—The expanse between the intellectual, knowledge based-questions, process, analytics, and thinking and the Higher intelligence of cocreative power

mind/Mind/MIND—The unified field that holds the unified field of shadow, intellect, and genius

mine/yours/theirs/ours—The collective in possessive

one—The individual

One—The individual in their power

ONE—The power and presence of many coming together

one/One/ONE—The unified presence of the many, from shadow to light, unconscious to conscious, demons to gods. The collective experience.

self—This expression of personhood is the unconscious, lower vibration and hidden shadow nature.

Self—This expression of personhood is the identity that surfs existence between lower and higher nature, unconscious to somewhat conscious.

SELF—This expression of personhood is of a higher nature that aspires to deeper presence and conscious living. This is the closest to divine presence that one can become in human form from the perspective of the mind.

Self/self—This expression of personhood is the merged experience and expression of the unconscious, shadow nature and identity that surfs between lower and higher nature, unconscious to somewhat conscious.

Self/SELF—This expression of personhood is the merging of identity that surfs between somewhat conscious and the higher nature that aspires to deeper presence and conscious living.

Self/self/SELF—This expression of personhood is the unified expression that soul came to experience, express, and witness.

truth—Distortion and perspective

Truth—What is believed on a larger scale; based on history, science, dogma, or heritage

TRUTH—What is… beyond intellect, knowledge, dogma, culture, or any manner of identification

Truth/TRUTH—Perspectives, beliefs, and wisdom held by a larger expanse of the collective mind, based on proof, science, spirituality, or the esoteric

truth/Truth/TRUTH—The merging of all thought, belief, and perspectives held in the field of consciousness. Everything—history, science, dogma, or heritage… beyond intellect, knowledge, dogma, culture, or any manner of identification—perspectives, beliefs, and wisdom—held by a larger expanse of the collective mind, based on proof, science, spirituality, or the esoteric.

you—This expression of personhood is the unconscious, lower vibration and hidden shadow nature.

You—This expression of personhood is the identity that surfs existence between lower and higher nature, unconscious to somewhat conscious.

YOU—This expression of personhood is of a higher nature that aspires to deeper presence and conscious living. This is the closest to divine presence that one can become in human form from the perspective of the mind.

You/you—This expression of personhood is the merged experience and expression of the unconscious, shadow nature, and identity that surfs between lower and higher nature, unconscious to somewhat conscious.

You/YOU—This expression of personhood is the merging of identity that surfs between somewhat conscious and the higher nature that aspires to deeper presence and conscious living.

You/you/YOU—This expression of personhood is the unified expression that soul came to experience, express, and witness.

Living —> Being —> Knowing
To live is to know.
To be is to live.
KNOWING comes through living… Living and LIVING.
in order to know being… Being and BEING.
An endless loop of Source
experiencing infinite choice
creates the embodiment of
KNOWING.

NOTES

about the author.

SIMRAN is a #1-rated, archived, syndicated host of Voice America's *11:11 Talk Radio* and publisher of the Nautilus Award–winning *11:11 Magazine*. Author of multiple books, including the Independent Publisher Book Awards (IPPY) and International Publisher Award (IPA) Gold Award–winning *Conversations with the Universe* and *Your Journey to Enlightenment,* and IPPY Gold Award–winning *Your Journey to Love*, SIMRAN creates art, books, and online courses to bridge humanity's experience and expression with devotion to the soul. Along with being a TEDx speaker, SIMRAN is a voiceover artist and the creator of the one-woman show *The Rebel Road. . . Connecting the Dots from What Was to What Is*.

Books by SIMRAN

Conversations with the Universe: How the World Speaks to Us
Your Journey to Enlightenment: Twelve Guiding Principles of Love, Courage, and Commitment
Your Journey to Love: Discover the Path to Your Soul' sTrue Mate
LIVING: The 7 Blessings of Human Experience
BEING: The 7 Illusions That Derail Personal Power, Purpose and Peace
KNOWING: The 7 Human Expressions of Grace

Simran's personal website: www.iamsimran.com
11:11 Magazine website: www.1111mag.com
11:11 Talk Radio website: www.1111TalkRadio.com

additional resources.

www.iamsimran.com
www.1111mag.com

Follow Simran and be in conversation:

YouTube—https://www.youtube.com/SimranSingh1111

Instagram for Simran—https://www.instagram.com/iamsimran1111/

Instagram for *11:11 Magazine*—https://www.instagram.com/1111_magazine/

Facebook for Simran—https://www.facebook.com/iamsimran1111

Facebook for *11:11 Magazine*—https://www.facebook.com/1111Magazine

Twitter for Simran—https://twitter.com/Simransingh1111

Twitter for *11:11 Magazine*—https://twitter.com/1111Magazine

LinkedIn for Simran:—https://www.linkedin.com/in/simransingh1111/

Pinterest for Simran—https://www.pinterest.com/simransingh1111/

Medium for Simran—https://medium.com/@iamsimran

Insight Timer—https://insighttimer.com/iamsimran

7 7 7

THE SELF-REALIZATION TRILOGY
is for individuals who desire to live beyond current
generalities, conditioning, and perceptions;
and for immersing within the subtle layers of Self in
conscious participation with the collective
as a Divine Creator
within the sacred vortex consciousness.
The moment has come...
for You to integrate the ONEness of
living/Living/LIVING... being/Being/BEING... and knowing/Knowing/KNOWING;
to up-level experience and expression;
and to embody divine inner authority and sacred sovereignty
through the unification of
Energy, Truth, Growth, and Wisdom.
In awakening to SELF-realized awareness...
***You* hit the jackpot!**

11:11
111
11
1

-

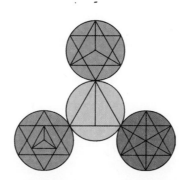

THE SELF REALIZATION TRILOGY

You are the gateway for...

7 BLESSINGS OF HUMAN EXPERIENCE.

to experience and express...

7 HUMAN EXPRESSIONS OF GRACE.

in order to absorb and dissolve

7 ILLUSIONS THAT DERAIL PERSONAL POWER, PURPOSE, AND PEACE.

NOTES

NOTES

NOTES

NOTES

NOTES